More praise for *Arms on the Market*

"The challenge of dismantling the weapons of the Cold War is firmly set forth and addressed in this volume edited by Gary Bertsch and Suzette Grillot. The flow of fissile material must be stopped at its source, and *Arms on the Market* lays the ground work to do just that."

—Harold P. Smith, Jr., *former Assistant to the Secretary of Defense, Department of Defense*

"As pioneers in research on export control issues, Gary Bertsch and his colleagues provide a very timely contribution to understanding the threats of weapons proliferation and global terrorism. *Arms on the Market* not only sounds an important warning about potential leakages of nuclear and other dangerous technologies from the former Soviet Union, but also highlights practical steps needed to contain the threats."

—Glenn Schweitzer, *Office Director, National Research Council*

"This book addresses one of the most serious threats to the national interests of the United States—the control of nuclear weapons-related material from the territories of the former Soviet Union. Written by a talented team of young analysts, *Arms on the Market* provides valuable and timely information for analysts and policymakers alike."

—Graham T. Allison, *Director, Belfer Center for Science and International Affairs, Harvard University*

ARMS ON THE MARKET

REDUCING THE RISK OF PROLIFERATION IN THE FORMER SOVIET UNION

EDITED BY

GARY K. BERTSCH AND SUZETTE R. GRILLOT

CENTER FOR INTERNATIONAL TRADE & SECURITY
THE UNIVERSITY OF GEORGIA

WITH A FOREWORD BY SAM NUNN

ROUTLEDGE
NEW YORK   LONDON

Published in 1998 by
Routledge
29 West 35th Street
New York, NY 10001

Published in Great Britain by
Routledge
11 New Fetter Lane
London EC4P 4EE

Library of Congress Cataloging-in-Publication Data

Arms on the market: Reducing the risk of proliferation in the former Soviet Union /
    edited by Gary K. Bertsch and Suzette R. Grillot.
        p. cm.
    Includes bibliographical references (p   ).
    ISBN 0-415-92058-2 — ISBN 0-415-92059-0
        1. Nuclear industry — Former Soviet republics. 2. Nuclear industry — security measures — Former Soviet republics. 3. Nuclear industry — Former Soviet republics — Safety measures. 4. Nuclear industry — Safety measures — International cooperation. 5. Nuclear nonproliferation. I. Bertsch, Gary K. II. Grillot, Suzette R.
    HD9698.F62A75   1998
    367.1'974—dc21   97-47647
                                                                                                                    CIP

10 9 8 7 6 5 4 3 2 1

CONTENTS

LIST OF ACRONYMS

AG	Australia Group
CFE	Conventional Forces in Europe Treaty
CIS	Commonwealth of Independent States
COCOM	Coordinating Committee for Multilateral Export Controls
CSCE	Conference on Security and Cooperation in Europe
CTR	Cooperative Threat Reduction (Nunn-Lugar) Program
CWC	Chemical Weapons Convention
DOE	U.S. Department of Energy
EBRD	European Bank for Reconstruction and Development
EU	European Union
FREEDOM	Freedom for Russia and the Emerging Eurasian Democracies and Open Markets
FSA	FREEDOM Support Act
FSU	Former Soviet Union
GDP	Gross Domestic Product
HEU	Highly Enriched Uranium
IAEA	International Atomic Energy Agency
ICBM	Inter-Continental Ballistic Missile
IC/DV	Import Certification and Delivery Verification
ITAR	International Traffic in Arms Regulations
MFA	Ministry of Foreign Affairs
MFER	Ministry of Foreign Economic Relations
MIC	Military Industrial Complex
MOD	Ministry of Defense
MOJ	Ministry of Justice
MOU	Memorandum of Understanding
MPC&A	Materials Protection, Control and Accounting
MTCR	Missile Technology Control Regime
NATO	North Atlantic Treaty Organization
NGO	Non-Governmental Organization
NIS	New Independent States
NNWS	Non-Nuclear Weapons State
NPT	Nuclear Nonproliferation Treaty
NSG	Nuclear Suppliers Group
SEED	Support for East European Democracy
SNM	Special Nuclear Materials
UN	United Nations
USSR	Union of Soviet Socialist Republics
WA	Wassenaar Arrangement
WEU	West European Union
WMD	Weapons of Mass Destruction

SAM NUNN

Today there is no greater threat to our nation or to the world than the illicit spread of weapons of mass destruction. During the Cold War our national security and that of the Soviet Union were premised upon a dangerous, but at least well-understood, balance of terror and upon well-traveled avenues of diplomacy.

Both the United States and the Soviet Union maintained formidable nuclear arsenals, so there was a high risk that conflict would result in certain and unacceptable losses no matter who the initial aggressor. If conflict appeared possible, diplomatic channels were available as a relief valve. Although living in a climate of high risk, we enjoyed a high degree of stability.

The collapse of Soviet communism and the end of the Cold War eliminated what many considered to be the greatest threat to world security. Certainly the threat of all-out war has gone down very significantly. Yet, today the concerns of the Cold War have been replaced with new and far different threats. We have moved from an era of high risks but also high stability to an era of much lower risk but also much lower stability.

Indeed, in many ways the world is far more unstable today than it was a decade ago. Ethnic, religious, racial, and political conflicts have led to an increasing level of violence and terrorism all over the globe. It seems no place is immune today. Not the subways of Tokyo, not the buses of Jerusalem, not the office buildings of New York City or Oklahoma City.

Zealotry in the name of a cause has led individuals, groups, and rogue nations to be increasingly willing to do the unthinkable, often for no other reason than to cause destruction and terror.

The breakup of the Soviet Union and the growth of democracy in Eastern Europe were hopeful signs for international tranquility. Yet never before has an empire disintegrated while in the possession of 30,000 nuclear weapons, at least 40,000 tons of chemical weapons, significant biological-weapons capability, tons of fissile materials, and tens of thousands of scientists and technicians who know how to make these weapons and their delivery systems but who do not know how to make a living for their families in a collapsing economy.

As the newly independent countries of the former Soviet Union struggle to achieve democratic reforms and build a free-market economy, thousands of weapons scientists and technicians, including nuclear scientists, now face unemployment and are looking for new ways to earn salaries with which to feed their families.

Military officers accustomed to being treated as among the country's elite now face economic hardships with which they are not familiar. Plant managers and workers at some of the most sensitive civilian research facilities, who had enjoyed a relatively high standard of living in the former Soviet Union, now labor under conditions which make it difficult for them to even feed their families.

The challenge facing the Russians and the rest of the world is to ensure that the former Soviet Union does not become a supermarket for the most deadly instruments and technology ever know to man.

Unfortunately, this threat is no longer theoretical. When my colleagues and I in the U.S. Senate began to address these issues several years ago, we were dealing with what we thought was a potential, a very high potential risk. Now we are dealing with reality.

The leakage of nuclear materials from the former Soviet Union is now fact. On several occasions Russian authorities recovered weapons-grade material, usable nuclear materials, which had been diverted from civilian research institutes by individuals who intended to sell the material abroad. In four other cases, weapons-usable material, including highly enriched uranium and plutonium, made its way from the former Soviet Union into Europe before authorities finally seized it.

But what we really are worried about is what we don't know. About three years ago I directed the staff of the U.S. Senate's Permanent Subcommittee on Investigations to conduct an in-depth examination of this issue in order to determine the likelihood of such diversion and trafficking occurring.

In May of 1994 their efforts led to a hearing which brought together for the first time before the Congress the director of the Federal Bureau of Investigation, the president of Germany's BKA, which is their equivalent of our FBI, and the head of Russia's organized crime control department, a rather unique three to have together.

The testimony of these officials revealed a high level of concern about the threat posed by organized crime in the former Soviet Union, and the possibility that under the right circumstances organized crime could become involved in either facilitating or creating a nuclear black market. In my view, this is almost inevitable.

Equally important as the leakage of fissile materials from the former Soviet Union is the disbursal of the technical know-how and expertise held by the 60,000 or so weapons scientists and technicians who were once part of a very formidable Soviet weapons program and aerospace program.

In 1996, my staff on the Permanent Subcommittee on Investigations obtained examples of various entities attempting to exploit this situation for money. The staff obtained a solicitation letter distributed in the Middle East by a Hong Kong company offering to sell nuclear expertise. The letter stated, "We have detailed files of hundreds of former Soviet Union experts in the field of rocket, missile and nuclear weapons. These weapons experts are willing to work in a country which needs their skills and can offer reasonable pay." This conveys an idea of the challenge.

You don't have to have too vivid an imagination to fathom the effect this brain drain can have on our national security and the national security of countries all over the world.

As economic conditions in the countries of the former Soviet Union continue to deteriorate (and I hope this situation will soon be remedied), we in this country have a real stake in seeing increased economic stability in those other countries. Whether we know it or not, we have a stake in their economic development, because as long as they are experiencing tremendous economic difficulties, then the pressure on all of these areas of proliferation, including the pressure on scientists and military officials, grows.

As economic conditions in these countries continue to deteriorate, we have to move more rapidly to give them incentives to secure and protect the lethal materials they have inherited. We have to bear in mind through all of this that 90 percent of the work in these areas has to be done by the countries themselves. We are not capable of solving their problems. We can help stimulate their efforts, we can help prioritize, we can help give them incentives, but we can't solve the problems for them. They have their own national security at stake here too and they have to realize it.

However, all experts agree that the wisest policy is to secure the materials at their source. When they get out into the world market, the degree of difficulty in dealing with the problem gets bigger and bigger. We must redouble our commitment to combat this threat. We have started, but we have a long, long way to go.

I, therefore, am pleased to see Gary Bertsch and his colleagues at the University of Georgia involved in this work. Gary and his associates at the University's Center for International Trade and Security are conducting in-depth research on nonproliferation export control developments in Russia and the newly independent states. Their efforts are of vital importance to the task of ensuring nonproliferation. They are based upon sound social-science research. They contribute to a better understanding of the important and complex set of nonproliferation export control issues in the former Soviet Union. They are policy-relevant and will help us deal with the nonproliferation challenge in the years ahead. I recommend this report of their work for your reading.

Sam Nunn

GARY K. BERTSCH

This book is part of a larger effort at the University of Georgia and Center for International Trade and Security. Several of us at the university started studying U.S. and Western strategic trade and export control policy in the 1980s. With the collapse of Soviet communism in the early 1990s and the disintegration of the USSR and the Warsaw Treaty Organization binding it and the East European states together, we shifted our attention to the strategic trade, export control, and security challenges facing the new, post-communist states of that region.

Senators Sam Nunn and Richard Lugar and a few other visionaries, in the United States and abroad, recognized early the emerging threat of weapons proliferation from the former Soviet Union (FSU). We at the Center for International Trade and Security decided to try to bring the resources of a major research university to bear. We developed an advanced research program to address the problem and to try to point policy-makers toward solutions.

We began by expanding our University of Georgia team and funding. We recruited experts like Igor Khripunov from Russia and Victor Zaborsky from Ukraine. We developed relationships with individuals and other programs like Graham Allison and Ashton Carter at Harvard University, Bill Potter and the Monterey Institute, and Sandy Spector, formerly at the Carnegie Endowment for International Peace and now director of arms control and nonproliferation at the U.S. Department of Energy. We engaged key officials and offices in the U.S. government responsible for dealing with the problem of weapons proliferation from the former Soviet Union. We traveled to Russia and the other newly independent states to meet with their governmental counterparts. We helped create indigenous programs and centers in Moscow, Kyiv, and Minsk and established a network of nonproliferation export control officials and experts in these countries. We put together a diversified program of collaborative research, workshops, and seminars, and organized a series of outreach programs and conferences designed to introduce government officials and enterprise managers to the threat of weapons proliferation and the need for responsible export control. We published a series of reports and papers on these issues and encouraged our counterparts in the FSU to do the same.

Perhaps the most important thing we did at the University of Georgia was to bring young scholars from the United States and abroad into our center and involve them in all aspects of this work. Because the threat of weapons proliferation is not only significant but *long-term*, we felt we needed to train *young and skilled analysts* who could devote much of their lives and careers to these issues. The contributors to this book fit this description and are part of the University of Georgia team. They are trained in the conduct of scientific research. They know the countries of the former Soviet Union well and have worked and conducted research on the ground in their countries of specialization.

These young scholars have immersed themselves in the details of nuclear and other weapons of mass destruction (WMD), nonproliferation, and trade and security issues. Most have been involved with a program of the Department of Energy (DOE) to spend time at Los Alamos National Laboratory, DOE, and other agencies of the U.S. government involved in nonproliferation export control. Some have spent time in the FSU working with such diverse organizations as the Kazakhstan Atomic Energy Agency, the Center for Export Controls in Moscow, and the Scientific and Technical Center in Kyiv. They have undertaken individual research and study in these countries and joined collaborative research and assistance projects that have expanded their experience and expertise in these issues. They have conducted personal interviews with key export control officials in all of the FSU countries represented in this volume.

The University of Georgia team has also worked to develop methodological tools that could make the study of these issues more objective and precise. The study of nonproliferation export controls has been traditionally "soft," with past work based upon considerable speculation. When describing the policy and administrative performance of states in the past, most resorted to observations and anecdotes. Country A's performance was weak because we had perhaps seen, or more likely heard, this or that, while country B's export controls were stronger because we thought we knew this or that. The University of Georgia team wanted to do better. Drawing upon their substantive expertise and scientific training, they developed a new methodology for evaluating nonproliferation export control development.

To help explain varying levels of export control development and performance in this book, the University of Georgia researchers utilize international relations and political science theory. This places their research findings in more rigorous structures of analysis and explanation, and moves their work to a higher level of interpretation and application. The research reported in the chapters that follow call attention to important differences in nonproliferation export control policy and practice in the FSU. More important, however, they help explain why these differences exist, and provide a better understanding of what is likely to happen, and what can be done to promote positive developments, in the future. The book, therefore, is not just an exercise in evaluating the development of nonproliferation export controls in the FSU, but also an attempt to contribute to a broader, ultimately global, explanation of the forces that drive such developments.

Accordingly, the research reported in this book is based upon the canons
of scientific inquiry. It draws upon the detailed knowledge of area studies.
In so doing, it recognizes the significance of contextual factors such as history, culture, politics, and economics. It recognizes the importance of con-
ceptual clarity and precision, the need for quantitative operationalization of
primary concepts and variables, the power of theoretical focus and explanation. It undertakes both detailed case studies and cross-national, comparative analysis.

Applying scholarly research to the threat of weapons proliferation is a
worthy enterprise. Although Senator Nunn's foreword to this book describes
the challenge clearly, I would like to take a few more paragraphs to outline
the problem further and the importance of scientific inquiry into these issues.

We can not ignore the fact that Russia and the new independent states of
the FSU remain the repositories of huge and destructive arsenals left from
the Cold War. These troubled and fragile states possess an extraordinary
amount of advanced weaponry and the capacity to produce much more. In
addition to the presence of existing weapons of mass destruction and materials, some have the personnel, know-how, industrial capacity, and economic incentives to produce more. Conversion to nonmilitary production,
unfortunately, is not succeeding. These and other realities present a critical
security challenge as we approach the twenty-first century. The proliferation threats from the territories of the FSU are real and require more attention and more effective responses. Scholarly research, such as that presented
in this book, can help.

Our research indicates that the growing economic crises in the new states
of the FSU heighten the threats of weapons proliferation week by week,
month by month, and year by year. Government officials work in political
environments where national export earnings are a necessity and where pro-
ducers are desperate to sell. Organized crime and corruption with international connections are rampant. Given the confusion associated with the
ongoing political transitions and moves toward privatization, it is increasingly difficult for government officials to control nuclear smuggling and
other forms of illicit weapons-related trade.

The research reported in this book also indicates that officials in Russia,
Ukraine, and the other new states are trying to address this challenge in in-
credibly difficult environments. There are limited budgetary resources to
put into defense conversion and nonproliferation policies and systems.
Agencies charged with export control responsibilities are severely underfinanced and understaffed. There is widespread corruption in business and
government, including customs and law enforcement agencies. The new
states lack nonproliferation cultures which might help restrain individuals

and enterprises from selling sensitive technology and items to countries and groups of concern. Some political leaders in the FSU often show little sensitivity to the national security threat of transferring strategic items to destinations and groups of concern.

Our research shows there are no comprehensive export control laws and enforcement systems in most of the new states of the FSU. Most customs and border controls are in poor condition. Given this and the economic environment, the export controllers are often a poor match for the pro-trade government, business interests, and criminals who want to sell or smuggle sensitive items, and who can benefit personally from the sometimes lucrative sales.

What can be done to restrain the spread of the Soviet arsenal? There are three major strategies for controlling the spread of weapons and associated materials, equipment, and technologies from the NIS: *physical protection*, *accounting and control*, and *export control*. *Physical protection* involves securing the weaponry and/or associated items in order to avoid illicit movement or use by unauthorized persons. *Accounting and control* involves keeping good records of all relevant weapons and associated items and assuring that they remain under authorized control. *Export controls* involve efforts to deny the illicit transfer or sale and to monitor and review the licensed sale of the controlled items. Because of privatization and other reasons outlined above, *export controls* are becoming of increasing importance. Unfortunately, the development and implementation of nonproliferation export controls are receiving far too little attention by both government officials and nongovernmental researchers.

The University of Georgia Center for International Trade and Security is committed to its long-term research, teaching, and outreach related to nonproliferation export controls. Many are assisting us. Numerous foundations have supported our work on proliferation challenges in the FSU, including (listed chronologically, earliest support first): W. Alton Jones Foundation, Ploughshares Fund, Carnegie Corporation, John Merck Fund, U.S. Institute of Peace, MacArthur Foundation, and the NATO Science Program. A grant from the National Council for Eurasian and East European Research allowed four of the contributors to this book to conduct field research in eight of the new states of the FSU.

We have also received considerable assistance from government officials who are responsible for nonproliferation export control programs in the United States and the new states in the FSU. In sharp contrast to the secrecy surrounding such policies and programs during the Cold War, officials were often willing to discuss details. Officials in the U.S. Departments of Commerce, Defense, Energy, and State were particularly helpful. The Department of Energy's International Nuclear Nonproliferation Graduate Program, administered by the Los Alamos National Laboratory, gave many of this book's contributors hands-on export control experience in Los Alamos, Washington, D.C., Moscow, and other cities and nuclear sites in the FSU.

There are also many to thank at the University of Georgia for supporting our efforts. Former Secretary of State and University of Georgia Professor Dean Rusk called our attention to the challenge of export controls in 1978 and provided inspiration for our early work. Martin Hillenbrand, former ambassador and assistant secretary of state, and the first Dean Rusk Professor of International Relations at the University of Georgia, contributed in many ways to our efforts over the past fifteen years. Richard Cupitt, Igor Khripunov, Jonathan Benjamin-Alvarado, Dmitriy Nikonov, and Victor Zaborsky of the Center for International Trade and Security contributed in critical ways to the research effort reported in this book. Colleagues in the political science department assisted us with a range of theoretical and methodological issues. Center researchers and staffers— such as Seema Gahlaut, Fangfang Gao, Linda Haygood, Lantian Ma, Jyotika Saksena, Anupam Srivastava, Milind Thakar, and Rong Yan—make our center an enjoyable and stimulating place to conduct our work.

Seeing this research project and book develop has been one of the highlights of my professional life.

ONE

EXPLAINING THE DEVELOPMENT OF NONPROLIFERATION EXPORT CONTROLS
Framework, Theory, and Method

SUZETTE R. GRILLOT

Since the demise of the Soviet Union and subsequent end of the Cold War, government and scholarly communities have paid increasing attention to the potential proliferation threat emanating from the former Soviet region.[1] Almost overnight, the massive military-industrial assets of the Soviet Union came under the jurisdiction of fifteen fledgling states instead of one established government. The question of who would inherit, safeguard, and control the stockpile of weapons of mass destruction (WMD) and the associated materials, equipment, technology, and expertise posed problems for the security relations of both the newly independent states (NIS) and the international community. Of special concern was how the fifteen successor states would control exports of military and dual-use items (goods, services, and technologies with both military and commercial applications) given both economic and political instability.

While only Russia, Belarus, Ukraine, and Kazakhstan inherited weapons of mass destruction from the Soviet Union, all but two of the fifteen states of the former Soviet Union can produce sensitive materials, technologies, equipment, or have requisite expertise related to weapons production. Moreover, all these states may serve as transit points for legal commerce and illegal smuggling of these items, and several border potentially undesirable end-user states.

All of the NIS did not, however, equally inherit the means by which to control and monitor these assets or the movement of sensitive materials and technologies.[2] Moreover, all of the NIS have difficulty controlling their borders. Consequently, sensitive items may find their way from or through these states to other regions of the world.[3] Developing effective export control systems (regulations, processes, and practices governing the transfer of

military or military-enabling dual-use items, technologies, or information)
for all the NIS, therefore, has become an important objective in the effort to
reduce the risk of proliferation of weapons of mass destruction.[4]

Given the perceived threat to international security these realities pose,
each former Soviet state pledged in some way to fight the problem of proliferation shortly after their independence.[5] Together, the NIS and key Western actors (namely the United States and a few West European countries)
have worked to tighten borders, provide for material protection, control,
and accounting, and establish effective systems of export control in the former Soviet region. Still, development of export control systems in these
countries varies considerably. Russia, for example, is developing a comparatively sophisticated export control system, while Uzbekistan has almost
no recognizable system. Others, such as Belarus, Kazakhstan, Latvia, and
Ukraine, have made substantial progress, but have yet to establish complete
systems of export control.

As borders within the NIS are very porous, weak export controls in any
single state threaten to undermine more successful efforts elsewhere. Given
that all NIS governments have expressed their commitment to control sensitive exports, why are there such great variations in policy development?
From another perspective, why would any of the NIS attempt to control any
export for which they could gain much needed hard currency? Similarly,
why would these countries feel obligated to add the administrative burden
of an export control system when their governments face severe financial
constraints and other pressing domestic challenges?

We find these questions to be puzzling for various reasons. First, nearly
all the NIS are dependent on exports for economic growth. Intuitively, one
could argue that a high level of export dependence would lead to a low priority being placed on export controls in general, and on subsequent progress
on export control development in particular. We have seen, however, all of
the NIS commit to such an endeavor and at least a few of these states making efforts to carry out their obligations. Second, the NIS that have experienced significant negative economic growth rates (Belarus 20 percent;
Ukraine 19 percent; and Russia 15 percent in 1996) are making significant
progress in developing systems of export control. This is counter-intuitive
because one would expect countries undergoing economic difficulties to
balk at any legal, institutional, or behavioral commitments that would hinder, rather than promote, economic activity (exports). This is especially true
in high value-added sectors of the economy typical of proliferation-related
WMD and dual-use technology.[6]

For many years, Western scholars have debated why states develop,
implement, and cooperate on systems of export control. Some have suggested that states cooperate on export controls through participation in multilateral fora because the United States compels them to do so, while others

have argued that security considerations or domestic political calculations motivate states to cooperate on these policies.[7] More recently, others have argued that a state's liberal identification affects export control cooperation.[8] Still others suggest that some mixture of these and other factors are most appropriate for understanding why states control sensitive exports.[9] Understanding how and why the variations in NIS export control systems emerged, therefore, should provide not only a basis for policy prescriptions to improve these systems, but also broader theoretical insights about international cooperation and NIS security and economic relationships.

This book examines the attempts of the fifteen Soviet successor states to develop and implement nonproliferation policies—specifically their export control policies. The study has two primary objectives: to explore why and to what extent these states have developed their export control systems; and to explain what drives export control behavior in these states. Ultimately, we seek to address the following questions: Are there determinable patterns in how and why these states have sought to control their exports, or are there divergent factors at work in these states that influence their export control behavior?

This introductory chapter is composed of three subsequent sections. We first review the various theoretical approaches that provide insight into why states develop systems of export control, and articulate the export control behavior that each approach would expect. We then present and discuss our method for analyzing export control development and outline our procedures for conducting our research. Finally, we offer concluding comments on the importance of establishing both a theoretical and a practical basis for analyzing the development of nonproliferation export controls.

WHY DO STATES DEVELOP SYSTEMS OF EXPORT CONTROL?

We find that at least four theoretical approaches (realism/neorealism, rational institutionalism, domestic political processes, and liberal identity) offer explanations as to why states would develop export control systems. Each of the perspectives differ in that they would lead us to expect observably different behavior. Our review of the four approaches is limited to how states would behave regarding export controls.

Realism/Neorealism

The realist/neorealist approach to international relations suggests that because of the lack of a central governing authority in world politics, whose role it is to execute and enforce rules, laws, and norms, states operate and interact in an international system characterized by anarchy.[10] In an anarchical system, therefore, states must rely on their own wits and abilities as they attempt to achieve national security and maintain survival. States are overwhelmingly motivated by their primary objective of guaranteeing their security through the pursuit of power. Acquiring military capability, then, is important for achieving this objective. Moreover, states are compelled to balance the power of other, potentially adversarial, states. To do so, they rely either on internal balancing measures by focusing on their own capabilities, or on external balancing by forming or joining military alliances.[11]

Because states operate in a "self-help" environment under anarchy, pursue power as a means for achieving security, and seek to balance against other powers, realists and neorealists suggest that states are necessarily concerned with the relative gains of both friends and foes. The anarchical nature of the international system, after all, breeds distrust. Security-minded states, in other words, are inherently wary of the actions of others as states may very well take advantage of each other in the daily struggle to survive. Because all states are striving to maintain their sovereignty, they find it difficult to be certain of other states' intentions. States must always anticipate the dangers of offensive actions and are, therefore, aware of and sensitive to the capabilities of others.[12]

According to the realist/neorealist perspective, we would expect states to have a more developed export control system if they are particularly concerned about external threats to their security and perceive export control development as a way to diminish those threats by limiting the diffusion of military-related items, technology, and know-how. We would also expect to see a greater commitment to export control development in those states that are seeking to balance the power of a particular state or group of states by controlling the flow of weapons, materials, and technology to them. States may, however, focus export control measures toward certain target states whom they wish to balance against, and away from allies who are participating in such balancing efforts. The realist/neorealist approach also leads us to expect that states concerned about the relative gain in other states'

TABLE 1

Realism/Neorealism: Expected Behavior

- Concern about external threats to security as a result of weapons, equipment, and technology proliferation;

- Desire to balance the power of others by controlling the export of military items, possibly steering controls toward particularly threatening states and away from friendly states;

- Interest in preventing gains in others states' military capabilities;

- Attempt to use export controls as a means for enhancing state security.

military capabilities would seek to stem the transfer of military relevant equipment and technology to others. Moreover, export control systems will be more developed in those states that see such behavior as a way to *enhance* their security in relation to others (see Table 1).

Rational Institutionalism

Contrary to the realist/neorealist notion that cooperation among states is limited, the rational institutional approach suggests that, even under anarchy, states can and do cooperate in the international system.[13] Rational institutionalist scholars have argued that together states create and maintain explicit patterns of behavior, from which emerge various rules and norms that constrain future policy choices.[14] These international institutions or regimes facilitate cooperation among nations for many reasons. They enlighten states as to the policy preferences of partners, thereby decreasing uncertainty in international interactions. Institutions reduce the transaction costs inherent in international relations as states may link issues from one area to another. Moreover, regimes provide opportunities for the use of side payments and enhance the credibility of state commitments.[15]

The rational institutional approach to international cooperation highlights how states rationally calculate the costs and benefits of cooperation based on their self-interests. Because state actors may better achieve their individual goals through collaborative action, states come together to solve common problems and maximize joint interests. Promises of future interaction based on reciprocity enhance state willingness to cooperate.[16] Furthermore, such interaction "spills over" into other issue areas, creating a wider array of opportunities for cooperation among nations. Ultimately, within the scope of international institutions, states are induced to develop more cooperative policies because their interests are tied to the interests of others;

TABLE 2

Rational Institutionalism: Expected Behavior

- Calculates costs and benefits that will be in favor of export control development;

- Acknowledges nonproliferation regime's rules and norms as constraints on behavior;

- Exhibits an interest in reducing transaction costs and uncertainty and in increasing future interaction and reciprocity;

- Receives material incentives in the form of direct and/or side payments.

---

international rules and norms limit their policy choices; the costs of defection and benefits of cooperation are increased; uncertainty is decreased; issues are linked; and material incentives in the form of side payments are used.[17]

From the rational institutional perspective we expect that states' systems of export control will be more developed when they perceive greater benefits and fewer costs (such as the benefit of access to markets and technology in the West versus the cost of developing and maintaining a bureaucracy) associated with export controls. We expect that states with more developed export control systems will emphasize the role the rules and norms of the nonproliferation regime played in constraining their policy choices.[18] We would also expect states to have more developed export control systems when they perceive that transaction costs and uncertainty in their future interactions with others may be reduced by joining, or adhering to, the international nonproliferation regime.[19] Moreover, we expect that states will have more developed systems of export control when they receive favorable material incentives in the form of side payments—even from one issue to another—to do so (see Table 2).

Concerning material inducements, we consider two types to be especially important. First, aid generally targeted toward nonproliferation policies, and specifically toward the development of nonproliferation export controls, should obviously affect state export control behavior.[20] Second, other types of aid (such as monies available via the U.S. Department of State's FREEDOM Support Act [FSA]) may be considered an inducement if it is *explicitly* linked to the development of nonproliferation policies, activities, or norms.[21]

Domestic Politics

Scholars have often found that various domestic political variables have a profound effect on foreign policy choices. To date, no single theory of domestic politics exists to explain state behavior, international cooperation, or (especially) export control policies. There are, however, at least four domestic political approaches that may enlighten and inform us as to the decision state leaders make and the policies they employ.[22] Below we review four domestic theories (pluralist, elitist, institutional, and bureaucratic theories), and elicit from each various expectations for state action regarding export control behavior in the NIS.[23]

Pluralist approaches to foreign policy suggest that domestic interest groups matter. Findings on the specific impact of interest groups have, however, been mixed. Some scholars argue that domestic pressure groups play a limited role in the construction of state policies, while others find that they significantly affect state behavior.[24] The pluralist approach centers on the competition and struggle between various groups with various interests,

each vying for influence over particular policy choices. In the realm of nuclear policy, for example, Etel Solingen explains state decisions to develop
and maintain nuclear weapons according to the relative strength or weakness of two broad interest groups—a "liberalizing coalition" and an "inward-looking coalition." The first group, which prefers less state
intervention in economic affairs and seeks economic opportunities outside
state boundaries, is less willing to support a state's nuclear status if it inhibits access to external markets. The second group, which supports the extension of state power into economic (and other) affairs and opposes state
openness beyond national borders, is more willing to herald nuclear weapon
status if such a stance enhances state independence and prevents the intru-
sion of external influences in state affairs.[25] These groups, therefore, struggle to influence state decisions. Ultimately, their pressure places constraints
on the choices and strategies of state decision-makers, and subsequently
shapes state behavior.[26]

Elite approaches to foreign policy focus on national decision-makers
themselves as the source of state behavior. According to this perspective, the
perceptions, beliefs, and interests of state leaders influence policy choices.
The approach emphasizes the goal-oriented behavior of elite decision-makers as they address both internal and external pressures in an effort to shape
policy in accordance with their preferences.[27] Their preferences are tied to
and define the "national interest," and rest on the belief of overall general
welfare.[28] Moreover, recent literature on "two-level games" and foreign policy choices suggests that elite decision-makers manipulate domestic constraints, including pressure groups. Where the pluralist approach
emphasizes the independent effect of societal groups, an elite approach emphasizes a leader's ability to construct coalitions among groups to serve her
needs, enhance her position, and enable her to select policies that are consistent with her preferences.[29]

An institutional approach to state behavior centers on the specific institutional characteristics of states and how they influence policies.[30]
According to this "domestic structures" approach, states "differ in the extent to which their states and societies are centralized, and in the range of
policy instruments available to state officials. . . . They also differ in the
degree of autonomy state officials enjoy relative to societal forces."[31] Based
on these differences, states can be placed along a continuum in which one
extreme is characterized as "weak" and the other as "strong." Weak and
strong states are differentiated as to the degree to which the state is centralized. Weak states, for example, are "decentralized and fragmented along
bureaucratic or institutional lines."[32] Due to the number of domestic constraints in weak states, policy-makers do not have the range of policy instruments available to them that policy-makers do in strong states. As a
result, decision-makers "find it difficult to act purposefully and coherently,

to realize their preferences in the face of significant opposition, and to manipulate or restructure their domestic environment."[33]

Finally, theories of bureaucratic politics highlight the effect that competition between governmental agencies and bureaucracies have on policy choices.[34] According to this approach, state behavior is the result of a tug-and-pull between government officials that represent various agency interests. Multiple governmental bodies engage in bargaining strategies to see that their institutions' interests are addressed in the policy process, thereby enhancing their relative position of power. Such intergovernmental struggles ultimately influence the array of policy options available to decisionmakers, as well as the policy selections.[35]

These various theories each highlight domestic political variables that have an effect on state foreign policy decisions. From these domestic perspectives, we may expect certain state behavior regarding export control policies in the NIS. We should see states have more developed systems of export control if domestic interest groups exist and seek to influence export control decisions. "Liberalizing coalitions," for example, may pressure the government to select policies that would allow greater access to international markets, while "inward-looking coalitions" would exert pressure to choose a course of action that enhances independence and prevents openness.[36] Moreover, we would expect the governments of the NIS to be responsive to such domestic pressure and act accordingly. We expect that states will have more developed systems of export control if the perceptions and beliefs of elite decision-makers suggest to them that the control of sensitive exports is consistent with their notion of the "national interest." From an institutional perspective, we expect "weaker," more decentralized and fragmented states may find it more difficult to commit to, develop, and coordinate export control activities. On the other hand, we expect that "stronger" states will have more developed export control systems. Finally, we expect

---

TABLE 3

Domestic Politics: Expected Behavior

- Interest groups pressure government to develop export control policies and procedures in line with international standards;

- Elite decision-makers perceive and believe export control policies to be in the "national interest";

- More centralized states will be better equipped to develop and coordinate export control activities;

- Agencies with export control functions are more powerful and influential than agencies with trade promotion functions.

---

that states with more influential export regulation agencies as actors (as opposed to the relative influence of agencies with competing functions, such as trade promotion) will have more developed systems of export control (see Table 3).

Liberal Identity

Finally, recent scholarship on state behavior suggests that states choose cooperative policies not because of some rational calculation of security threats, costs, or benefits, but because they "identify" with others in a community of states.[37] Borrowing from theories of social identity, some international relations scholars argue that states, like people, can and do come to share a common identification.[38] Just like individuals, states develop a group identity and a "sense of community" through interaction, communication, and "transaction flows."[39] Group identity enables individual actors to act collectively in solving common dilemmas. Moreover, group identity allows members of the group to behave toward one another in a cooperative manner. Partners in a community, in other words, operate based on "mutual obligation," loyalty, and trust.[40]

In 1957, Karl Deutsch and his colleagues offered one of the first significant pieces of research on community in the security arena to help understand, explain, and proscribe behavior for the elimination of violent conflict.[41] "Security communities," they suggest, differ in the degree of integration and institutionalization they exhibit—from fully integrated (amalgamation) to fully autonomous (pluralistic). Either way, members of a security community achieve a sense of common identity, and believe that they together can solve common problems in a peaceful manner.[42] Recently, scholars have employed this concept of security-community to explain the so-called "democratic peace."[43] They suggest that states do create communities based on a common identification, but more often than not it is liberal states that form such communities. Liberal democratic governments feel a common bond with other liberal democratic states based on similar normative and institutional foundations. The belief that domestic conflict should not be resolved with violence, for example, is extended to relations with other democratic states—for leaders in one state are more certain that their democratic partners also value nonviolent conflict resolution, and can, therefore, be more certain of their partners' potential actions.[44]

Because individuals, as do states, gain self-satisfaction and esteem from group membership, they also tend to discriminate based on their group identities.[45] Psychologically, the concepts of self and other are important to one's mental well-being. Further distinguishing between self and other only enhances that well-being. Group identity, being an extension of individual identity, predisposes one to specifically target members of your group (ingroup) with cooperative behavior, or members of another group (outgroup) with noncooperative behavior.[46] Members of a community of liberal states, therefore, may target illiberal states with more restrictive behavior than they would liberal states.

From the perspective of liberal identity, then, we can expect that states who interact regularly on export control matters may develop a "sense of community" and a common group identification. As members of the liberal community tend to preach the virtues of nonproliferation export controls, we expect that those states in the NIS who interact regularly with the liberal community will have more developed systems of export control. We expect that those in the NIS who are developing the normative and institutional bases of a liberal democratic government may see themselves as part of the liberal security community, and will, therefore, have more developed export control systems. Finally, we expect that the budding democracies of the NIS who are interested in focusing export controls on illiberal states will have more developed export control practices (see Table 4).

TABLE 4

Liberal Identity: Expected Behavior

- Acknowledges a "sense of community" in export control matters;

- Places importance on regular interaction with the liberal community, and its advocation of nonproliferation export controls;

- Develops the normative and institutional bases of a liberal, democratic government;

- Favors targeting the control of sensitive materials toward illiberal states.

RESEARCH PROCEDURE

To analyze and examine the expectations highlighted in the previous section, this study employs the comparative case study method. The case study method is most appropriate for this project as it is preferred when researchers: (1) ask "how" and "why" questions; (2) do not and cannot control the subjects and/or events being studied; and (3) focus on contemporary events in their natural context.[47] Moreover, case studies are useful when investigators attempt to illuminate particular decisions, processes, institutions, and events, why and how each of these operated and/or are made, and what resulted.[48] In this book, we offer seven case studies (Russia, Ukraine, Belarus, Kazakhstan, the Baltics, Transcaucasia, and Central Asia) through which we compare the behavioral expectations (outlined above) against the empirical record of their export control development. We then provide a cross-case comparison that suggests the strengths and weaknesses of each approach. Our objective is to determine which approach, if any, best explains the development of nonproliferation export control measures in each of the states of the NIS.

Important for case study analysis is the use of multiple sources of evidence. The individual investigators have gathered data from many open sources including published books and articles; official government documents and reports; and other primary news and information sources such as the *Foreign Broadcast Information Service Daily Reports*, which offer English translations of news reports and official documents for the entire former Soviet region. Data were, however, collected from Russian, Ukrainian, Belarusian, Kazakh, and other language sources. More importantly, the investigators independently conducted a number of personal interviews with officials, researchers, and other experts involved in and/or knowledgeable of NIS export control policy development, as well as with their key counterparts in the United States who have been integrally involved in promoting and assisting NIS export control activities.[49] The behavioral expectations served as a common guide for data collection and analysis.

Specifically concerning our measurement of export control development (our dependent variable), we analyzed and evaluated NIS export control measures using a general quantitative tool that we created based on Western nonproliferation export control "common standards" that have emerged over the past several decades.[50] Because individual states develop and implement national systems of export control, it is possible that states may inconsistently create and apply export control measures. Such inconsistencies or gaps in export control systems decrease the effectiveness of export control as an international nonproliferation tool. Multilateral action is, therefore, necessary.

For export controls to be a useful tool for preventing proliferation, states (especially regime member states) must interpret and implement controls with some degree of uniformity.[51] Accordingly, "common standards" for export control development and implementation, which emerged thoughout the Cold War era, serve as a basis for state export control systems. In particular, the earliest export control regime, the Coordinating Committee for Multilateral Export Controls (COCOM), began to establish in 1949 the rules, norms, and procedures that permit member states to manage their economic competition while focusing on the security threats posed by common enemies.[52] Through their participation in COCOM, states were encouraged to develop common lists of controlled commodities, as well as other national procedures that evolved into the "common standards" for national systems of export control. The standards provided COCOM members a guide for the creation of comprehensive and consistent national export control practices and allowed for the evaluation of national export control systems.[53] These "common standards," therefore, serve as a point of departure for our measurement of export control development.[54]

From various questionnaires that Western government officials have in the past used to describe levels of national export control development, particularly a COCOM questionnaire used to evaluate member and cooperating states, we elicited ten elements of an export control system.[55] The ten elements are distinct from one another, but mutually reinforce and complete an effective export control system (see Table 5).

TABLE 5

Elements of an Export Control System

- Licensing System
- Regime Adherence
- Training
- Customs Authority
- Penalties

- Control Lists
- Catch-All Clause
- Bureaucratic Process
- Import/Export Verification
- Information Gathering/Sharing

Each element consists of three subparts: (1) policy and/or legal foundation; (2) institutions and procedures; and (3) behavior (implementation). The first subpart concerns the existence of nonproliferation export control laws and decrees that provide a legal basis for the country's control of sensitive exports. The second subpart rests on the notion that policies may be effective only if institutions and procedures exist for implementing them. Do officials and/or bureaucracies, for example, exist that are responsible for export control development and implementation? The third subpart reflects the necessity for actual export control behavior. Are export control policies and procedures, in other words, actually in use?

With the ten elements of an export control system in mind, we devised a questionnaire for the measurement of export control development in a given country. The seventy-two-item questionnaire allowed us to calculate levels of export control development with the use of a rating scheme that ranges from no development (0) to some development (.5) to compliance with Western standards (1) (see Appendix 1 for the questionnaire, and Appendix 2 for evaluation criteria). Because some export control elements may be more significant in the effective operation of an export control system, we developed relative weightings that indicate the importance of certain elements. We created the weightings based on surveys of governmental officials, nongovernmental experts, and industry representatives. We asked the respondents to list the ten elements according to their importance using a scale from 1 (most important) to 10 (least important).[56]

To calculate the weights we averaged the rank scores for each element and subtracted that number from 10. The "Licensing System" element, for example, received the highest score (2.53), and the "Catch-All Provision" element received the lowest average score (8.8). The relative weights, therefore, calculated to be 7.47 and 1.2 respectively (see Appendix 1 for the remaining weights). To arrive at a total weighted score that represents a country's level of export control development based on common standards, we averaged the tallies for each element, multiplied the averages by the weights, then added the weighted scores for a total measurement that may then be compared to the "ideal" or "perfect" score,[57] as well as to the scores of other states.[58] Using our method for measuring export control development, we were then able to determine the level at which each state of the FSU complies with Western, common standards in export control (see Table 6).

TABLE 6

Development of NIS Nonproliferation Export Controls (Percentage Compliance)

Country	Export Control System Status in 1997
Russia	.83
Ukraine	.78
Belarus	.74
Latvia	.74
Estonia	.70
Lithuania	.65
Kazakhstan	.64
Armenia	.50
Kyrgyzstan	.36
Georgia	.30
Azerbaijan	.29
Uzbekistan	.17
Turkmenistan	.10
Tajikistan	.10

The remainder of the book examines these various levels of export control development in light of the theoretical approaches discussed earlier. Each chapter presents an in-depth examination of the behavioral expectations derived from the four approaches. Because Russia, Ukraine, Belarus, and Kazakhstan each inherited a significant portion of the Soviet weapons complex, they are treated individually in chapters 2 through 5. The Baltic, Transcaucasian, and Central Asian states are analyzed regionally in chapters 6 through 8. Finally, we conclude this collection of case studies with a cross-case comparison of FSU export control developments, an analysis of the four theoretical approaches, and a set of recommendations concerning future export control efforts.

SIGNIFICANCE

Nonproliferation export controls have played, and continue to play, an important role in the realm of international security. Because the new states of the former Soviet Union inherited vast stockpiles of weaponry as well as sensitive materials and technologies, but did not equally inherit the means for controlling such an inheritance, it is important to evaluate, examine, and explain nonproliferation export control behavior in the region. This book seeks to do just that. Through our analyses, we hope and expect to provide practical and theoretical insights regarding NIS export control behavior, specifically, and worldwide export control practices, generally. Our enhanced understanding of export control development should in turn enhance our ability to further control and prevent the proliferation of the world's most deadly weapons.

APPENDIX 1: ELEMENTS OF AN EXPORT CONTROL SYSTEM QUESTIONNAIRE

Below is a list of ten elements that contribute to an export control system. For each element there is a series of questions that generally elicit (a) policies; (b) institutions; and (c) behavior (in that order) concerning each element. Every starred (*) question that ends in a question mark (?) should be scored with either a 1, 0, or .5 (1 being a positive answer, 0 being a negative answer, and .5 being a negative or positive answer with a caveat) in the blank following the question. You should then average the scores for each element and multiply that average by the weight provided at the end of the questionnaire. Sum the weighted scores for each element for a total weighted export control system score. The perfect or ideal score is 41.82.

1. Licensing: exports
                                   reexports

    a. Are there export control laws or decrees and
       regulations that:
         * provide authority to license sensitive goods?   _____
         * provide authority to control reexports?   _____

    b. Are there standard licensing procedures for:
         * the control of sensitive exports?   _____
         * the control of reexports?   _____

    c. Are licensing procedures actively at work for:
         * the control of sensitive exports?   _____
         * the control of reexports?   _____

2. Lists

    a. Do laws, decrees, or regulations provide for
       the establishment of control lists?   _____

    b. Are there procedures and personnel responsible
       for control lists?   _____

    c. Are control lists created and maintained?   _____

3. International Regimes: member/
                                  adherence

    a. Does the country intend to become a member
       or adherent (in terms of policy) to the:
         * Australia Group?   _____
         * Nuclear Suppliers' Group?   _____
         * Missile Technology Control Regime?   _____
         * Wassenaar Arrangement?   _____

b. Does the country have a bureaucracy for
  participating in the:
    * Australia Group? _____
    * Nuclear Suppliers' Group? _____
    * Missile Technology Control Regime? _____
    * Wassenaar Arrangement? _____

c. Is the country a member or adherent to the:
    * Australia Group? _____
    * Nuclear Suppliers' Group? _____
    * Missile Technology Control Regime? _____
    * Wassenaar Arrangement? _____

4. Catch-all

a. Is there policy to provide a "catch-all" mechanism? _____

b. Are there procedures for the "catch-all" provision? _____

c. Are the procedures actively pursuing items
  that would fall under a "catch-all" provision? _____

5. Training: licensing officials
                      border guards
                      customs officials

a. Are there provisions for training the following
  in areas of export control:
    * licensing officials? _____
    * border guards? _____
    * customs officials? _____

b. Are there training procedures in place for:
    * licensing officials? _____
    * border guards? _____
    * customs officials? _____

c. Are the following actually trained in the
  areas of export control:
    * licensing officials? _____
    * border guards? _____
    * customs officials? _____

6. Bureaucratic process: agency review
                               agency cooperation

a. Are there policy provisions for:
    * interagency review of licenses? _____
    * interagency cooperation on licensing decisions? _____

b. Are there various agencies in place that:
   * review licenses?   _____
   * cooperate on decisions?   _____

c. Do various agencies actually:
   * review licenses?   _____
   * cooperate on decisions?   _____

7. Customs Authority: border control
                                       transit

a. Do laws, decrees, or regulations provide authority
   to control:
   * borders?   _____
   * transits?   _____

b. Is there a bureaucracy in place, and functioning
   equipment available, to control:
   * borders?   _____
   * transits?   _____

c. Are there actual checks being made:
   * at borders?   _____
   * of transits?   _____

8. Verification: Import Certificate/Delivery Verification
                                end-use/end-user
                                pre-license/post-license

a. Do laws, decrees, or regulations provide authority for:
   * Import Certificate/Delivery Verification?   _____
   * end-use/end-user checks?   _____
   * pre-license/post-license checks?   _____

b. Are there procedures for providing and checking:
   * Import Certificate/Delivery Verification?   _____
   * end-use/end-user?   _____
   * pre-license/post-license?   _____

c. Are the following being conducted:
   * Import Certificate/Delivery Verification?   _____
   * end-use/end-user checks?   _____
   * pre-license/post-license checks?   _____

9. Penalties: criminal
                                civil

a. Are there the following provisions for penalties
   for export violations:

    * criminal?   _____

    * civil?   _____

b. Are there agencies or people responsible for
   conducting investigations and making arrests in
   correspondence with the following penalties:
     * criminal?   _____
     * civil?   _____

c. Is there evidence of the following penalties
   being enforced with actual prosecution:
     * criminal?   _____
     * civil?   _____

10. Information: gathering—international/domestic
                          sharing—international/domestic

a. Are there provisions for the:
    * gathering of information on exporters and
      export violations (using international and/or
      domestic sources)?   _____
    * sharing of information on:
       * export control procedures (with
         international and/or domestic parties)?   _____
       * exporters (with international and/or
         domestic parties)?   _____
       * export violations (with international
         and/or domestic parties)?   _____

b. Is there a bureaucracy for:
    * gathering information on exporters and export
      violations?   _____
    * sharing information on:
       * export control procedures?   _____
       * exporters?   _____
       * export violations?   _____

c. Is information concerning export control procedures,
   exporters, and export violations actually:
    * gathered on exporters and export violations?   _____
    * shared on:
       * export control procedures?   _____
       * exporters?   _____
       * export violations?   _____

Overall Composite Score (Perfect Composite Score = 72)   _____

Overall Weighted Score

Elements	Avg. Score		Weight	Score
1. Licensing	_____	x	7.47	_____
2. Lists	_____	x	6.34	_____
3. Regimes	_____	x	3.20	_____
4. Catch-All	_____	x	1.20	_____
5. Training	_____	x	3.87	_____
6. Bureaucratic Process	_____	x	3.47	_____
7. Customs Authority	_____	x	6.60	_____
8. Verification	_____	x	3.67	_____
9. Penalties	_____	x	1.80	_____
10. Information	_____	x	4.20	_____

TOTAL (Perfect Weighted Score = 41.82)   _____

APPENDIX 2: EVALUATION CRITERIA

For our evaluation tool, we assigned scores of 0, .5, or 1 depending on the level of development of a specific aspect of the state's export control system. Based on these values, three levels of development are delineated. This helps to simplify matters to a point at which it is possible to create a quantitative evaluation of a state's export control system while also providing enough detail to not lose slight differences between the level of development of systems in different states. The following general criteria were used for assigning the scores to a given question.

Score of 0 (zero). A score of 0 was given when the answer to the question as judged by the expert was no. In other words, 0 would be the appropriate score when a clear-cut answer of no was possible. Below this is explained for each series of questions.

The first series of questions, "series a," involves policy issues. This means, does a policy exist for a given element? For licensing, this would be: "Are there export control laws or decrees and regulations that provide authority to. . ." Thus, for this series, if laws, decrees, or regulations do not exist, then a score of 0 is given. It is a basic have/have not dichotomy.

The second series of questions, or "series b," refers to the existence of institutions responsible for a given element. For licensing, this would be: "Are there standard licensing procedures for . . ." Again, it is a question of whether or not this element exists. If no procedures or institutions exist, then a score of 0 is given.

The third series of questions, "series c," takes this a step further to actual behavior. Not only is the question about the mere existence of a policy (series a) or institution or standard procedures for the implementation of a policy (series b), but also whether or not this policy is actually implemented as designed. For licensing, such a question would be: "Are licensing procedures actively at work for . . ." A score of 0 is given if there is no evidence that a particular element is being implemented.

Score of .5 (one-half). The score of .5 is the most difficult to explicate, but is also the most critical for the evaluator. We admit that on many of these issues, there is often less than a clear-cut and simple answer to a given question. Thus, we allow for an evaluator to score a question as a .5. An answer of .5 is given in general when the answer to a question is most appropriately "yes, but . . ." or "no, but . . ." In other words, some element may well exist on paper, but in reality it is handled in a different manner; or the opposite—something does not exist officially, but events generally are handled in such a way to point to a positive response. Further explanation is needed for the separate series of questions.

For the group of "series a" questions (policy issues), the answer of .5

would be appropriate when a general policy indeed does exist, but there is some caveat. For example, a question such as: "Are there provisions that allow for the gathering and sharing information on exporters?" can easily result in a score of .5. This would occur in a situation when there are provisions in existence, but there is some inhibiting factor that prevents the adequate operation of such provisions. Maybe the government has created a provision, but has not in any way delineated how it is to be carried out. On paper, the provision exists, but in reality, no sharing of information will be possible. If voicing an answer to such a question is likely to begin with "yes, but . . . " or "no, but . . . " a score of .5 is appropriate.

Scoring becomes somewhat clearer when moving on to the "series b" questions on institutions. A score of .5 may be given for these questions perhaps when a given institution does exist to implement a policy as stated in its regulations, but the organization may not be capable of such a task. For example, a score of .5 may be assigned for the question, "Does the country have a bureaucracy for participating in the NSG?" if a specific bureaucracy is appointed for participation, but within that bureaucracy there exists no capability to follow through. Perhaps there is no funding provided by the state to allow for participation or the responsible agency does not have the staff to represent the state in a given regime. In other words, while on paper an organization is assigned a certain responsibility, in reality it is not able to participate. The opposite may also be true in a case where there is no official policy statement, but an institution takes responsibility for participation in and monitoring of a particular regime. Yet another possibility deserving a .5 score would be a situation where there is no clear responsible institution, and rather, there are several organizations that see it as their responsibility to represent the state. All these decisions must be made by the evaluating expert.

For "series c" questions, a score of .5 becomes even more critical because oftentimes a policy exists and a responsible institution exists to implement the policy, but somewhere along the line the policy is never fully implemented. A score of .5 is given when the policy is only partially implemented. For instance, on the question, "Are end-use/end-user checks being conducted?" it is plausible that while they are being conducted in some instances, for many cases no checks are being made. For this scenario, a score of .5 accurately reflects a system that conducts end-use/end-user checks, but not as consistently as international standards would require.

Score of 1 (one). A score of 1 is given when the answer to the question as judged by the expert is yes. In other words, a score of 1 would be the appropriate score when a clear-cut answer of yes was possible. This is in all likelihood the clearest judgment for evaluators to make. They reward a 1 when the question can be answered that the existing component exists fully.

For example, if the country has developed control lists, then the answer to the question concerning the existence of such lists would be assigned a 1. This logic can be followed throughout.

NOTES

1. See, for example, Graham Allison et al., *Avoiding Nuclear Anarchy: Containing the Threat of Loose Russian Nuclear Weapons and Fissile Material* (Cambridge: MIT Press, 1996); Gary K. Bertsch, ed., *Restraining the Spread of the Soviet Arsenal: NIS Nonproliferation Export Controls 1996 Status Report* (Athens: University of Georgia, 1997); William Potter, "Before the Deluge: Assessing the Threat of Nuclear Leakage from the Post-Soviet States," *Arms Control Today* 25, 8 (October 1996), pp. 9–16; Zachary Davis and Jason Ellis, "Nuclear Proliferation: Problems in the States of the Former Soviet Union," *CRS Report for Congress* IB91129 (June 28, 1995); United States General Accounting Office, "Weapons of Mass Destruction: Reducing the Threat From the Former Soviet Union: An Update," GAO/NSIAD-95–165 (June 1995); United States General Accounting Office, "Nuclear Nonproliferation: U.S. Assistance to Improve Nuclear Material Controls in the Former Soviet Union," GAO/NSIAD/RCED-96–89 (March 1996); and U.S. Congress, Office of Technology Assessment, *Proliferation and the Former Soviet Union*, OTA-ISS-605 (Washington, D.C.: U.S. Government Printing Office, September 1994).

2. See Potter, *Nuclear Profiles of the Soviet Successor States* (Monterey, CA: Monterey Institute of International Studies, 1993).

3. Many cases have been reported. In Ukraine, for example, 100 kilograms of mercury was confiscated along with falsified documents from Armenia, Tajikistan, Moldova, and Russia. See "Attempt to Smuggle Radioactive Material Thwarted," *Radio Ukraine World Service*, 22 December 1993, *JPRS*-TND-93–003, 31 January 1994, p. 28. Reportedly, an Azerbaijani who made his way to Turkey via Armenia was detained in Istanbul as he attempted to sell 750 grams of enriched uranium. See "Azeri Detained in Turkey with Uranium for Sale," *Reuters*, 20 October 1994. For cases of smuggling throughout the former Soviet region, see Craig Whitney, "Germans Seize More Weapons Material," *New York Times*, 17 August 1994, pp. A1, A13; Julia Rubin, "Nuclear Nightmare: A Soviet Legacy," *Sunday Age*, 27 November 1994, p. 16; and the Statement of Potter Before the Permanent Subcommittee on Investigations, Committee on Government Affairs, United States Senate, 13 March 1996 (especially Appendix 1).

4. On the importance of export control as a long-term challenge requiring continuous development and modification to address the changing domestic and international environment, see Gary Bertsch and Igor Khripunov, *Restraining the Spread of the Soviet Arsenal: Export Controls as a Long-Term Nonproliferation Tool*, Center for International Trade and Security, University of Georgia, March 1996; and the Statement of Bertsch Before the Permanent Subcommittee on

Investigations, Committee on Government Affairs, United States Senate, March 13, 1996.

5. All former Soviet states have committed themselves to nuclear nonproliferation by signing the Nuclear Nonproliferation Treaty and have promised to control sensitive exports by signing some export control agreements such as the Minsk Accord, the *Atomredmetzoloto* agreement, or the Cooperative Threat Reduction (CTR) agreement. See Potter, *Nuclear Profiles*.

6. For the likelihood of business lost due to export controls, see Kathleen Bailey, "Nonproliferation Export Controls: Problems and Alternatives," in Kathleen Bailey and Robert Rudney, eds., *Proliferation and Export Controls* (New York: University Press of America, 1993), pp. 49–55. Bailey also argues that there are opportunity costs to developing export control systems, so that such development may come at the expense of other defense (or even nonproliferation) activities.

7. See Gunnar Adler-Karlsson, *Western Economic Warfare* (Stockholm: Alquist and Wiksell, 1968); Michael Mastanduno, *Economic Containment: CoCom and the Politics of East-West Trade* (Ithaca, NY: Cornell University Press, 1992), or Hendrik Roodbeen, *Trading the Jewel of Great Value: The Participation of the Netherlands, Belgium, Switzerland, and Austria in the Western Strategic Embargo versus the Socialist Countries* (Leiden, The Netherlands: Rijksuniversiteit, 1991).

8. See Richard Cupitt and Suzette Grillot, "COCOM is Dead, Long Live CO-COM: Persistence and Change in Multilateral Security Institutions," *British Journal of Political Science* 27 (July 1997), pp. 361–89.

9. See Bertsch et al., eds., *International Cooperation on Nonproliferation Export Controls: Prospects for the 1990s and Beyond* (Ann Arbor: University of Michigan Press, 1994); and Claus Hofhansel, *Commercial Competition and National Security: Comparing U.S. and German Export Control Policies* (Westport, CT: Praeger, 1996).

10. On the anarchical nature of the international system, see Kenneth Waltz, *Man, the State, and War: A Theoretical Analysis* (New York: Columbia University Press, 1959); Waltz, *Theory of International Politics* (Reading, MA: Addison-Wesley, 1979); Raymond Aron, *Peace and War: A Theory of Peace and War*, translated by Richard Howard and Annette Fox (Garden City, NY: Doubleday, 1966); and Stanley Hoffmann, *The State of War: Essays in Theory and Practice of International Politics* (New York: Praeger, 1965). For a complete explication of realism see Hans Morgenthau, *Politics Among Nations: The Struggle for Power and Peace*, 5th ed. (New York: Alfred A. Knopf, 1973); and Edward Carr, *The Twenty Years Crisis, 1919–1939* (New York: Harper Torchbooks, 1964).

11. See Waltz, *Theory of International Politics*, pp. 117–23; and Waltz, "The Emerging Structure of International Politics," *International Security* 18, 2 (Fall 1993), pp. 44–79. Stephen Walt argues that states not only balance the power of other states, but they balance specific threats. See Stephen M. Walt, *The Origins of Alliances* (Ithaca, NY: Cornell University Press, 1987); and Walt, "Alliance Formation and the Balance of Power, " *International Security* 9, 4 (Spring 1985), pp. 3–43.

12. See Joseph Greico, *Cooperation Among Nations: Europe, America, and Non-Tariff Barriers to Trade* (Ithaca, NY: Cornell University Press, 1990), p. 46; John Mearsheimer, "The False Promise of International Institutions," *International Security* 19, 3 (Winter 1994/95), pp. 7–11; and Robert Gilpin, "The Richness of the Tradition of Political Realism," in Robert Keohane, ed., *Neorealism and Its Critics* (New York: Columbia University Press, 1986), pp. 304–05.

13. Kenneth Oye, ed., *Cooperation Under Anarchy* (Princeton, NJ: Princeton University Press, 1986); Oye, "Explaining Cooperation Under Anarchy: Hypotheses and Strategies," *World Politics* 38 (1985), pp. 1–24; Robert Axelrod, "The Emergence of Cooperation Among Egoists," *American Political Science Review* 75 (June 1981), pp. 306–18; Axelrod, *The Evolution of Cooperation* (New York: Basic Books, 1984); and Robert Axelrod and Robert O. Keohane, "Achieving Cooperation Under Anarchy: Strategies and Institutions," *World Politics* 38 (October 1985), pp. 226–54.

14. International regimes are commonly defined as "set[s] of implicit or explicit principles, norms, rules, and decision-making procedures around which actors' expectations converge in a given area of international relations." See Stephen D. Krasner, ed., *International Regimes* (Ithaca, NY: Cornell University Press, 1983), p. 2.

15. Robert O. Keohane, "The Demand for International Regimes," *International Organization* 36 (Spring 1982), pp. 325–56; Keohane, *After Hegemony*; Krasner, ed., *International Regimes*; and Lisa L. Martin, "Institutions and Cooperation: Sanctions During the Falklands Island Conflict," *International Security* 16 (Spring 1992), pp. 143–78.

16. On the importance of future interaction and the "shadow of the future," see Axelrod, *The Evolution of Cooperation*; and Oye, ed., *Cooperation Under Anarchy*. On the importance of reciprocity see Robert Keohane, "Reciprocity in International Relations," *International Organization* 40 (Winter 1986), pp. 1–27. Keohane highlights two kinds of reciprocity—specific and diffuse. Specific reciprocity centers on expectations of exact returns for that which is given, and diffuse reciprocity focuses on an actor's willingness to give more and receive less from issue to issue. Nonetheless, both specific and diffuse reciprocity highlight the state's rational actions based on future returns.

17. Robert O. Keohane, *International Institutions and State Power* (Boulder, CO: Westview Press, 1989); Robert O. Keohane and Joseph Nye, Jr., *Power and Interdependence: World Politics in Transition*, 2nd ed. (Boston: Little, Brown, 1989); and Keohane and Nye, "*Power and Interdependence* Revisited," *International Organization* 41 (1987), pp. 723–53.

18. The international nonproliferation regime comprises various international arms control treaties (e.g., the Nuclear Nonproliferation Treaty [NPT], Biological Weapons Convention [BWC], and Chemical Weapons Convention [CWC]), and supplier organizations that control the proliferation of weapons of mass destruction and their component parts, material, equipment, and expertise (e.g., the Nuclear Suppli-

ers Group [NSG], Australia Group [AG], Missile Technology Control Regime [MTCR] and Wassenaar Arrangement).

19. Activities such as signing and ratifying the NPT and joining such institutions as the International Atomic Energy Agency (IAEA), Wassenaar Arrangement, AG, MTCR, NSG, BWC and CWC.

20. Aid from the United States for nonproliferation activities, for example, comes from the Cooperative Threat Reduction/Safe and Secure Dismantlement program (CTR), and/or the Nonproliferation Disarmament Fund (NDF).

21. Section 498A(a)(6) of the FREEDOM Support Act requires each state to "implement responsible security policies, including":

(A) adhering to arms control obligations derived from agreements signed by the former Soviet Union; (B) reducing military forces and expenditures to a level consistent with legitimate defense requirements; (C) not proliferating nuclear, biological, or chemical weapons, their delivery systems, or related technologies; and (D) restraining conventional weapons transfers.

22. It is not our intention in this project to determine the value (strength or weakness) of each domestic approach, but rather to establish whether domestic variables matter concerning state export control behavior.

23. This study examines only these four domestic political approaches. We acknowledge that these are not the only domestic politics approaches available for analysis, but appear to be the four that are more often employed in the study of foreign policy and international cooperation. See Helen Milner, "International Theories of Cooperation Among Nations: Strengths and Weaknesses," *World Politics* 44, 3 (April 1992), pp. 494–95.

24. See, respectively, Steven Miller, "Politics Over Promise: Domestic Impediments to Arms Control," in Charles Kegley, Jr., and Eugene Wittkopf, eds., *The Domestic Sources of American Foreign Policy: Insights and Evidence* (New York: St. Martin's Press, 1988), pp. 166–77; and Etel Solingen, "The Political Economy of Nuclear Restraint," *International Security* 19, 2 (Fall 1994), pp. 126–69.

25. Solingen, "The Political Economy of Nuclear Restraint."

26. See Peter Gourevitch, *Politics in Hard Times* (Ithaca, NY: Cornell University Press, 1987); Helen Milner, *Resisting Protectionism* (Princeton, NJ: Princeton University Press, 1988); David Truman, *The Governmental Process: Political Interests and Public Opinion* (New York: Knopf, 1951); and Robert Dahl, *Who Governs?* (New Haven, CT: Yale University Press, 1963).

27. Andrew Moravcsik, "Introduction: Integrating International and Domestic Theories of International Bargaining," in Peter B. Evans, Harold K. Jacobson, and Robert D. Putnam, eds., *Double-Edged Diplomacy: International Bargaining and Domestic Politics* (Berkeley: University of California Press, 1993), pp. 3–42; especially p. 30. The notion behind elite approaches to foreign policy are similar to Kenneth Waltz's concept of the "first image." See Waltz, *Man, the State, and War.*

28. Stephen D. Krasner, *Defending the National Interest: Raw Materials*

Investments and U.S. Foreign Policy (Princeton, NJ: Princeton University Press, 1978); and John Odell, *U.S. International Monetary Policy* (Princeton, NJ: Princeton University Press, 1982).

29. Moravcsik, "Introduction," p. 436.

30. See, in particular, G. John Ikenberry, David A. Lake, and Michael Mastanduno, eds., *The State in American Foreign Economic Policy* (Ithaca, NY: Cornell University Press, 1990); Peter J. Katzenstein, *Between Power and Plenty: Foreign Economic Policies of Advanced Industrialized States* (Madison: University of Wisconsin Press, 1978); Peter J. Katzenstein, *Small States in World Markets: Industrial Policy in Europe* (Ithaca, NY: Cornell University Press, 1985); and Hofhansel, *Commercial Competition and National Security*.

31. Ikenberry, et al., *The State in American Foreign Economic Policy*, pp. 10–11.

32. Ibid., p. 11.

33. Ibid.

34. See Graham Allison, *Essence of Decision* (Boston: Little, Brown, 1971); and Morton H. Halperin, *Bureaucratic Politics and Foreign Policy* (Washington, D.C.: The Brookings Institution, 1974).

35. Allison, *Essence of Decision*, pp. 162–77.

36. Arguably, in the area of export control development, both "liberalizing coalitions" and "inward-looking coalitions" may or may not pressure state actors to develop systems of export control. "Liberalizing coalitions" may perceive export controls as consistent with international nonproliferation standards that may place their state in favor and open access to new markets with new partners; or they may see export controls as an obstacle and constraint on trade and, therefore, will pressure government to forgo export control practices. "Inward-looking coalitions" may disregard the importance of export controls as trade with the world is not a priority; or they may support them in an attempt to control economic activity. Regardless, these are empirical questions with which our project is not concerned at this point. We are simply evaluating whether domestic pressure groups did indeed influence state officials to choose one export control strategy over another, and whether the officials did indeed respond.

37. For an excellent overview of this approach see Emanuel Adler and Michael Barnett, "Governing Anarchy: A Research Agenda for the Study of Security Communities," *Ethics and International Affairs* 10 (1996), pp. 63–98.

38. On theories of social identity, see Glynis M. Breakwell, ed., *Social Psychology of Identity and the Self Concept* (London: Surrey University Press, 1992).

39. For one of the earliest and most influential works on community among states, and the importance of transactions in the development of such communities, see Karl Deutsch, Sidney A. Burrell, Robert A. Kann, Maurice Lee, Jr., Martin Lichterman, Raymond E. Lindgren, Francis L. Loewenheim, and Richard W. Van Wagenen, *Political Community and the North Atlantic Area: International Organization in the Light of Historical Experience* (Princeton, NJ: Princeton University

Press, 1957). Also see Bruce Russett, *Power and Community in World Politics* (San Francisco: W.H. Freeman and Company, 1974); and Claudio Cioffi-Revilla, Richard L. Merritt, and Dina A. Zinnes, eds., *Communication and Interaction in Global Politics* (Beverly Hills, CA: Sage Publications, 1987).

40. Alexander Wendt, "Anarchy is What States Make of It: The Social Construction of Power Politics," *International Organization* 46 (1992), pp. 395–421; Wendt, "Collective Identity Formation and the International State," *American Political Science Review* 88 (1994), pp. 384–96. See also, Joseph S. Nye, Jr., *Peace in Parts: Integration and Conflict in Regional Organization* (Boston: Little, Brown, 1971), pp. 16–44.

41. Deutsch et al., *Political Community and the North Atlantic Area.*

42. Ibid., pp. 5–6.

43. See Bruce Russett, *Grasping the Democratic Peace: Principles for a Post-Cold War World* (Princeton, NJ: Princeton University Press, 1993); Michael Doyle, "Kant, Liberal Legacies, and Foreign Affairs," Parts I and II, *Philosophy and Public Affairs* 12, 3–4 (Summer/Fall 1983); and Doyle, "Liberalism and World Politics," *American Political Science Review* 80, 4 (December 1986), pp. 1151–70.

44. Ibid.

45. Jonathan Chase, "The Self and Collective Action: Dilemmatic Identities," in Breakwell, ed., *Social Psychology of Identity and the Self Concept*, pp. 101–27, especially p. 107.

46. H. Tajfel, "Social Identity and Intergroup Behavior," *Social Science Information* 14 (1974), pp. 101–18; and Tajfel, "Differentiation Between Social Groups: Studies in the Social Psychology of Intergroup Relations," *European Monographs in Social Psychology, No. 14* (London: Academic Press, 1978).

47. Robert Yin, *Case Study Research: Design and Methods* (Newbury Park, CA: Sage Publications, 1989), p. 4. For more on the case study method, see Harry Eckstein, "Case Study and Theory in Political Science," in Fred I. Greenstein and Nelson W. Polsby, eds., *Handbook of Political Science, Volume 7: Strategies of Inquiry* (Reading, MA: Addison-Wesley, 1975), pp. 79–137; and Alexander L. George, "Case Studies and Theory Development: The Method of Structured, Focused Comparison," in Paul Gordon Lauren, ed., *Diplomacy: New Approaches in History, Theory, and Policy* (New York: The Free Press, 1979), pp. 43–68.

48. Joe R. Feagin, Anthony M. Orum, and Gideon Sjoberg, eds., *A Case for the Case Study* (Chapel Hill: University of North Carolina Press, 1991).

49. Interviews were conducted primarily with NIS representatives from the Ministries of Foreign Economic Relations, Foreign Affairs and Defense. In the United States, interviewees were situated primarily in the U.S. Departments of Commerce, Customs, Defense, Energy, and State. All interviewees were promised anonymity in that their comments would not be attributed to their names and titles in our written report.

50. For a complete and detailed description of this measurement tool for export control development, see Cassady Craft and Suzette Grillot with Liam

Anderson, Michael Beck, Chris Behan, Scott Jones, and Keith Wolfe, "Tools and Methods for Measuring and Comparing Nonproliferation Export Control Development," Occasional Paper of the Center for International Trade and Security (Athens: University of Georgia Press, 1996); and Grillot and Craft, "How and Why We Evaluate Systems of Export Control," *The Monitor: Nonproliferation, Demilitarization and Arms Control* 2, 4 (Fall 1996).

51. On the importance of transparent compliance among regime members, see Oran Young, *International Cooperation: Building Regimes for Natural Resources and the Environment* (Ithaca, NY: Cornell University Press, 1989); Karl Deutsch, "Power and Communication in International Society," in Anthony de Reuck and Julie Knight, eds., *Conflict in Society* (Boston: Little, Brown, 1966); and Arthur Stein, "Governments, Economic Interdependence, and International Cooperation," in Philip E. Tetlock et al., eds., *Behavior, Society, and International Conflict* (New York: Oxford University Press, 1993).

52. COCOM was created in 1949 to control the transfer of military-related materials, equipment, technology, and know-how to the Soviet Union, its allies and (later) China. Original COCOM members included Belgium, Canada, Denmark, France, Italy, Luxembourg, the Netherlands, Norway, the United Kingdom, the United States, and West Germany. Portugal joined in 1951, Japan in 1952, Greece and Turkey in 1953, Spain in 1985, and Australia in 1989. In 1995, COCOM members disbanded the informal organization and replaced it with the Wassenaar Arrangement on Export Controls for Conventional Arms and Dual-Use Goods and Technologies, which continues to control sensitive, militarily relevant exports to questionable end-users. "Common standards" for export control practices were also enhanced by the Nuclear Nonproliferation Treaty (NPT) in 1968, the Nuclear Suppliers' Group (NSG) in 1976, the Biological and Toxin Weapons Convention (BWC) in 1972, the Australia Group (AG) in 1985, the Missile Technology Control Regime (MTCR) in 1987, and the Chemical Weapons Convention (CWC) in 1993. Each of these treaties and arrangements contributes to the overall nonproliferation regime, which seeks to prevent the spread of nuclear, chemical, and biological weapons, technologies, material, and equipment, as well as their means for delivery. For a discussion of these arrangements, see Leonard S. Spector and Virginia Foran, "Preventing Weapons Proliferation: Should the Regimes be Combined?" A Report of the Thirty-Third Strategy for Peace, U.S. Foreign Policy Conference, October 22–24, 1992.

53. The "common standards" approach was also employed to assess and evaluate "third countries" who were seeking to cooperate with COCOM controls. On COCOM's "third country initiative" program, see Panel on the Future and Design and Implementation of U.S. National Security Export Controls, Committee on Sciences, Engineering and Public Policy, *Finding Common Ground: U.S. Export Controls in a Changed Global Environment* (Washington, D.C.: National Academy Press, 1991), p. 123; and Bertsch, Cupitt, and Elliott-Gower, *International Cooperation on Nonproliferation Export Controls*, pp. 34–39, 50.

54. The nonproliferation regime's common standards serve as a reasonable model of internationally accepted export control practices, policies, and procedures. We do not suggest, however, that such a model is a perfect example of export control practices, nor that it is without flaws. Nonetheless, the multilaterally accepted export control procedures that COCOM and the other regimes established have been and continue to be well accepted and can, therefore, serve as a basis for evaluation and comparison.

55. For a description of the COCOM and other export control evaluation questionnaires, see Richard T. Cupitt and Yuzo Murayama, "Nonproliferation and Export Controls: Malaysia, Singapore, and Taiwan," paper presented at the annual meeting of the International Studies Association, San Diego, April 1996; and Richard T. Cupitt, "The Emergence of Security Regimes: Export Controls in East Asia," *The Journal of East Asia Affairs* 11, 2 (Summer/Fall 1997), pp. 452–80.

56. For a different weighting method that focuses on control list items, see "Some Details on the Proposed Method for List Construction and Review," Appendix J of *Finding Common Ground: U.S. Export Controls in a Changed Global Environment.*

57. The "perfect" weighted score of 41.82 represents 100 percent compliance with Western common standards. This score does not suggest, however, that the system itself is "perfect" or that such a system would allow zero proliferation. A perfect score suggests simply that a country's export control system consists of Western-style export control policies, institutions, and procedures that are in place and in practice. The score does not reflect, in other words, an individual level of export control *effectiveness*—only an individual level of development.

58. For details concerning the various avenues of comparison, which are not employed in this study, see Craft et al., "Tools and Methods"; and Grillot and Craft, "How and Why We Evaluate Systems of Export Control."

TWO

RUSSIA'S RATIONALE FOR DEVELOPING EXPORT CONTROLS

MICHAEL BECK

As the Soviet Union gave way to a disordered Russia, the most militarized of the former Soviet republics, Western policy makers fretted over the impending proliferation threat. Questions surrounded the ability of Russia to control and safeguard its vast stockpiles of weapons of mass destruction, related technologies, and sensitive design information possessed by weapons scientists and engineers. The multiple layers of the Soviet security system designed to protect military secrets, technologies, and information was abandoned and many in the West feared that Russian exporters of high-technology and military-enabling items would sell anything in an attempt to earn desperately needed funds and capitalize on Russia's domestic turmoil. Personnel in Russia's military-industrial complex faced low wages or even went unpaid, thereby adding to the proliferation concern.[1] At the same time, privatization in Russia resulted in the appearance of enterprises and joint ventures with increasing autonomy, anxious to find partners in the West for Russia's weaponry and high technology. While the proliferation threat from Russia has not been eradicated, and in many ways is more pressing in 1998 than in 1992, important steps have been taken by the Russian government to establish a system for controlling the transfer of sensitive exports.[2]

EXPORT CONTROL DEVELOPMENTS

Russia has developed a relatively sophisticated export control system in comparison to the other states of the former Soviet Union. Although Russia did inherit much of the Soviet export control bureaucracy, the Soviet experience was not capable of coping with Russia's privatizing economy which provided exporters with increased autonomy including the opportunity to negotiate and sign contracts with foreign companies. In 1992, Russia's export control system was only 40 percent compatible with the ideal type outlined in our methodology section. However, since 1992, Russia has made significant strides toward enhancing its system to meet the challenges of a market economy and increased international high technology trade. By 1997, the Russian system was 83 percent compatible with the ideal export control system.

The legal basis of Russia's export control system hinges upon a series of presidential directives that are then approved by governmental decree. From 1992 to 1997, Russia developed control lists for missile, biological, chemical, nuclear, and dual-use related items and issued regulations governing the export of these items.[3] These regulations outline the procedures required of enterprises seeking a license to export controlled commodities and technologies. Specifically, exporters are required to obtain the approval of *Exportkontrol*, Russia's interagency export control commission, whose working arm is the Federal Service for Currency and Export Control. The Federal Service for Currency and Export Control takes into account the end-user or recipient of the exported item and the declared end-use of the export. The importing country is also usually required to provide a certificate or pledge with assurances that the item being imported will be used for civilian purposes and will not be reexported without permission of the Russian Federation Government. If the license application is approved by the Federal Service for Currency and Export Control after a review of documents and occasionally upon consultation with other relevant ministries, the Ministry of Foreign Economic Relations issues a license. If exporters of controlled technologies or articles are under the jurisdiction of a government ministry or agency such as the Ministry of Atomic Energy (MINATOM) or the Russian Space Agency, they are often subject to additional requirements. For example, the Ministry of Atomic Energy has issued guidelines which require each of its enterprises to appoint an administrator with responsibility for ensuring that the enterprise is in compliance with national export control regulations. If an enterprise under the jurisdiction of a state body wishes to enter negotiations with a foreign entity on the sale of controlled commodities, a consultation frequently is required with officials at the relevant government agency. This measure was established ostensibly to prevent enterprises from investing time in pursuit of contracts that would not be sanctioned by the government.[4]

Russia's lists of controlled technologies and weaponry correspond to those advocated by the multilateral export control arrangements which include the Nuclear Suppliers Group (NSG), the Missile Technology Control Regime (MTCR), the Wassenaar Arrangement, and the Australia Group. Russia inherited the Soviet Union's status as a member of the NSG, and its representatives have been active within the arrangement since Russia's independence. In 1993, following the settlement of a conflict with the United States over a contract to transfer missile technology to India, Russia signed a memorandum of understanding that stated its intention to comply with MTCR guidelines. In 1995, Russia was accepted as a member of the MTCR. Russia's pledge to curtail arms transfers to Iran also paved the way for Russia's admission into the Wassenaar Arrangement.[5] Prior to this, Russia participated in the COCOM Cooperation Forum, a multilateral arrangement that was established to aid the states of the former Soviet Union in formulating export control policies in the wake of the Cold War. Although Russia is not a member of the Australia Group, it is an adherent to the guidelines of the arrangement following the issuance of decrees in 1992 regulating exports that can be used for developing chemical and biological weapons.

While the Federal Service for Currency and Export Control (previously the Department of Export Control at the Ministry of Economics) is the agency with principal responsibility for review of license applications and maintenance of control lists, and the Ministry of Foreign Economic Relations issues licenses, other agencies on Russia's export control commission also have important roles. The Ministry of Foreign Affairs takes the lead in articulating Russia's interests at multilateral fora and coordinates bilateral negotiations on export control issues. For example, it has taken some steps to coordinate export control efforts within the Commonwealth of Independent States (CIS), albeit with few resources. These efforts prompted two meetings of export control officials from states of the CIS and led to the signing of a CIS agreement to coordinate export control policy.[6] The Ministry of Foreign Affairs has also overseen numerous bilateral seminars and exchanges with Western governments, especially the United States, in order to learn more about foreign export control practices and procedures.[7] The Ministry of Atomic Energy also has a separate export control council within its division of international relations, which considers whether contracts with foreign entities can be pursued and which also reviews license applications of nuclear-related exports. The Ministry of Defense takes an interest in export control because of its concern for preventing sales of technology or weapons systems that might threaten Russian troops and because of its interest in promoting technical cooperation and commercialization of dual-use technologies.[8] Other agencies that are less active on the commission, but that nevertheless maintain export control functions, include the Federal Security Service, the Foreign Intelligence Agency, and the State Customs Committee. The commission meets approximately twice a year with other contacts taking place on an informal basis.

From 1992 to 1996, Russia also took numerous other steps to implement a system of nonproliferation controls. Customs and licensing officials received training by the United States and other Western governments.[9]

Customs laboratories were opened in locations around Russia for analyzing seized materials. Equipment was installed at various customs posts for detecting illicit transfers of radioactive materials.[10] An amendment was added to Russia's Criminal Code which renders export of materials or equipment that can be used to make weapons of mass destruction punishable by three to twelve years imprisonment.[11] In 1994, the government established procedures for issuing import certificates and conducting end-user checks, both of which are elements of an effective nonproliferation verification system.[12] Finally, conferences have been organized to inform industrialists about export control procedures and regulations.[13]

Despite Russia's progress, there are several challenges that must be addressed in order for Russia to further enhance its export control system. First, government agencies tasked to control strategic exports are both underfinanced and understaffed. For example, the Federal Service for Currency and Export Control has only a small cadre of about twenty-five employees to review licenses and has difficulty retaining them because of low salaries that cannot compete with jobs in the private sector. The Ministry of Foreign Affairs often finds it difficult to send the desired representation to international conferences because of budget limitations.[14] Furthermore, the Russian Federal Border Service was allotted less than half of what it requested for 1996 and remains ill-equipped to thwart smuggling operations.[15] Overall, Russia's agencies involved in export control have only a small fraction of the staff that their Western counterparts possess.

Organized crime and government corruption render attempts to control sensitive exports from Russia especially difficult. Agencies charged with enforcing controls, the Interior Ministry and the State Customs Committee, are reported to be among the most corrupt.[16] The Russian General Prosecutor's Office recorded over 1,700 violations by customs officials in 1994, which led to 138 criminal cases brought against officers charged with accepting bribes and misusing their offices.[17] Officials charged with licensing exports and personnel responsible for guarding borders face the temptation of lucrative bribes offered by exporters and importers wanting to circumvent the system and avoid duties. According to estimates by Russia's Customs Committee, about 30 percent of all exports bypass customs.[18] As state enterprises of the military-industrial complex privatize or form side ventures to promote export, the risk of such activity increases. Russia has not effectively coped with such illegal activity either. There is no evidence that violators of export control have been identified and punished.[19] Russia also lacks trained personnel within its embassies to carry out inspections to ensure that technologies originating in Russia are being used for declared civilian purposes.[20] The enforcement of export control regulations in Russia will likely suffer until the general political and economic environment stabilizes.[21]

WHY EXPORT CONTROL DEVELOPMENT?

In spite of the significant challenges that remain, Russia's progress toward developing an advanced export control system is surprising given many factors that would lead us to expect Russia to balk at the need for controls over strategic exports. First, enterprise directors of Russia's expansive military-industrial complex lobbied for relaxing all barriers that inhibit trade, especially export controls. After the Soviet breakup, Russia was left with 1,200 purely military enterprises at which 4 million people worked.[22] The failure of defense conversion meant that exports of military and military-related items were the only way to earn hard currency given drastic reductions in defense expenditures. Not surprisingly, many Russian industrialists and policy-makers ardently oppose cooperation with multilateral export control regimes because they hamper trade to Soviet-era markets. In fact, some of Russia's former trade allies, including Iran, Iraq, North Korea, India, and Libya, are states now targeted by the Western export control arrangements with which Russia has joined forces. Russian officials have also noted the growing share of the U.S. arms market and argued that export control is an attempt to deny Russia legitimate market share while "capitalizing on a Cold War victory."[23] Finally, Communists and nationalists in Russia's parliament have opposed cooperation with the West in the area of export control because some Western states, namely the United States, maintained controls on the transfer of certain dual-use technologies to Russia.[24] Members of Yeltsin's foreign policy team were especially irritated by continued COCOM controls on trade to Russia and the appearance of Russia on various "blacklists."[25]

These countervailing forces coupled with Russia's political and economic turmoil from 1992 to 1996 raise questions as to why and how Russia was able to develop a relatively advanced export control system and cooperate with international export control institutions. In order to explain and analyze export development in Russia and Russia's cooperation in multilateral export control arrangements, the rest of this chapter examines behavioral expectations derived from the realist, domestic political, liberal identity and rational institutionalist approaches. These approaches (outlined in the book's introduction) provide us with plausible explanations for Russia's development of export controls. First, I examine the realist/neorealist school and demonstrate its shortcomings for explaining Russia's export control development because the threats to Russia's security would not motivate export control development.[26] Next, theories of domestic politics are explored to demonstrate the impact that bureaucratic politics and competing domestic interests have had on shaping policy. I then show that liberal identity theory, which directs attention to Russia's democratization and economic reform, is sufficient for explaining Russia's cooperation and export control development in the "honeymoon" period of the early 1990s, but not so for explaining continued export control development after 1993, following Russia's shift away from a pro-Western orientation toward a more independent and assertive foreign policy. Finally, I turn to rational institutionalism, which I contend best explains Russian export control development because access to markets and other side payments played a principal role in motivating the development of export control in Russia. Here I draw special attention to the decision of Russia to renege on its decision to sell rocket technology to India, which represented an important turning point in Russia's export control system and its cooperation with international export control arrangements.

REALISM CHALLENGED

During the Soviet era, security interests, understood as military security, took primacy over economic and other interests. The Soviet Union sought to control proliferation because it threatened to undermine the bipolar order of the Cold War period, which they deemed preferable to a multipolar world with many unaligned nuclear powers. Despite conflictual relations on many fronts, both the Soviet Union and the United States found cooperation in nonproliferation possible because of this mutual security interest in maintaining the nuclear status quo and preventing the emergence of new nuclear states.[27] However, with the passing of the Soviet empire, Russia emerged as a state without well-defined security interests and without specific security threats that might motivate comprehensive nonproliferation efforts.[28]

Realism suggests that states with security threats will develop export control as a way to counter that threat. However, few in Russia have identified external security threats that would motivate the development of export controls. According to Russia's military doctrine, Russia has "no enemies."[29] This view was especially prevalent in the early 1990s among foreign policy elites. Even President Yeltsin, on Soviet Army Day in the spring of 1993, said, "We do not consider any country or coalition of countries, either in the West or in the East, to be an enemy."[30] Such a position is difficult for realism to address because it presumes that states find themselves in a self-help environment, in other words without reliable security, and therefore ever attentive to threats from others and the need to counter such threats. Nonetheless, for Russia, internal security issues, such as ethnic conflicts within its borders and on its periphery, are a much higher priority.[31] In fact, Russia's national security doctrine points primarily to internal threats to Russia's security, and realism would suggest that such states would be likely to have a less developed export control system, since such measures would not be a tool for addressing domestic conflicts or instability.[32]

While the expansion of NATO has emerged as a principal concern for many in Russia, it is not an external threat that would prompt the development of export controls as a means of preventing military or proliferation-related items from reaching these states because the membership of NATO is generally consistent with that of the multilateral supply-side nonproliferation arrangements (MTCR, Wassenaar, NSG). Moreover, NATO members are already equipped with the most advanced weapons and possess weapons of mass destruction. Furthermore, while Russia objects to the stationing of nuclear weapons, troops, and other arms on the territories of new NATO members, export control measures are not a tool for addressing the problem.

One might contend that the security concern motivating the development of export control is Russia's southern periphery, namely Iran. This argument finds some support. According to one of Russia's leading export control officials, "The majority of the existing and potential conflicts are located in close proximity to Russian borders."[33] A former official from the Ministry of Foreign Affairs argued that "Russia has inherited from the Cold War perhaps the worst periphery."[34] On the other hand, Russian officials argue against attempts to target states as "rogue" regimes and rarely identify any state that presents a proliferation threat to its territory.[35] Thus, the Russian system is not one which is steered toward any states considered threatening. A 1993 report produced by Russia's Foreign Intelligence Agency, which assesses proliferation developments in countries around the globe, fails to cite any country as a proliferation threat to Russia. According to most officials dealing with security issues in Russia, it is the job of the United Nations to identify proliferation threats and attempts to target states outside of this forum, especially by the United States, are unwarranted.[36] In fact, many Russian officials argue that nonproliferation efforts are best supported by consultation rather than isolation of countries of proliferation concern.[37] It appears that this approach is favored by Russia as it allows it to declare that it is meeting its international obligations while leaving the door open for ensuring maximum flexibility in the pursuit of its trade interests.

Russia's behavior in the area of strategic exports also suggests that there is little concern for sensitive transfers to states that are deemed proliferants by the West. It has signed agreements to complete the Bushehr nuclear power plant in Iran, and it had plans to transfer cryogenic rockets to India until the United States intervened and swayed Russia with threats of sanctions and promises of cooperation in space research.[38] Russia has also sold advanced conventional arms to Iran, including the Mig-29 Fulcrum, the T-72 battle tanks, and Kilo diesel-electric submarines.[39] Russian plans to sell several billion dollars worth of new arms in coming years appeared to contradict pledges made by Yeltsin at a 1994 summit with President Clinton to curtail future arms sales to Iran. It was this concession that paved the way for Russia's admission into the Wassenaar Arrangement, which was set up to control arms transfers to "rogue states" and unstable regions.[40] Russia has also sought to expand arms sales to China and India. One might contend that Russia's position and other sales, which raise eyebrows in the West, do not reflect an entire lack of proliferation concern by Russia; rather, they simply reflect the preference to favor short-term economic gains over the more distant threat of an emergent proliferant in the region. Nonetheless, such a position does not adhere to expectations derived from realism, which would lead one to expect military-security concerns to be a higher priority motivating Russian nonproliferation efforts and export control development.

OPENING THE BLACK BOX: COLLIDING BUREAUCRATIC INTERESTS

The lack of a consensus on Russia's role in the wake of the Cold War has been evident on numerous policy fronts in Russia, including in the nonproliferation and export control realms. Russia's export control system, like systems in other states, is prone to interagency conflicts. These conflicts have pitted elites and agencies with competing notions of Russia's national interests against one another. Here we will address why and how these conflicts have resulted in significant progress in export control development.

Although competing actors do vie for influence in Russia, those groups that shape export control policy and development lie almost exclusively within the state realm. We cannot yet speak of independent interest groups in Russia outside of government that are synonymous with a Western understanding of interest groups. Therefore, a pluralist approach to examining policy is not appropriate. In Russia, most exporters of controlled technologies and items maintain some link to the state. For example, the enterprises of the nuclear complex fall within the jurisdiction of the Ministry of Atomic Energy, and most enterprises involved in missile and space activity are governed by the Russian Space Agency. However, like their Western counterparts, most Russian exporters favor more lax controls and largely see export control as an obstacle to trade.

The reasons that individual enterprises have not more actively inhibited the development of export controls and lobbied for a lax system are manifold. First, directors of individual enterprises often have competing interests concerning Russia's foreign economic policy orientation. Those who rely on Western contracts are more likely to support cooperation with the West in nonproliferation efforts. For example, Energomash, a Russian producer of jet engines, has developed a system to monitor exports of sensitive technologies within the enterprise in part because of encouragement from its Western partner Pratt & Whitney.[41] On the other hand, those enterprises that have not successfully landed contracts in Western markets or that have potential partners with Western-tagged "Pariah" states are most likely to oppose export controls or other efforts to sanction such states.

A second reason that enterprises do not effectively block export control is that the bureaucracies that oversee sectoral interests and represent them (e.g., MINATOM, the Russian Space Agency, Ministry of Defense Enterprises) have not prioritized export control. Although these agencies are represented on the interagency Export Control Commission, which sets policy, their participation is minimal. However, like the enterprises that fall under them, those government agencies who favor integration with Western economic institutions or who have benefited from cooperation with the West are prone to favor cooperation with the West in export control and compliance with multilateral export control arrangements. On the other hand, agencies representing interests that have failed to garner much Western assistance or contracts in the West are apt to oppose cooperation. For example, the Russian Space Agency, whose enterprises have had relative success in landing contracts with the West to launch commercial satellites, favors cooperation with the West in export control.[42] Many of the institutes affiliated with space research and development believed that Russia's observance of Missile Technology Control Regime principles and norms would enhance their opportunities to cooperate with the West in space technologies and attract investment from the West for Russia's space technology sector.[43] The Russian Space Agency has even worked with a Moscow-based NGO to establish guidelines that are designed to ensure that its enterprises comply with national legislation governing exports of controlled missile technology.[44] The Ministry of Defense Industries, whose enterprises have struggled to compete with their more market-savvy counterparts in the West for arms markets, have largely opposed export control, which they see as inhibiting access to markets, especially to states such as Iran and India. Not surprisingly, the Ministry of Defense Industries lobbied against Russia's participation in the Wassenaar Arrangement on the grounds that the costs of membership in terms of lost markets outweighed any promised benefits of cooperation with the West.[45] With the growing need of Russian enterprises to boost exports of technology and arms, a stronger lobby seeking to limit the scope of export control is likely to emerge.

The lack of serious attention to export control by these agencies, which represent sectors of the defense establishment, has left export control policy to proponents of export control, namely to the Ministry of Foreign Affairs and the Federal Service for Currency and Export Control. These and other agencies that are responsible for regulating the export of military-related items, see export control as vital for obtaining resources and also favor export control on the grounds that it promotes the "national interest" by integrating Russia into Western economic and security institutions and by providing Russia access to high-technology imports from the West. Both of these agencies have been instrumental in promoting export control development.[46] Because the Federal Service for Currency and Export Control and the Ministry of Foreign Affairs have a virtual monopoly on information surrounding the work of international nonproliferation regimes and a greater stake in export control (for other agencies, export control is a secondary function), they have effectively lobbied for the development and implementation of export control regulations. These agencies' position is also strengthened because many Western states, especially the United States, have elevated nonproliferation on their foreign policy agendas and stressed its importance for positive bilateral relations. Nonproliferation issues, including export control matters, were frequently raised within the Gore-Chernomyrdin Commission and at bilateral summits such that there was a regular demand for agencies armed with information on Russia's stance and prepared to defend Russia's record as a "trustworthy" partner worthy of further integration into Western trade and security institutions.

The lack of attention that some agencies give to export control has provided its defenders the opportunity to promote the development of an export control system with fewer obstacles. Nevertheless, there have been debates between agencies over how stringent controls should be.[47] One interagency conflict emerged after MINATOM signed the aforementioned contract to supply nuclear reactors and training to Iran.[48] MINATOM pursued this contract without first consulting with other agencies involved in export control, which resulted in MINATOM loosing its ability to approve certain nuclear exports unilaterally. Moreover, MINATOM's director, Victor Mikhailov, signed a protocol to begin discussions on supplying Iran with a gas centrifuge, which could be used for acquiring enriched uranium for a nuclear weapon and which would have violated Russia's international nuclear export obligations. The Ministry of Foreign Affairs rejected the possibility of supplying the gas centrifuge and used the decision in negotiations with the United States as a concession and apparently as a ploy that allowed Bill Clinton to "save face" in light of Russia's refusal to back down from the deal to complete the Iranian reactors at Bushehr.[49] As a result of bureaucratic debates that followed the Iranian contract, the Federal Service for Currency and Export Control was granted greater oversight of sensitive nuclear exports, and MINATOM's position within Russia's system diminished.[50] Without cooperation from MINATOM, however, nonproliferation initiatives may be threatened because the agency continues to oversee Russia's immense nuclear complex.

Another potential obstacle to export control development in Russia was the parliament, which has primarily consisted of political parties, namely Zhirinovsky's Liberal Democratic Party and Zyuganov's Communist Party, that opposed cooperation with the West in almost any international setting. Preoccupation with other domestic and international issues, however, has meant that representatives of Russia's Duma (The Lower House) and Federation Council (The Upper House) rarely delved into export control matters except in the most publicized and controversial cases, such as the decision to abort the sale of cryogenic rockets to India and the subsequent decision to join the Missile Technology Control Regime and Wassenaar Arrangement.[51] In fact, aside from a small group within Russia's Duma that follows security issues, export control is not well understood. While most within the Duma support nonproliferation as a concept, export control, if it results in the loss of international sales, is seen as counter to the national interest.[52] If the Russian president did not possess such preponderant power relative to other government bodies in Russia, it is likely that several publicized decisions on nonproliferation policy taken by the Yeltsin administration would have been blocked. The relative impotence of the legislative branch to block executive decisions and policies, however, often diminishes its role in issues of export regulation to one of rhetorical dissenter.[53]

Unlike insights from bureaucratic politics models, the expectation derived from theories of domestic politics that suggests more centralized states are better equipped to develop and coordinate export control does not seem to hold much validity in the Russian case. Russia has managed to make progress in issuing export control regulations and licensing procedures despite increased regionalization. Moscow's ability to maintain some semblance of control is certainly aided by the fact that industries of the military-industrial complex fall under the jurisdiction of agencies in Moscow (MINATOM, Russian Space Agency, etc.) that are aware of export control. Moves for greater autonomy in the foreign economic realm by regional governments could, however, pose a future challenge for the national government, especially with implementation and enforcement efforts. If Russia's regions, such as Chechnya, are allowed to operate their own customs body or even license their own exports as some regions wish to do, it is unlikely that one could speak of an effective Russian export control system. The problem is aggravated by the lack of export control knowledge outside of major cities. In addition, the central government has not made compliance easy for enterprises outside of Moscow that seek licenses for controlled commodities. In some cases, exporters from other cities must take their license application to Moscow and hand deliver them to the necessary agencies for approval because export control officials do not accept faxes or other electronic communications as official documents.[54] Although this measure is explained as an attempt to ward off corruption, it may undermine export controls and encourage exporters to work around the system, given the many bureaucratic hurdles that require clearing in order to obtain a license.

THE IMPACT OF RUSSIA'S SEARCH FOR AN IDENTITY

According to the liberal identity approach, states with a strong liberal identification, democratic institutions, and a market economy are expected to interact more frequently with other liberal states and to share certain norms and practices—in this case, those related to nonproliferation. Russia represents an interesting and difficult case for the liberal identity approach. In the case of Russia, one is hard-pressed to speak of any one state identity that predominates.[55] Instead, since the demise of the Soviet Union, Russia has struggled to define its place in the post–Cold War era, resulting in a foreign policy that lacks consistency and is characterized by confusion and unpredictability.[56] In psychological terms, Russia might be best characterized as possessing multiple identities as there are vastly differing views of what Russia's role in the post–Cold War world should be.

During the first years of Russia's independence, Russia's foreign minister Kozyrev pursued a foreign policy which sought to integrate Russia into the "civilized" or Western community of states. Kozyrev and other "pro-Westerners" or "Atlanticists" who were at the helm of Russian foreign policy during this "honeymoon" period, as it was tagged, identified with the Western value system and saw integration with the West as the path toward restoring Russia's status as a "great power."[57] Kozyrev and other pro-Westerners saw Russia's fate closely linked to the West and argued that Russia defended its economic interests by cooperating with the West.[58] There was also the belief that Russia's security would be enhanced through integration into a European Security System stretching from "Vancouver to Vladivostok" within the framework of the Conference of Security and Cooperation in Europe (CSCE).

Russia's identification with the West in the early years of Russia's independence also allowed for unprecedented cooperation in arms control and nonproliferation. At the 1993 Vancouver Summit with President Clinton, Yeltsin noted that cooperation was possible on a range of issues, including nonproliferation, because the United States and Russia "are now democratic partners."[59] A foreign policy adviser to Yeltsin at the time also noted that Russian cooperation in stemming proliferation was possible only because Russia was a "member of the democratic community."[60] During this period Russia also moved to coordinate export control policy with the West and demonstrated its reliability as a new "partner."

Russian foreign policy, however, was increasingly scrutinized by nationalists and Communists who argued that Kozyrev was capitulating to the West. The warm relations that characterized Russia's relations with the West soured in late 1993 with the success of Zhirinovsky's Liberal Democratic Party in parliamentary elections. Although the new Constitution, adopted in a referendum in December 1993, strengthened the role of the president in foreign policy, Kozyrev was forced to recognize his tenuous position in light of criticism from the opposition within the new parliament and even from within his own ministry.[61] Russia's foreign policy-makers, including Kozyrev, were forced to increasingly contrast Russia's interests with those of the West. The views of "geopoliticians" within Yeltsin's camp who argued that Russia's foreign policy should be dictated by geography and that it should prioritize relations with the CIS and neighboring China and Islamic states as a balance against the West gained saliency. Eurasianists who held that Russia had a unique value system and culture which made integration with Europe futile, joined the call to favor relations with the CIS and advocated the view that Russia should serve as a bridge between East and West.[62] The shift in foreign policy also led to increased acrimony between Moscow and the West especially over the expansion of NATO to the East, a move that many policy-makers denounced as an attempt by the West to isolate Russia.

A liberal identity approach would suggest that this reorientation in Russian foreign policy and turn away from the West would result in fewer steps to establish export controls. Yet, in fact, export control development and cooperation advanced even more quickly despite a shift toward a more independent foreign policy following opposition party success in Russia's parliamentary elections of December 1993 and despite Russia's move away from what critics called Kozyrev's "moralist" foreign policy.[63] Russia's cooperation with the United States and other states has expanded in the export control arena despite this reorientation of foreign policy.[64] For example, most of Russia's progress in implementing a nonproliferation export control system has been made during this shift away from a Western orientation. Russia issued numerous implementing regulations and became a full member of the Missile Technology Control Regime and the Wassenaar Arrangement after December 1993.

While Russia was taking steps to enhance its export control system, it also began to seek closer ties with states that the West and especially the United States deemed proliferants. Russia made overtures to have trade sanctions lifted against Iraq, and economic and political relations with Iran have warmed, suggesting that it does not share Western, and especially U.S., concerns with such illiberal states. There were also many in Russia's policy circles who believed that the decision of Russia to join the United States in imposing U.N. sanctions against Iraq, Libya, and Yugoslavia were "concessions" inconsistent with Russia's national interest and decisions which needed to be altered.[65] Some in Russia saw U.S. efforts to promote export control and nonproliferation as an attempt to steal Russian technologies and gather secrets about its military capabilities.[66] In particular, some Russian officials saw the International Science and Technology Center, a West-financed effort to employ Russian scientists in nonmilitary activities, as an effort to uncover Russian technological secrets and not a nonproliferation program designed to prevent Russian scientists from assisting the military ambitions of rogue states.[67] Furthermore, some Russian agencies, most notably MINATOM, accused the West of conspiring to take control of Russia's nuclear industry by asserting that Russia could not manage its nuclear assets.[68] Cooperation in nonproliferation was also aggravated by Russian apprehension that the United States was attempting to simply reorient export controls from East-West controls to North-South controls, thereby limiting Russia's trade opportunities. All of this suggests that those in charge of Russia's foreign policy and nonproliferation stance do not strongly identify with Western interests and that a liberal identity approach is insufficient for explaining Russia's continued efforts to develop export control and participate in multilateral nonproliferation efforts, especially given that much of Russia's progress on export control came as its relations with the West became strained.

An explanation based upon liberalism's tenets must also grapple with the extent to which we can speak of Russia as a liberal state; or, for that matter, to what extent we can speak of any identity in Russia. Russia has liberalized, as is reflected by its privatization efforts and multiparty elections, but it is not clear that Russia can be classified as a liberal democratic state because it meets only the most minimal requirements of such, and the presence of even some of these democratic institutions is in doubt. For example, questions surround the fairness of the 1996 presidential elections given the coverup of Yeltsin's heart attack between the first and second rounds and media bias favoring Yeltsin. Attempts to quell unrest in Chechnya also raised doubts about the Russian government's commitment to human rights. Critics have also noted Yeltsin's forceful dismantlement of the Supreme Soviet in 1993 and general treatment of domestic opponents as evidence that Russia is an authoritarian state.

In summary, a liberal identity approach fails to account for continued export control development and cooperation with the West in light of Russia's move away from a pro-Western foreign policy. The expansion of NATO strengthened the position of those in the foreign policy establishment who argue that Russia must pursue an independent foreign policy and perhaps seek closer relations with China and Iran, including sensitive trade, as a countermeasure. These measures, however, did not prevent Russia from developing export controls, but they did call into question the extent to which Russia actually shares Western nonproliferation norms and values.

MARKET ACCESS AND TRADE AS INDUCEMENTS

Rational institutionalism leads us to direct our attention to the ways in which states are induced to cooperate. In the case of export control behavior, we are especially interested in the actions taken by the United States and others in the Western community to further export control development in Russia. Did inducements offered or promised by these states promote the development of export control regulations and Russia's participation in multilateral nonproliferation export control regimes?

Because Russia has received little assistance directly linked to export control development, one might dismiss rationalist explanations. Although Russian officials involved in export control have hosted delegations from many countries and have been involved in numerous delegation trips abroad, they have not received significant funding to finance the work of agencies involved in export control and have received limited help to support training of export control officials.[69] This is despite high expectations in some circles that millions of dollars would be provided to support Russian work through the U.S. Cooperative Threat Reduction (CTR) program.

Promises of access to Western markets and technology, however, did affect Russia's decision to pursue export control development. The former member states of COCOM, most notably the United States, emphasized from the period immediately following the disintegration of the Soviet Union that normalization of trade relations and the lifting of restrictions on certain high-technology transfers were dependent upon the implementation of an export control system.[70] This message did not fall upon deaf ears because Russia recognized the economic costs suffered as a result of COCOM sanctions during the Cold War and continued restrictions on trade with Russia in its wake.[71] COCOM was not only effective at denying military-related technologies to the Soviet Union, but also dual-use and other technologies that were vital for building an economic infrastructure. As a result, the desire to have all trade controls directed at Russia lifted, especially those of COCOM, took on special significance.[72] The lifting of these "discriminatory" controls was seen as important to the economic development of the country because of the benefits that were expected to follow from increased high-technology trade with the West.[73] Addressing this issue, Gennady Voronin, deputy chairman of the Committee on Defense Industries remarked: "Russia is interested in cooperation with the U.S. and other developed countries in the sphere of high technology, including dual-use technologies. Such cooperation would allow more effective use of the technological culture and intellectual potential of the defense sectors in the interests of both states. A basic obstacle to such cooperation is the discriminatory restrictions put in place at one time by COCOM countries in relation to the USSR and automatically transferred to Russia."[74]

Other statements by Russian officials reflected an appreciation of the importance of export control development for normalizing trade relations with the West.[75] A deputy director of the Federal Service for Currency and Export Control emphasized that Russia "cannot join the world market as an equal partner without participating in international organizations and export control regimes."[76] He also noted that "the Russian Federation policy for integration into the world market system, increasing participation in international trade by businesses producing high-technology products, and more active economic, trade, scientific, and technical cooperation with foreign countries leads to a need to significantly increase the quality of export control."[77] Another official from the same agency explained that Russia's international cooperation in export control integrates Russia's national system of export control in the international system and "has a favorable effect on the trade and economic cooperation of the Russian Federation with other countries."[78] An official from the Russian Ministry of Foreign Affairs argued that participation in the Wassenaar Arrangement offered Russia "new opportunities for the widest cooperation with partners in the high-tech sphere."[79]

Russian officials also acknowledged the desire to have West-imposed barriers lifted on all trade and understood that such a move hinged on Russian progress in export controls. In bilateral meetings with the United States and at conferences, Russian officials continually pressed their desire to have all controls withdrawn, arguing that Russia's system was sufficiently "effective" and developed to warrant decontrol and Russia's inclusion in all international regimes.[80] Russian officials also understood that if Russia gained admission to international regimes (MTCR, Wassenaar Arrangement), it was likely that Western countries would lift trade controls and that membership would provide an extra degree of legitimacy to the system. In explaining the advantages of Russia's participation in international export control institutions, an official from the Ministry of Foreign Affairs noted that such involvement provides Russia with an additional tool for "removing discriminatory barriers to trade."[81]

In addition to the role that promises of improved trade relations played in prompting export control development, Russia's decision to cancel the sale of cryogenic rockets to India offers one glaring case in which inducements, in this case those offered by the United States, led Russia to alter its policy. It was only after the United States offered Russia the "carrot" of joint space cooperation that Russia reneged on the $800 million deal, thereby paving the way for Russia's entry into the MTCR. The United States charged that the sale to India violated MTCR rules and vowed to impose sanctions because of the deal. Russian officials argued that the contract should be fulfilled because it was concluded before Russia agreed to abide by MTCR principles. In bargaining that ensued, the United States insisted that Russia show progress in developing an export control system and comply with MTCR regulations, namely by canceling the transfer of cryogenic rockets to India, and in return the United States would lift controls on high-technology trade. Russian officials insisted that the United States first lift controls and then Russia would agree to abide by MTCR. From the time that the MTCR was established in 1987, its Western members were concerned that the regime's effectiveness would be undermined without Soviet and later Russian participation. The Soviets were offered membership in the MTCR when it was established but declined because of continued COCOM-imposed controls. According to Gennady Khromov, the Soviet message was the following: "Abolish COCOM, and the Soviet Union will join the MTCR."[82]

Ultimately, the issue of Russia's membership in the MTCR was resolved first. When Bill Clinton became president, the United States's strategy appeared to Moscow to be more flexible. Although many within the foreign policy community opposed cancellation of the Indian cryogenic deal, they successfully negotiated a deal that allowed them to fulfill parts of the contract and to gain promises of joint U.S.-Russian cooperation in space exploration, which would provide the Russian Space Agency with millions of dollars in contract work. Some have pointed out that Russia simply calculated that cooperation with the United States would be better for the space industry in the long run and that continued U.S.-imposed sanctions would be detrimental to economic growth.[83] One U.S. official stated that the decision for Russia was one of "simple mathematics" and that Russia simply stood to gain much more by canceling parts of the contract with India.[84] In addition to the material benefits gained, one Russian analyst noted that the decision to alter the contract paved the way for Russia's admission into the MTCR and COCOM successor regime which assured removal of West-imposed trade restrictions which were "extremely negative" for the development of Russia's economy.[85]

In the end, Russian foreign policy-makers determined that the advantages of developing export controls and pursuing membership in international export control institutions, if it was an "equal partner," outweighed the costs.[86] By participating in the export control arrangements of the nonproliferation regime, Russia achieved some recognition as a responsible international player and gained the ability to shape the direction of these multilateral institutions. Above all, however, Russian policy-makers were motivated to develop export controls because it was a necessary means to gain access to Western technology and international markets that were previously denied Russia. According to a Russian analyst who follows nonproliferation and export control issues closely, "Russia's penetration into Western markets, above all Western markets of weapons and technology, its close cooperation with developed countries and, most importantly, the abolition of discriminatory restrictions on trade of high-technology goods directly depended on resolving the issue of membership in the international export control organizations."[87] In the absence of Western policies which linked high-technology trade to Russian progress in developing export control, it is unlikely that Russia would have pursued membership in the international export control arrangements or assigned adequate resources to promote development of a system. Given other pressing domestic and international issues, the development of export controls would likely have dropped off the policy agenda without a foreign-imposed rationale motivating their development and implementation.

CONCLUSION

Analysis of Russia's efforts to develop controls on strategic trade were motivated in large part by a belief that implementation of such a system was necessary for gaining access to Western technology and markets. This belief was based upon the message underscored by Western officials in numerous meetings: "No export control, no high-technology trade." (The member states of COCOM insisted that Russia develop a system of export control before its removal from the COCOM list of proscribed destinations.) Because Russia was largely moved by these warnings and other inducements, rational institutionalism appears best equipped to explain Russian nonproliferation behavior. The fact that this is so does not entirely debunk the other approaches analyzed. Realism directed our attention to potential security threats, which may motivate export control behavior if Russia's security environment worsens or if states with weapons of mass-destruction emerge on its border. Russia's behavior suggests that it does not yet view proliferation as the highest priority given internal security threats and the expansion of NATO (loss of regional influence), which are deemed more ominous. The expectations derived from the liberal identity approach are not entirely evident either. However, if a communist identity had not been abandoned by Russia, West-imposed trade restrictions would have continued, and there would be no need to speak of Russian export control cooperation or export control development designed to meet nonproliferation objectives for a market economy.

Domestic political approaches focused attention on the role that bureaucratic politics plays in shaping trade policy. In the case of Russia, two factors seem especially significant for explaining development and implementation of export controls. First, the agencies with greater responsibility for export control, hence those whose existence depended upon export controls, were able to promote development of a system in line with Western standards in spite of opposition from governmental agencies who had export promotion functions, because the latter agencies assigned fewer resources to export control or possibly did not see export control as an impediment to their ability to pursue international contracts. Second, the industry sectors and enterprises that viewed export control as a means to Western markets and investment were more apt to favor export control than industry sectors that believed export control inhibits trade to states that the West finds undesirable. Some enterprise directors viewed membership in export control arrangements as an attempt to deny Russia traditional markets. One shortcoming of domestic approaches to international politics, however, is that they are often overspecified and as such may not be useful for developing *generalizations* that would contribute to a theory of export control or nonproliferation. It seems plausible, nonetheless, that similar trends may be present in other states of the FSU and Eastern Europe, which are also in the process of developing export control systems.

While the measures that Russia has taken to control sensitive exports are noteworthy, there are several shortcomings related both to the economic environment in Russia and to Russia's rationale for pursuing export controls. Proliferation is perceived by many policy-makers in Russia as largely an American problem. Therefore, some in Russia feel that if the United States wants Russian assistance in nonproliferation efforts, the United States should provide compensation or concessions on issues that are of greater priority to Russia.[88] Also, many of the Russian government's efforts have clearly been directed at convincing the West that it has an export control system in place in an effort to speed the removal of trade barriers initiated during the Cold War. Hence, enforcement is the weakest element of the system to the extent that Russian officials have developed it in order to garner the benefits of membership in multilateral regimes and to obtain other Western carrots. There are serious doubts about the ability of Russia's border control and customs to interdict illegal transfers, and the criminal justice system is ill-prepared to enforce regulations.[89] The Russian state recognizes that goods smuggled in and out of the country represent a loss in revenues and have increased the Russian customs service from approximately 7,000 to 54,000 employees.[90] Nonetheless, it is unclear whether or not the extra staff are needed to prevent illegal export and import or to self-police what is widely known to be one of the more corrupt government agencies. Customs officers are frequent targets of bribes by importers and exporters seeking to bypass tariffs and bureaucratic red tape. Enforcement also suffers because corruption is rampant in both industry and government sectors.

The fact that some policy makers in Russia do not share the United States's and other Western perceptions of proliferation threats may also undermine the efforts of some multilateral arrangements. One of the reasons that COCOM effectively inhibited transfers of technology was the broad consensus about the Soviet threat. Now, although most states that are party to various international regimes agree that it is essential to slow the spread of weapons of mass destruction to other countries and limit transfers of advanced conventional arms to unstable regions, there is disagreement over precisely what needs to be controlled and to whom. Until Russia senses a pending security threat due to weapons proliferation to and from particular states in its region, and stabilizes both economically and politically, export control may be limited as a nonproliferation tool.

Several policy implications can be drawn from this analysis of export control development in Russia, which may be applicable to efforts to promote export control development in other states of the FSU and Eastern Europe. First, Western policy-makers should use access to important technologies and technology trade and investment as carrots in efforts to promote export control. Without some bargaining leverage, there will be little incentive to develop tight controls, especially in states that are undergoing economic hardship. At the same time, domestic support for export control needs to be fostered within the FSU. This support should include both government bodies and technology and weapons exporters who face tremendous economic pressures. In order to gain this support, it would be wise to promote joint venture projects and Western investment in high-technology and defense sectors as a way to deter them from trading with less savory partners in proliferant states. These ventures and investments can be conditioned upon enterprise and state support for export control. Finally, the Russian case suggests that export control systems will be more effective if states can be convinced that it is in their *security* interests, and not just economic interests, to develop export controls, and if a consensus can be reached among members of export control arrangements on what states or end-users should be the targets of export control. Achieving a consensus on what states constitute a threat, however, may become more rather than less difficult because of the decision of NATO to expand eastward. After 1993, the foreign policy establishment in Russia embraced a more pragmatic orientation by attempting to balance this expansion with a shift toward improving military and economic ties with its Eastern neighbors. This does not bode well for the work of multilateral institutions which seek to build common policies on technology transfers. If other states of the FSU are brought into a multilateral regime but do not share a common sense of threat, the effectiveness of multilateral nonproliferation efforts could be significantly diminished.

NOTES

1. For a discussion of the disorder within Russia's military industrial complex and the proliferation threat it poses, see the National Research Council Report *Proliferation Concerns: Assessing U.S. Efforts to Help Contain Nuclear and Other Dangerous Materials and Technologies in the Former Soviet Union* (Washington, D.C.; National Academy Press, 1997), pp. 32–48.

2. See D. L. Averre, "Proliferation Export Controls and Russian National Security," *Contemporary Security Policy*, Vol. 17, No. 2 (August 1996), pp. 185–226. Also see Michael Beck, Gary Bertsch, and Igor Khripunov, "The Development of Nonproliferation Export Control in Russia," *World Affairs Quarterly* 157, 1 (Summer 1994), pp. 3–18.

3. For a complete listing of all of Russia's export control regulations, see *Nat-*

sionalnaya Sistema Eksportnovo Kontrolya, a compendium issued by the Moscow Center on Export Controls, 1996. Also see Gary Bertsch and Igor Khripunov, eds., *Russia's Nonproliferation and Conventional Weapons Export Controls: 1995 Annual Report* (Athens: Center for International Trade and Security at the University of Georgia, 1996).

4. See Averre. For detailed information on the licensing process, see Gary Bertsch and Igor Khripunov, eds., *Russia's Nonproliferation and Conventional Weapons Export Controls: 1995 Annual Report* (Athens: Center for International Trade and Security at the University of Georgia, 1996). Also see Elina Kirichenko, "Russia's Export Control System: The Mechanism of Executive Branch Cooperation," *The Monitor*, Vol. 1, No. 2 (Spring 1995), pp. 1, 19.

5. Rustam Safaraliev, "Russian Export Control Is Taking Its Place in the Multilateral System," *The Monitor*, Vol. 1, No. 3 (Summer 1995), p. 3.

6. Beck et al., pp. 11–13.

7. For details about U.S. efforts in promoting export control see the National Research Council Report *Proliferation Concerns: Assessing U.S. Efforts to Help Contain Nuclear and Other Dangerous Materials and Technologies in the Former Soviet Union* (Washington, D.C.: National Academy Press, 1997), pp. 97–99. In 1996 alone, Russia hosted export control delegations from Israel, Japan, the United States, and the United Kingdom.

8. "Export Control in Russia," in Yu. Drugov, ed., *Reforms in Russia* (Moscow: Interdepartmental Analytical Center, 1993), pp. 56–72.

9. *Customs Today*, Vol. 31, No.1, (Winter 1996) pp. 9–13.

10. Ibid.

11. *The Monitor*, Vol. 1, No. 2 (Spring 1995), pp. 12, 24–25.

12. See Gary Bertsch and Igor Khripunov, eds., *Russia's Nonproliferation and Conventional Weapons Export Controls: 1995 Annual Report* (Athens: Center for International Trade and Security at the University of Georgia, 1996), p. 10.

13. Several industry outreach conferences were organized by the Moscow Center on Export Controls in 1995–97. The author attended several of these conferences while working at the center in 1996 for Los Alamos National Laboratory.

14. Discussion with official of the Ministry of Foreign Affairs, 10 June 1997.

15. *Nezavisamaya Gazeta*, 30 December 1995.

16. Testimony of Gary Bertsch, director of the Center for International Trade and Security at the University of Georgia, before the Permanent Subcommittee on Investigations, Committee on Government Affairs, 13 March 1996.

17. Ibid.

18. Ibid.

19. Michael Beck, Gary Bertsch, and Igor Khripunov, "Russia," in Gary Bertsch, ed., *Restraining the Spread of the Soviet Arsenal: The Development of Export Controls in the NIS*, (Athens: Center for International Trade and Security at the University of Georgia, 1997).

20. National Research Council Report, p. 95.

21. However, political and economic stability do not necessarily ensure an effectively enforced system. Many states of Western Europe who contributed to Iraq's programs went undetected until the end of the Gulf War.

22. Mikhail Gersaev and Victor Surikov, "Krizis Rossiiskoi Oboronnoy Promyshlennosti I Perspectivy Eksporta Vooruzheniya," in Andrew Pear and Dmitri Trenin, eds., *Rossiya v Mirovoy Torgovle Oruzhiyem: Strategiya, Politika, Ekonomika* (Moscow: Carnegie Endowment for International Peace, 1996).

23. Sergei Rogov, "Russia and the U.S.: Partnership or Another Estrangement?" *International Affairs* (July 1995), p. 10.

24. See "Export Control in Russia," pp. 56–72. Also see Pyotr Litavrin, "Rossiya I Noviy Forum Na Zamenu KOKOM," in Pear and Trenin, eds., *Rossiya v Mirovoy Torgovle Oruzhiyem: Strategiya, Politika, Ekonomika,* pp. 143–57.

25. Litavrin, pp. 143–57.

26. Here we have chosen to derive expectations from a mainstream conception of realism which suggests that states are most concerned with defending the state from external threats.

27. See Joseph S. Nye, "U.S.-Soviet Cooperation in a Nonproliferation Regime," in Alexander L. George, Phillip J. Farley, and Alexander Dallin, eds., *U.S.-Soviet Security Cooperation: Achievements, Failures, Lessons* (New York: Oxford University Press, 1988), pp. 336–52.

28. For a discussion of Russia's disoriented foreign policy, see Leszek Buszynski, *Russian Foreign Policy After the Cold War* (Westport, CT: Praeger, 1996).

29. *Official Kremlin International News Broadcast, Federal Information Systems Corporation* (LEXIS-NEXIS), 9 June 1994.

30. *UPI* (LEXIS-NEXIS), 22 February 1993.

31. See Dmitri Yestafiev, "Limited Armed Conflicts and Problems of Russia's Security," *Nauchniye Zapiski,* No. 2, (Moscow: Center for Political Studies in Russia, 1996).

32. *Moscow Times,* 31 August 1996.

33. Rustam Safaraliev, "Russian Export Control Is Taking Its Place in the Multilateral System," *The Monitor: Nonproliferation, Demilitarization and Arms Control* (Athens, GA: Center for International Trade and Security at the University of Georgia), Vol.1, No. 3 (Summer 1995).

34. Sergei Kortunov, "The National Export Control System in Russia," *Comparative Strategy,* Vol. 13 (May 1994), pp. 231–38.

35. Some officials identified weapons programs in Iran, Pakistan, Libya, and Israel of concern, but officials rarely identify states, or their weapons' programs, as a threat to Russia.

36. Presentation by official from the Ministry of Foreign Affairs at the Industry-Government Relations in Export Control conference in Moscow, 9 December 1996. This position is frequently noted at international seminars and meetings by Russian officials.

37. Discussions with officials from Russia's Ministry of Foreign Affairs, 10 December 1996 in Moscow.

38. See Shahid Alam, "Some Implications of the Aborted Sale of Cryogenic Rocket Engines to Russia," *Comparative Strategy* 13, No. 3,(July-September 1994), pp. 287–99. Also see D. L. Averre, "Proliferation, Export Controls and Russian National Security, *Contemporary Security Policy*, Vol.17, No. 2 (August 1996) pp. 203–05.

39. Derek da Cunha, "Russian Arms Sales Skyrocket Amid Western Complacency," *The Straits Times* (LEXIS-NEXIS), 21 November 1996.

40. Michael S. Lelyveld, *Journal of Commerce*, 20 February 1996, p. 14.

41. Profile of the Center on Export Controls, October 1996.

42. The Russian Space Agency was involved in signing agreements for joint cooperation in space with U.S. agencies after the Russian contract to transfer space technology to India was altered.

43. A. V. Ustinov, "Export of Missile Technology, Will Russia Enter the World Market?" *Comparative Strategy*, Vol. 13, p. 285.

44. Profile of the Center on Export Controls, October 1996.

45. Interview with Russian official, 9 December 1996.

46. These agencies possess a virtual monopoly on information because they attend international meetings of the multilateral groups and are knowledgeable of practices in other states.

47. For a discussion of competing interests among export control agencies see "Export Control in Russia," in Yu. Drugov, p. 58.

48. For a comprehensive account of Russia's nuclear deal with Iran, see Stuart D. Goldman, Kenneth Katzman, and Zachary S. Davis, *Russian Nuclear Reactor and Conventional Arms Transfers to Iran*, U.S. Library of Congress, CRS Report for Congress, 95–641 F, 23 May 1995. Also see John C. Baker, "Non-proliferation Incentives for Russia and Ukraine," *Adelphi Paper* 309, International Institute for Strategic Studies (New York: Oxford University Press, 1997).

49. According to Vladimir Orlov, in the agreement between MINATOM and Iran, the two sides agreed to discuss issues related to supplying the gas centrifuge. However, the Ministry of Foreign Affairs aborted this item when it learned about the agreement.

50. Michael Beck, Gary Bertsch, and Igor Khripunov, "Russia," in Gary Bertsch, ed., *Nonproliferation Export Controls in the Former Soviet Union: Status Report* (Athens Center for International Trade and Security at the University of Georgia, 1997).

51. Rhuslan Khasbulatov, former Speaker of the Supreme Soviet, called the decision to scrap the Indian contract a "national disgrace," and the Supreme Soviet attempted to assert its authority to consider ratification of Russia's decision to join the MTCR. See *Defense News*, 26 July–1 August 1993.

52. Interview with researcher from Moscow's Carnegie Center, 13 June 1997.

53. The parliament does have some powers in foreign policy. According to Article 106 of the Constitution, the Federation Council is to ratify and denounce treaties and was concerned with the "status and defense of the state borders of the Russian Federation."

54. Interview with enterprise director at Moscow conference "Industry-Government Relations in Export Control," 18 December 1996. Interview with directors of various MINATOM enterprises at Obninsk, Russia, 10 June 1997.

55. See James Richter, "Russian Foreign Policy and the Politics of National Identity," in Celeste Wallander, ed., *The Sources of Russian Foreign Policy After the Cold War* (Boulder, CO: Westview Press, 1996): 69–94.

56. See Leszek Buszynski, *Russian Foreign Policy After the Cold War* (Wesport, CT: Praeger,1996): ix–xii. The author refers to this as a "foreign policy of disorientation."

57. See Buszynski, pp. 1–48.

58. *RFE/RL Daily Report*, 27 May 1993.

59. "Excerpts from Clinton-Yeltsin News Conference," *Washington Post*, 5 April 1993.

60. Robin Wright, "Dmitri Ryurikov Creating a National Security System for a New Democracy That Is Russia," *Los Angeles Times* (NEXIS), 5 September 1993.

61. Buszynski, pp. 34–40.

62. Ibid., pp. 4–15. Buszynski presents the views of four foreign policy groups: pro-Western, Geopoliticians, Eurasianists, and a final group which includes Nationalists, Communists, and neo-Bolsheviks.

63. For a critique of Russia's foreign policy under Kozyrev, see Sergei Kortunov and Andrei Kortunov, "From 'Moralism' to 'Pragmatics.' New Dimensions of Russian Foreign Policy," *Comparative Strategy*, Vol. 13, No. 3, pp. 261–77.

64. For example, in 1996 Russia hosted export control delegations from the United States, United Kingdom, Japan, and Israel.

65. Alexei G. Arbatov, "Russian Foreign Policy Priorities for the 1990s," in Teresa Pelton Johnson and Steven E. Miller, eds., *Russian Security After the Cold War*, (Cambridge: Center for Science and International Affairs John F. Kennedy School of Government, 1994), p. 11.

66. Averre, p. 196.

67. Comments by Gennady Yevstafiev, director of the Foreign Intelligence Agency, at the Industry-Government Relations in Export Control conference held in Moscow, 18–19 December 1996. Yevstafiev expressed greater concern with Western intentions than emerging proliferants.

68. Averre, p. 193.

69. Between 1992 and 1996 most U.S. funds to promote export control in Russia went toward governmental exchanges, funding visits to Washington, D.C., by Russian export control officials and trips by U.S. officials to Moscow.

70. Gary K. Bertsch and Richard Cupitt, "Nonproliferation in the 1990s: Enhancing International Cooperation on Export Controls," *Washington Quarterly*, Vol. 16, No. 4, p. 62. This message was stressed by U.S. officials at one of the first meetings between U.S. and Russian export control officials at the US-NIS Dialogue on Nonproliferation Export Controls conference, Airlie, VA, 15–17 June 1993.

71. Averre, p. 201.

72. Litavrin, pp. 143–57.

73. See *RFE/RL Daily Report*, 18 August 1993.

74. Gennadi Petrovich Voronin, "How Russia's Defense Industry Responds to Military Technical Policy," *Comparative Strategy*, Vol. 13, 1994, p. 84.

75. See Rustam Safaraliev, "Export Controls as a Tool in Implementing the Russian Federation's Nonproliferation Policy," in Gary Bertsch and Igor Khripunov, eds., *Russia's Nonproliferation and Conventional Weapons Export Controls: 1995 Annual Report* (Athens: Center for International Trade and Security at the University of Georgia, 1996), p. 12. Igor Khripunov, "Report from the St. Petersburg Conference on Foreign Economic Activity and Export Control in Russia," *The Monitor*, Vol. 2, No. 1–2 (Winter-Spring 1996), p. 41.

76. Rustam Safaraliev, "Russian Export Control System Is Taking Its Place in the Multilateral System," *The Monitor*, Vol. 1, No. 3 (Summer 1995), p. 3.

77. Safaraliev, in Bertsch and Khripunov, p. 12.

78. Comments of Andrei Pinchuk, head of the Department at the Federal Service for Currency and Export Control in Washington, D.C., at the Symposium for Foreign Export Control Officials, July 1996.

79. Anatoli Antonov, "The Wassenaar Arrangement: Russia's Perspective on the New Regime," *Nonproliferation Export Control in Russia*, Newsletter of the Moscow Center on Export Controls, No. 2 (October 1996), p. 4.

80. Russian officials cited their progress in developing export controls as a reason for its inclusion as a founding partner in a new post-COCOM regime at the international conference in Moscow "Export Control: Political Aspects—Will West-East Restrictions Continue After COCOM?" 11 April 1994. Also see Sergei Kortunov, "Nonproliferation and Counterproliferation," *Comparative Strategy*, Vol. 13, 1994, pp. 235–37.

81. See Khripunov, p. 41.

82. Gennady Khromov, "Missile Nonproliferation and Russia's State Interests," *The Monitor*, Vol. 2, No. 3 (Summer 1996), p. 3.

83. Shahid Alam, "Some Implications of the Aborted Sale of Cryogenic Rocket Engines to India," *Comparative Strategy*, Vol. 13, 1994, pp. 287–300.

84. Interview with U.S. State Department Official, 25 July 1995.

85. Alexander Pikayev, "Problems of Nonproliferation and Disarmament," *Nauchniye Dokladi* (Moscow: Carnegie Endowment for International Peace, 1996), p. 16.

86. Russian officials frequently complain that they are not treated as "equal partners" within the nonproliferation regime and press the case that they deserve greater recognition.

87. Litavrin, p. 149. Author's translation.

88. Interview with staff of the Center on Political Studies in Russia, 8 June 1997. One researcher of the center noted that there are even some in Russia who advocate proliferation as positive because it implicitly challenges U.S. hegemony.

89. William K. Domke, "Proliferation, Threat, and Learning: The International and Domestic Structures of Export Control," in M. van Leeuwen, ed., *The Fu-*

ture of the International Nuclear Non-Proliferation Regime (Netherlands: Kluwer Academic Publishers, 1995), p. 226.

    90. Beck et al., "Russia," in Bertsch, ed., *Restraining the Spread of the Soviet Arsenal: The Development of Export Controls in the NIS.*

THREE

THE EVOLUTION OF THE UKRAINIAN EXPORT CONTROL SYSTEM
State Building and International Cooperation

SCOTT A. JONES

The dissolution of the Soviet Union shifted U.S. and Western security concerns from political-economic containment to the proliferation of weapons of mass destruction (WMD). Upon independence, the former Soviet republics—Russia, Ukraine, Belarus, and Kazakhstan foremost among them—confronted a considerable military-industrial legacy in different degrees.[1] Western policy-makers, alarmed at the proliferation threat posed by the FSU, began a financial, material, and informational campaign to address this emerging danger. Ukraine, long a Western security concern owing to its nuclear weapons inheritance, has been an object of such international nonproliferation efforts.

Unlike the Russian Federation, Ukraine did not inherit the export control apparatus of the Soviet Union. Ukraine did, however, fall heir to a considerable dowry of nuclear weapons, special nuclear material (SNM), equipment, expertise, missile manufacturing and technological capabilities, dual-use items and technologies, and a substantial military-industrial complex.[2] Shortly after independence, Ukraine, after much internal debate, declared its status as a non-nuclear weapons state (NNWS) by acceding to the Nonproliferation Treaty (NPT) in November 1994. Concomitant with its avowed NNWS status, Ukraine declared its intent to implement nonproliferation measures—export controls foremost among them.[3] Nevertheless, Ukraine, and the international security community, continues to face a chronic proliferation dilemma arising from political, economic, and social instability.[4]

Addressing the resultant proliferation threat, Ukraine, with Western assistance, focused its nonproliferation activities in primarily two areas: materials protection, control, and accounting (MPC&A) and export controls.[5]

The former consisted almost exclusively of donor-led and financed projects and involved minimal bureaucratic changes and negligible direct costs to the Ukrainian government. Export control development, on the other hand, involved considerable changes to government structure and significant direct and indirect costs.[6] Nevertheless, despite the attendant costs, the Ukrainian government has continued to develop its export control system in the midst of considerable political and economic adversity.

This chapter is organized in three sections: Section I will summarize the development of the Ukrainian export control system since independence in 1991, paying particular attention to the elements constituting an effective system. Section II examines the various theories seeking to account for export control development. Evidence is provided as to why rational institutionalism, by and large, best explains the Ukrainian experience. Section III, the concluding section, summarizes the preceding two parts and assesses the respective and collaborative explanatory power of the four approaches in explaining Ukrainian export control development. Although rational institutionalism is quite persuasive in accounting for development, it is not in and of itself an adequate explanatory device, but instead must rely in part on liberal identity and domestic politics approaches to complete our understanding of the still unfolding phenomenon.

EXPORT CONTROL DEVELOPMENTS: 1992–1997

Along with nuclear weapons, Ukraine inherited substantial WMD and dual-use materials and technologies, as well a sizable conventional military-industrial complex.[7] On 31 May 1996, the last former-Soviet strategic nuclear warheads located on Ukrainian territory were removed to Russia. While this act alleviated immediate international concerns regarding Ukraine's nuclear status, numerous proliferation concerns remain unresolved. To address the lingering proliferation threat, the Ukrainian government has undertaken an effort to establish a system by which to control the transfer of sensitive exports. The following section will summarize export control developments in Ukraine.

The system of nonproliferation export controls in Ukraine has undergone major changes since its inception in 1992. Given the deleterious political and economic environment, the progress since 1992 has been remarkably steadfast. As noted, despite inheriting WMD materials and technologies, Ukraine did not fall heir to, as did the Russian Federation, a system of export controls. Consequently, relative to Western export control systems, moderate and confined development is to be expected, in spite and because of Western assistance. The evolution of the system, however, continues to be part and parcel of the overall state-building process.

Assessing Development: The Elements

This study of the Ukrainian nonproliferation export control system—in correspondence with other chapters in this book—employs an assessment methodology derived from COCOM's "common standards."[8] The common standards were then modified, resulting in a measurement tool that allows for multiple perspective analyses. The tool consists of weighted elements, elements regarded as distinct but mutually reinforcing aspects of an effective export control system. By examining each of the elements, we are able to chart progress, stasis, or decline in the development of an export control system.

Overall, lacking an institutional history upon which to draw reference, Ukraine encountered and continues to face many challenges to its export control development effort. Nevertheless, substantial progress has been made.[9] For example, based on a quantitative analysis of export control development, Ukraine's export control system was 39 percent compliant with Western export control standards in 1992, and was 78 percent compliant in 1997.[10] Compared with other newly independent states (NIS), Ukraine ranked below only Russia and Belarus. Furthermore, when examining overall development over time, a longitudinal study reveals a progressive pattern.[11] In other words, since 1992, Ukraine has evinced a steady evolutionary path in the development of its export control system. This development is all the more remarkable when considering the political, economic, and social difficulties inherent in the transition from a communist political-economic system to a modern state *ex nihilo*.

Despite Ukraine's progress, problems and proliferation risks remain to be overcome. Several reports have chronicled illicit transfers of sensitive goods and technologies to such destinations as China, Iraq, and Libya.[12] The export control agencies are understaffed, underequipped, and undertrained. Furthermore, owing to parliamentary wrangling over the 1997 budget, funds were not disbursed until July of that year, thereby impeding export control activities. Organized crime and government corruption remain formidable obstacles to export control development. For example, in late 1993, top officials in the Ministry of Foreign Economic Relations were arrested for taking bribes and for issuing licenses to export "strategic raw materials."[13] The exporting community is not well versed in its export control obligations. For example, internal compliance mechanisms are not a common feature of Ukrainian enterprises.[14] Additionally, porous, understaffed borders add to the dilemma. Lax enforcement and limited overseas representation diminish export control developments.

Ukraine is well endowed with sensitive technologies, materials, and equipment. In the absence of a large domestic consumer market and owing to its interdependent structure, the Ukrainian economy is export oriented.[15]

Consequently, economic privation brings considerable pressure to bear on the export imperative, which in the Ukrainian case involves many internationally controlled items. These economic pressures translate into direct political pressures. For example, the Soviet Union's defense enterprises provided a broad range of social services, such as housing and health care, for their employees and families.[16] Furthermore, Ukraine is home to some 1,870 defense-related enterprises, comprising some 70 percent of the industrial sector, and therefore employing a substantial portion of the working population. In many cases, such enterprises comprise entire towns or regions. Thus, enterprise managers and regional politicians are under considerable pressure to maintain jobs by seeking out clients on the international market.[17]

International Nonproliferation Regime Adherence

Since 1992, Ukraine has joined or adheres to all nonproliferation supplier regimes. Nuclear, chemical, biological, and conventional weapons and dual-use control lists are now harmonized with those of the international regimes.[18] In April 1996, Ukraine became a member of the Nuclear Suppliers Group (NSG).

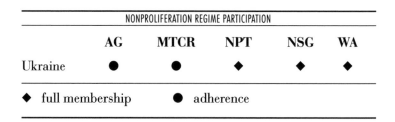

NONPROLIFERATION REGIME PARTICIPATION					
	AG	MTCR	NPT	NSG	WA
Ukraine	●	●	◆	◆	◆

◆ full membership   ● adherence

The Missile Technology Control Regime (MTCR) has proved to be the most elusive nonproliferation objective. On 13 May 1994, Ukraine signed a memorandum of understanding with the United States in which it pledged to respect MTCR guidelines. However, membership negotiations have stalled over Ukrainian reservations regarding elements in the arrangement that would adversely affect Ukraine's ability to continue producing Category I missile systems. Washington and Kyiv were attempting in 1997 to move past the impasse to an agreement acceptable to both sides.[19]

Institutional Developments

The bureaucratic framework of the Ukrainian export control system was not inherited from the Soviet Union. Lacking a vestigial control system and the accompanying personnel trained and conversant in such matters, the present structure has emerged in what can be described as an "adaptive" manner.[20] The present structure is the result of a continuing process by which Ukraine seeks to balance its international obligations, resource capabilities, and political, security, and economic idiosyncrasies and interests.

In early 1992, export control responsibilities rested with the Ministry of Foreign Affairs, the Ministry of Foreign Economic Relations, and the Ministry of Defense. Prior to the creation of specific export control agencies, much of the licensing and coordination between buyer and seller was still conducted in Moscow.[21] Subsequently, Ukrainian export control authorities were consolidated into the Governmental Commission on Export Controls (GCEC) and the Expert and Technical Committee (ETC) of the Cabinet of Ministers. Furthermore, there are sections responsible for export control in a number of ministries and agencies.

The Governmental Commission on Export Controls, now the Governmental Commission on Export Control Policy (GCECP), is a broad managerial organ responsible for coordinating state policy in the area of export control, licensing, determining quotas for export and import of commodities subject to export control, and arranging control over legislation implementation. The commission consists of representatives, usually at the head or deputy head level, from the State Export Control Service and various state ministries.[22]

The Expert and Technical Committee of the Cabinet of Ministers, now the State Export Control Service (Gosexportcontrol) is the main state executive organ on export control. The committee conducts its activities in compliance with the decisions of the GCECP and functions as a permanent body.

Gosexportcontrol examines applications and issues licenses for export, import, and the transit of goods subject to export control; submits proposals for renewing the list of commodities subject to export control; provides reports on the implementation of export control legislation; and organizes and maintains cooperation with appropriate organs on export control in foreign countries. Gosexportcontrol is also responsible for export control enforcement. Enforcement is hampered by finite resources, lack of qualified personnel, and the limited number of overseas missions capable of conducting end-user verification checks. Recently, Gosexportcontrol expanded its battery of technical experts by establishing a formal working relationship with the Kyiv Institute for Nuclear Research of the Ukrainian Academy of Sciences for the purpose of license, policy, and control lists review.[23]

Cooperation continues between the Ukrainian and U.S. export control communities. Cooperative exchanges, technical and policy seminars, workshops, and working agreements (such as the U.S. Department of Energy *Lab-to-Lab* agreements) have increased since early 1996. Activities involving the U.S. Departments of Commerce, Defense, Energy, and State, as well as Customs include licensing automation plans, border post automation equipment and training, industry outreach programs, and technical exchanges. Finland, Germany, Japan, and Norway have also provided export control assistance to Ukraine.[24]

A clearly identifiable export control culture and community is emerging in Ukraine. Gosexportcontrol is in the process of developing regional export control offices that will serve local exporters. A center for export control information and assistance, the Ukrainian Scientific and Technical Center, was created in March 1997. Initiated by Ukrainian exporters and Gosexportcontrol, the center will assist Ukrainian enterprises by providing export control information and assistance on developing internal compliance mechanisms.

The continued development of an "objective" (i.e., a system managed by a state body devoid of portfolio and, therefore, of parochial interest) export control structure is proceeding as quickly as the difficult political and economic environment allows. Since its institutional inception, a clearly progressive line of development through centralization and further empowerment of the export control organs has been discernible.

Although the Ukrainian Customs Authority has been substantially augmented since independence—personnel have increased from 2,000 to 17,000 in four years—smuggling and corruption remain formidable problems.[25] Enforcement authority remains weak owing to the uncertain legal environment. Training efforts and equipment upgrades are limited by the acute financial strains facing the government. Border postings are understaffed, ill-equipped and, in most cases, isolated from the central authorities in Kyiv. Borders with Russia and Belarus are not tightly monitored.[26] Furthermore, detection and interdiction efforts are primarily aimed at duty collection. Consequently, customs officials are more apt to focus on volume rather than types of imports and exports.[27]

Legal and Regulatory Developments

The legal basis for the Ukrainian export control system continues to be executive branch decrees (issued by both the president and Cabinet of Ministers). A legal basis for export control in Ukraine was initiated by the "Act on Foreign Economic Activity" adopted by the Verkhovna Rada (Parliament) in 1991. Article 20 of the act specifies that the export and import of weapons, special components for their manufacture, explosive agents, nuclear material, technologies, equipment, and installations, as well as other kinds of goods, technologies, and services that could be used for the production of weapons require authorization by the Ukrainian state. The Cabinet of Ministers of Ukraine, in coordination with appropriate standing commissions of the Rada, oversees the nomination of foreign economic policy executives and the regulation of related export and import activities.[28]

As of late summer 1997, an effort was under way to implement a comprehensive export control law. With the assistance of the Department of Commerce (DOC) Bureau of Export Administration and the Lawyers Alliance for World Security, Gosexportcontrol has drafted the "Temporary Provision on Export Controls in Ukraine." Already circulated to the appropriate ministries for review and comment, the national provision was undergoing a second examination in 1997 before it was to be recirculated to the ministries and to the parliamentary committees (Committee on Foreign Economic Relations and Standing Committee on Defense and Security) for a second perusal. This draft provision will be a prototype of national export control legislation. Until such legislation is drafted and adopted by the Rada, it will have the power of law and was slated to be signed by President Kuchma by late 1997.

The draft national export control provision is intended to solidify the legal structure of the export control system by fixing the administration division of labor, consolidating the various control lists, detailing the legal procedures surrounding import and export licensing, specifying criminal and civil violations, and establishing an international agreements protocol. Furthermore, the law is to contain a "catch-all" provision which has heretofore been lacking. An enacted comprehensive export control law would be the most significant advance in the development of the export control system to date.

Given the limited success, if not large-scale failure, of defense conversion efforts,[29] an active military-industrial complex lobby [30] (especially in the fields of dual-use and missile-related technologies and equipment), an unstable, still unfolding political environment, and overall economic hardship, why would Ukraine devote its limited resources to developing a system that would ostensibly limit its ability to address pressing economic and political issues?[31]

In order to explain export control development in Ukraine since its 1991 independence, this section will examine the four theoretical approaches delineated in the introductory chapter: realism, rational institutionalism, domestic politics, and liberal identity. Each approach, with its accompanying behavioral expectations, will be applied to the Ukrainian case with the express aim of exploring the variables driving nonproliferation export control development. The final section summarizes the theoretical findings.

EXPLAINING UKRAINIAN EXPORT CONTROL DEVELOPMENT
Realism: Evolving Security Concepts

The realist approach to international relations is of limited explanatory utility in accounting for Ukrainian export control developments. According to this approach, we would expect to see states develop export controls as a means of enhancing their security, of balancing the power of others, or of addressing external threats. Ukraine's geopolitical position is such that it sits astride a critical European juncture.[32] Ukrainian history is replete with periods of foreign occupation, the most recent being Russian, veiled under the veneer of Soviet social engineering. Moreover, pitted between a Russia wary of NATO expansion and a Europe and United States ambivalent over extending full security guarantees, the resultant political-military pressures complicate Ukraine's avowed neutrality.[33] Furthermore, since independence, Russian-Ukrainian relations have been strained over such issues as border demarcation, energy arrears, nuclear weapons divestiture and indemnity, division of the Black Sea Fleet, and the political status of Crimea, conferred to Ukraine by Khrushchev in 1954. Generally speaking, Russia is seen as the only viable external threat to Ukrainian national security.[34]

With the exception of Russia, Ukraine has not articulated the presence of external threats to its physical security.[35] Ukraine enjoys generally good relations with its immediate and regional neighbors. For example, Ukraine and Romania recently signed a Treaty on Friendship and Cooperation which addressed issues such as border disputes and nationality questions. Furthermore, Ukraine interacts politically, economically, and militarily on a regular cooperative basis with Iran, a country the West deems a "rogue" and proliferant.

In 1996, the Ukrainian parliament (Verkhovna Rada) approved the legislation of the *Ukrainian Security Concept*. This document sets out Ukraine's priorities as: ensuring state sovereignty, preserving its territorial integrity, and upholding the inviolability of borders. It also calls for overcoming the economic crisis, developing democratic institutions, and integrating into the world and European community. Listed among the threats to Ukraine's security are interference in the country's internal affairs, territorial claims, instability and conflicts in neighboring states, separatism, and violations of the constitutional system. The document emphasizes acute and prolonged economic instability as being the primary threat to national security.[36] The Ukrainian economy is, owing to its structural inheritance, vulnerable to Russian and regional factors.[37] For example, Russian supplies of oil and gas have been used to pressure Ukraine on such issues as the division of the Black Sea Fleet.[38] Furthermore, a recent $500 million sale of 320 T-80 tanks to Pakistan prompted a Russian response threatening to deny Ukraine vital tank parts because Moscow believes Ukraine to be undercutting its arms market in South Asia.[39]

Despite the potential menace of Russian economic and political hegemony, external threats, however, do not explain Ukraine's relatively advanced export control system.[40] Russia and the NIS, once being a coherent political-economic unit, represent parts of a military-technological whole.

Consequently, many sensitive items, technologies, and equipment are still, perforce, exchanged, sold, and transferred between former republics, thereby resuming erstwhile division-of-labor patterns. For example, Ukraine's advanced missile and rocket industry is deeply integrated into the Russian space and missile program, as evidenced by a recent agreement to work on jointly modernizing SS-18 ballistic missiles so they can carry satellites.[41] Consequently, both Ukraine and Russia are dependent on the comparative expertise of the other, thus highlighting the need of continual technological and material exchange.[42] Export controls, therefore, could hardly be expected to assuage Ukrainian security concerns in seeking to balance the power of others, Russia specifically. Furthermore, confronting decision-makers is the sheer novelty of the nonproliferation issue. Nonproliferation export controls have not been linked by Ukrainian officials, unaccustomed to global security issues, with national security.[43]

Ukraine has not identified the presence of regional threats.[44] Because Ukraine's security concerns incorporate Russia, already substantially endowed with advanced sensitive materials and technologies, then any attempt to preclude Russia from strategic trade would be both ludicrous and self-defeating. Nonetheless, if not a regional concern, Ukrainian leaders maintain that WMD proliferation is a *global* security issue, and Ukrainian export control development as a means by which to address the *international* proliferation threat.[45] That proliferation concerns are addressed at all is testament to the perseverance of the international community, the United States specifically, and Ukraine's cooperative response.

The *Ukrainian Security Concept* articulates internal threats as being the foremost obstacle to achieving Ukrainian security. Economic and political instability are real and immediate threats to Ukrainian sovereignty. Regional and ethnic frictions threaten to undermine the overall coherence of the territorial state.[46] For example, separatist pressures in Crimea and ethnic tensions in the ethnically Russian-dominated Donbas could be future points of conflict and instability. Export controls, costly and ostensibly unrelated to the immediate dictates of economic and political perils, seem ill-suited to addressing Ukrainian security concerns, such as they are.

According to the realist approach, state behavior is best explained in terms of its respective security concerns. As such, security issues occupy high priority in a state's political agenda. Were export controls seen as a viable and effective means by which to decrease security threats, then we would expect to see export controls figured prominently in the affairs of state. This is not the case in Ukraine.[47] In fact, concepts such as the dangers arising from nuclear proliferation were noticeably absent from the Ukrainian nuclear debate.[48] Ukrainian government officials clearly recognize the value of more effective export controls. However, while they recognize the importance of improving their current capabilities, they also acknowledge that export controls are only one among many political and economic priorities.[49] As, at best, second-tier concerns, export controls are not seen as redressing security imbalances or minimizing security threats. Furthermore, Ukraine has sought Western security guarantees and the strengthening of its own military—and not export controls—as the primary vehicles by which to address its security concerns.[50] Thus, the realist approach offers little explanatory power in accounting for the evolution of Ukrainian nonproliferation export controls.

Rational Institutionalism: The Success of Incentives

Of the approaches examined in this study, the rational institutional approach most effectively explains the continued development of export controls in Ukraine. According to rational institutional expectations, a state will develop a nonproliferation export control system if it values future interactions with nonproliferation regime member states, is interested in engendering reciprocity and reducing transaction costs and uncertainty, receives side payments, and otherwise calculates the associated costs and benefits.

Ukraine, with advanced missile and nuclear industries, believes its economic salvation lies in Western markets and through increased foreign direct investment.[51] Ukrainian political leaders recognize the link between international nonproliferation norms compliance and access to Western technology and markets.[52] For example, in August 1996, the United States removed Ukraine from the International Traffic in Arms Regulations (ITAR) list. This means that U.S. policy no longer prevents the issuance of licenses for the sale or purchase of military equipment or services to and from Ukraine. The change in policy is contingent upon assurances that an adequate export control system is in place. Furthermore, nonproliferation regime membership (e.g., Nuclear Suppliers Group) and/or adherence (Missile Technology Control Regime) suggests that Ukraine realizes the long-term economic benefits accruing to compliance with the international nonproliferation regime.[53]

The rational institutional approach contends that states will have more developed export control systems when they perceive that transaction costs and uncertainty in their future interactions with others are reduced by joining or adhering to the international nonproliferation regime. Having joined or adhered to the supplier regimes, Ukraine cooperates on a regular basis with other states, thereby stabilizing and giving structure to subsequent interactions in an increasingly wider array of issue areas.[54] Gradually, a wider representation of Ukrainian policy-makers has been included in export control technical and working exchanges on a bilateral and multilateral basis, thus ensuring broader support and understanding of export control norms and initiatives amongst state officials. As most Ukrainian government officials are unfamiliar with export control norms—as all export control issues were formerly handled in Moscow—nonproliferation regime norms and rules are conveyed via routine interactions between an increasingly wider array of Ukrainian government officials and regime members. In this capacity, for example, stereotypes about the supplier "cartels" are disabused and, consequently, uncertainty between states reduced.[55] Nevertheless, it remains to be seen how effectively regime norms will constrain future export behavior, as adherence does not guarantee compliance.[56]

The costs of noncompliance can be considerable. Because Ukrainian economic reformation depends upon access to Western markets and aid disbursements, uncooperative behavior could jeopardize long-term economic and political objectives. For example, allegations were made against Kyiv involving Ukrainian arms and missile transfers and technology exports to Libya.[57] According to a 2 October 1996 CIA report, two Ukrainian "entities" concluded separate agreements, estimated to be worth $510 million, with the regime of Libyan leader Moammar Gadhafi. Congressional restrictions require a halt on U.S. aid to Ukraine if that nation is found to be trading military goods to Libya. The allegations, if proved, could affect $225 million earmarked for Ukraine in fiscal year 1997 and up to $900 million already appropriated. An initial payment of $3 million was allegedly made to "Ukrainian officials" in July 1996 for what the CIA report said were SS-21 or Scud B missiles that will be dismantled before delivery to Libya. When completed, the transfer will be worth $500 million, the report said. A second deal, concluded in May 1996 between another Ukrainian firm and Libya, called for Ukraine to provide maintenance services and spare parts for Libya's four Soviet-era Foxtrot submarines and other surface ships, the report said. The service agreement grew out of a visit to Tripoli in May 1996 by a group of Ukrainians and will be worth $10 million if completed, the report said. A third agreement outlined in the report involves Iran's purchase in August of a large shipment of unspecified Ukrainian weapons "with the intention of transferring them to Libya."[58]

The military sales would violate UN sanctions imposed on Libya for its failure to turn over two Libyan agents wanted in the 1988 bombing of Pan Am Flight 103 over Lockerbie, Scotland. If the missiles are Scud-Bs, the transfer would violate the MTCR, which bans exports of missiles with ranges greater than 300 miles. The SS-21s would be illegal under the MTCR even if not fitted with chemical or biological warheads, government experts noted. Defense Department officials said Libya is believed to have the capability to produce chemical warheads.[59]

In response, Ukraine set up a parliamentary commission to investigate charges of a strategic partnership between Tripoli and Kyiv. Secretary of the National Security and Defense Council, Volodymyr Gorbulin, said the Ukrainian investigation confirmed that the charges were groundless. Nevertheless, in a meeting with U.S. State Department director for CIS affairs,

James Collins, Gorbulin confided that he "hopes the affair would not affect the U.S. Congress in dispensing aid to Ukraine."[60] The U.S. Senate passed the foreign aid bill on 17 July 1997. The Senate's version of the bill maintained a $225 million earmark for Ukraine, for fiscal year 1998. Included were several subearmarks for specific programs needed in Ukraine: Chernobyl-related safety assistance, commercial law and legal reform, democratic initiatives, and law enforcement procedures. As he introduced the bill on the Senate floor on 16 July 1997, Foreign Operations Subcommittee Chairman Mitch McConnell (R-Ky.) stated: "We must use foreign aid to promote American values as well as American interests." However, the bill contained language that "held" half of the earmarked funds until the secretary of state certified that economic and political progress would continue in Ukraine (including continued nonproliferation cooperation), corruption was being dealt with appropriately, and American investor-business problems were being resolved. [61]

Ukraine has received broad side payments, both for export control development specifically and in the form of general material and financial assistance.[62] Thus, Ukraine recognizes lesser costs in conforming to nonproliferation norms for its attendant benefits (e.g., access to Western markets and technologies).[63] The amounts and types of side payments, both those assisting specific export control efforts and those giving general assistance under the auspices of Ukrainian compliance (e.g., U.S. Freedom for Russia and the Emerging Eurasian Democracies and Open Markets [FREEDOM] Support Act), correlate strongly to Ukraine's relatively advanced export control development among the NIS. Furthermore, Ukraine has received export control system material assistance in the form of computer hardware and software, enforcement and licensing training, and numerous U.S. and internationally sponsored nonproliferation export control workshops and seminars.[64] Thus, Western material and financial assistance offsets many of the costs associated with the erection and maintenance of the export control system.[65]

There is some evidence to suggest that international nonproliferation norms have constrained Ukrainian export control behavior. For example, under direct U.S. pressure, Ukraine reneged on its plans to assist the Russian reactor project in Bushehr, Iran. Ukrainian state-owned Turboatom, working as subcontractor for the Russian Ministry of Atomic Energy (MINATOM), was to provide generator turbines. Believing the reactor to be part of the Iranian nuclear weapons program, officials in Washington said that such an arrangement would preclude U.S.-Ukrainian nuclear cooperation on commercial nuclear technology, and would threaten the increasingly warm U.S.-Ukrainian relationship. Pressure from Israel and Germany also influenced Kyiv's decision not to participate in the Bushehr project.[66] Nevertheless, some U.S. government officials contend that Ukraine regularly ignores international norms with its exports.[67]

Given the acute economic crisis currently plaguing Ukraine, we would expect any obstacle to selling readily marketable goods and technologies would be summarily removed. Regarding the development of export controls, such is not the case in Ukraine. Through regime membership, foreign financial and material export control assistance and training, enhanced access to much needed previously restricted technologies, and increased interactions with Western security and economic organizations, Ukraine has developed a significant export control system. Therefore, the rational institutional approach indicates that Ukrainian officials in fact derive greater benefits by conforming to international nonproliferation norms and rules than they would by ignoring them. Although Ukraine may not share the exact battery of security concerns as the West (e.g., labeling some countries as "rogues"), export controls are viewed by many in Kyiv as a means for ensuring continued security and economic interaction.[68]

The Ukrainian government officials responsible for implementing and developing the export control system are also those attempting to reform the economy and government.[69] The reform effort is modeled and dependent on the West.[70] As such, nonproliferation norms and rules violations would jeopardize this relationship. Therefore, compliance with international standards is crucial to the Ukrainian economic stabilization and government reform effort. For example, the current debate over Ukrainian MTCR membership illustrates the complexities involved in determining a state's weighing the respective costs and benefits inherent in balancing international cooperation with the requisites of national interest. The MTCR case reveals how the cost-benefit process operates in Ukraine.

Being a critical and integral part of the former-Soviet missile, space, and satellite industry, Ukraine is rich in material, manufacturing, and technological expertise. Furthermore, Ukraine is having limited success in its arms sales abroad.[71] As such, Ukraine hopes to compete in the global space launch market. However, owing to stringent—some would argue discriminatory—membership requirements enacted by the United States, Ukraine has balked at full MTCR membership.[72]

In a memorandum of understanding (MOU) dated 13 May 1994, Ukraine agreed to conduct its missile-related exports according to MTCR criteria and standards. Under the MOU terms, Ukraine was to develop a control list in compliance with MTCR requirements. To this end, the Cabinet of Ministers approved the "Regulation Guiding the Control Over Export, Import, and Transit of Missile Technology Items, As Well As of Equipment, Materials and Technology used in the Manufacture of Missile Weapons" on 27 July 1995.

The prospects of Ukraine's full membership in the regime are still unclear due to U.S. criteria. Nevertheless, Ukraine has enacted a control list in complete compliance with MTCR standards. Additionally, Ukraine has professed not to have engaged in illicit missile trade with proliferant countries.[73] Lucrative trade with the West via a highly capable indigenous space industry necessitates full export control compliance. Despite the strict criteria applied to MTCR membership, seen by many in Ukraine as economic discrimination, Ukraine and the United States signed, during a state visit by President Kuchma, a Commercial Space Launch Agreement in February 1996. This agreement, operating on the assumption that Ukrainian export controls are in full compliance with international nonproliferation norms, allows Ukrainian access to the potentially lucrative U.S. space and satellite market.

Control of missile-related exports is of particular concern to the president and his administration, as President Kuchma was former director of the Yuzhnoye aerospace complex in Dnipropetrovsk.[74] The Kuchma administration has been indispensable in brokering aerospace business deals with foreign firms and governments. For example, the Sea Launch project—an international joint venture between Boeing Commercial Space Company (United States), Energia (Russia), Kvaerner Maritime (Norway), and Yuzhnoye (Ukraine)—formed to launch commercial satellites, represents the type of space activities in which Ukraine can prosper. The World Bank recently approved two partial-risk guarantees of $100 million each in support of commercial bank loans to Sea Launch. The Sea Launch Project will foster substantial economic benefits for Russia and Ukraine by generating close to an estimated $2 billion of incremental exports for Russia and Ukraine over the life of the project, thereby helping to maintain 20,000–30,000 high-wage, high-skill jobs in Energia, Yuzhnoye, and their subcontractors throughout Russia and Ukraine. Other benefits for Ukraine include: enhancing the development of a high-tech sector in which Yuzhnoye has a clear comparative advantage; introducing local, high-tech firms to the international marketplace; teaching local firms how to structure international joint ventures by exposing them to international business and financial practices; promoting cooperative ventures between Ukrainian and other international firms; and promoting additional guarantee operations for other high-priority investment projects in Ukraine. [75] All manufacturing agreements and launches will be licensed, regulated, and monitored by the U.S. government.

The MTCR issue illustrates Ukrainian awareness of the rewards accruing to compliant behavior—most recently evidenced in Kyiv's response to the Libyan affair and regime cooperation in deciding not to supply key parts to the Russian Bushehr project (see above). Thus, the powerful Dnipropetrovsk political clique, staffing much of the government and presidential administration, is certain to continue pursuing commercial space technology as a means of revitalizing the reforming economy, thereby necessitating an export control system cognate with those in the West. As understood through the rational institutional approach, Ukrainian export control behavior makes clear why export control developments continue: cost and uncertainty reduction through cooperation with the nonproliferation regimes, ongoing engagement with Western security and economic organizations, recognition that the benefits accruing to export control development outweighs the costs of developing such a system, and receipt of material incentives. These developments, moreover, are the result of a pro-active president and government—the primary political source enacting export control development in Ukraine.

Domestic Politics: Executive Engagement

Domestic political expectations regarding export control behavior offer only marginal assistance in explaining the Ukrainian case. The domestic political environment in Ukraine conforms to a pattern similar amongst the majority of the successor states governments: liberalizing executive pitted against a reactionary and leftist legislature.[76] As such, the political situation is fractious and highly variable. Legislation, executive action, and bureaucratic initiatives have been uncoordinated and, as a result, often inconsistent and contradictory. Consequently, the government is in a state of irresolution, a condition wherein the divisions of power and formal relations within the central government and between Kyiv and the regional governments have yet to be firmly established.[77] The decentralized trajectory of government reforms have complicated the overall political and economic climate. Nevertheless, as a consequence of a weak civil society and entrenched Soviet-era political culture, the Ukrainian state remains highly centralized.[78]

Owing to governmental immaturity and the uncertain political environment, the Ukrainian export control system has developed largely without the influence of interest groups or firmly established institutional structures outside of the government. Interest groups cannot, at this time, be said to exist as viable political forces in Ukraine because there is no institutional pattern by which extragovernment groups come to influence policy.[79] As noted above, export controls do not figure prominently in state policy-making. Save for well-publicized issues, such as talks over MTCR membership criteria, export controls are not an issue area around which a clearly identifiable interest group or public organization has coalesced. Moreover, civil society is still weak, leaving politics to a narrow circle of regional and central elites.[80] As all sensitive and military industries are state-owned, export control activities transpire solely within the government. Although attempting to decentralize, political power is still vested largely in the state—specifically in the executive, which happens to be the locus of export control development initiatives. Therefore, we see that as a centralized state, Ukraine is better equipped to develop and coordinate export control activities.

The Ukrainian export control system exists solely on the basis of presidential and government decrees. As such, the elite approach offers a rich explanatory means as to how and why the present system emerged and continues to develop. For example, a December 1996 presidential decree established the creation of a new ministry (Gosexportcontrol) dealing exclusively with implementing export control policy. By conferring ministerial status to the state export control organ, President Kuchma enabled export control officials to solidify and rationalize their power base. Prior to this decree, the export control agency operated under the Cabinet of Ministers and was frequently superseded by interagency conflicts.[81]

Various ministries—primarily the Ministry for Foreign Economic Relations; the Ministry of Defense; the Ministry of Machine Building, the Military-Industrial Complex, and Conversion; and the Ministry of Foreign Affairs—have vied for control over sensitive exports, mostly in the conventional weapons area.[82] Because the Ukrainian government structure is an amalgam of Soviet-era and liberalizing institutions, departmental or agency interests have not articulated a clear, consistent position on export control development. Parliamentary involvement is minimal with only desultory, *ad hoc* involvement by two Rada committees addressing export control issues: the Commission on Defense and State Security and the Commission on Foreign Affairs. In terms of the domestic politics approach, the Rada is dominated by "inward-looking coalitions."[83] However, the Rada has demonstrably little involvement in export control policy. The "liberalizing coalitions," moreover, are to be found in the executive.

In 1994, then Prime Minister Leonid Kuchma was elected the second president of Ukraine. Under the Kuchma administration, Ukraine increased its reformist pace by radical privatization plans and by a demonstrably Western bias in its foreign and economic policies. Indeed, since Kuchma's 1994 election, a discernible Western-centric complexion has emerged in Kyiv.[84] Former director of the Yuzhnoye aerospace complex, President Kuchma built his early career in Dnipropetrovsk and drew its leaders to his administration.

President Kuchma has overcome a series of political obstacles to enact his liberalizing reform policies.[85] Packing the administration and government with allies has been a difficult and exacting struggle.[86] Nevertheless, since passage of the post-Soviet constitution in June 1996, Kuchma continues to strengthen economic and political ties with the West while seeking to minimize Ukraine's involvement in the Commonwealth of Independent States (CIS).[87] Furthermore, Western assistance in general, from the United States in particular, has influenced the policy choices made by the Kuchma administration. For example, donor stipulations have shaped presidential economic reforms.[88]

The export control system structure has undergone a series of reorganizations which have involved removing export-promoting agencies from issuing licenses.[89] The reorganization is meant to establish strict control over international transfers of arms and military technology as well as raw materials and skills that might be used for the production of weapons and other military technology. The presidential efforts to strengthen export controls are also seen in the recent decision to control conventional arms exports.

The three main arms-export firms in Ukraine, Progress, Ukrinmash, and Ukroboronservice, have merged into one new company, Ukrspetsexport, to increase state control of weapons sales abroad.[90] Previously, the State Security Service, Ministry of Defense, and the Ministry of Foreign Economic Relations, respectively, independently managed the three firms.[91] These ministries have sought to retain exclusive control over exports, particularly the Ministry of Defense, which, with its surplus armaments and direct links to the military industry, views arms exports as a viable means of generating revenues for conversion efforts, equipment upgrades, and salaries.[92] For example, the Ministry of Defense was also quite vocal with its concerns over sales disclosure protocols in the Wassenaar Arrangement, but were nevertheless persuaded by the Ministry of Foreign Affairs that Ukraine's membership was crucial to the legitimacy of future military sales.[93]

As part of his military and government reorganization plan, President Kuchma appointed the first civilian defense minister in the FSU, Valery Shmarov, shortly after gaining office. Shmarov, a Kuchma colleague from the military industry, was also deputy prime minister for the military-industrial complex. As deputy prime minister, he headed the Governmental Commission on Export Controls (GCEC) and, as such, with the president, had the final say on all sensitive exports. Shmarov was actively involved in promoting Ukrainian non-nuclear status and closer ties with NATO. Shmarov was eventually replaced by a young general, Olexander Kuzmuk. Many believe that Kuzmuk's appointment was Kuchma's attempt to consolidate his military reform programs by circumventing older, established elements in the Ministry of Defense.[94]

Coupled with the recent export control system reorganizations, the ability of export control opponents to influence the direction of export control developments has been substantially curtailed. The State Export Control Service (Gosexportcontrol), the lead export control agency, has expanded in powers and responsibility under the Kuchma administration. However, its ability to effectively implement export control laws and procedures is hampered by insufficient funding and inexperience. Gosexportcontrol has received substantial U.S. financial and technical assistance, thereby instilling an awareness of export control issues and international obligations that are otherwise lacking in other ministries. The export control agencies are, however, limited in their autonomy given that much of the political elite hails from the military-industrial complex. For example, the former and present directors of Gosexportcontrol are former military procurement specialists with close ties to the Ministry of Defense. Thus, the evidence attesting to the influence of the export control agencies is mixed.

Liberal Identity: Forging National Interests

Explaining export control development as a function of identity dynamics, the liberal identity approach partially accounts for the Ukrainian case. This approach posits that states will develop export controls as a consequence of increased interaction and institutional and normative affinities with the Western, liberal community of states. As such, interacting states come to regard themselves as intrinsic parts to the liberal whole, of which export controls are part of a larger battery of expected behaviors. Ukraine, however, poses several challenges to the derived expectations concerning export control development. These challenges are the difficulty in determining the overall political disposition in Ukraine, a country without, arguably, a definitive sense of a uniform political-national identity outside of the government. Nevertheless, the Ukrainian government clearly evinces a "liberal" predilection in both its political rhetoric and state-building efforts. This section explores the identity issue and how the liberal community has influenced export control development in Ukraine.

The history of the Ukrainian people and of the Ukrainian territory does not abound with continuity and constant lines of development throughout the centuries. The dominant continuity in the history of Ukraine is the absence of an independent state in modern times. Ukrainian history thus deviates from the European pattern of state building.[95] Furthermore, Ukraine itself is internally divided. Galicia, or western Ukraine, tends to be more nationalistic than the south and east of the country. The latter, the regions of the Donbas and Crimea, are composed primarily of ethnic Russians. These regions clearly differ in demographic, economic, and religious-denominational terms. This informal dividing line is the source of chronic political tensions, thereby making consensus on political identity complex and laborious.[96]

Ukrainian political identity is further confounded by its shared political, cultural, religious, and linguistic history with Russia. From the days of the Kyivan-Rus, Ukrainian and Russian histories have been inseparably linked.[97] In 1654, control over the Ukrainian region was formally ceded to the Russian Tsar. Both the Russian and Soviet yoke enfeebled any latent national aspirations. Until independence, Ukraine existed as a Russian province.[98] Subsequently, both Ukraine and Russia have sought to determine the nature of their relationship, and, perforce, Ukraine has sought to differentiate itself from Russia as befits its newfound sovereignty.

Ukrainian national and political identity has been, at best, a problematic issue arising fundamentally from the difficulties attendant to the creation of a new state.[99] However, Ukraine, under the direction of the president, evinces a decidedly Western disposition in its domestic and international policies. Economic liberalization efforts, democratic political reforms, and courting the Western security communities have been clear indications of the pro-Western political complexion holding sway in Kyiv.[100] According to one Ukrainian export control official, regular interaction with Western states specifically addressing export control issues has resulted in palpable advances in export control advancements.[101]

Relations with the West have gradually evolved into the current state of positive engagement. After Ukraine undertook its nuclear divestiture, the West ostensibly lost interest in continued engagement. However, the inchoate economic and political reform efforts, waning relations with Russia, and the continued proliferation threat quickly refocused Western attention on this country of 51 million. To this end, the Kuchma administration and government actively courted Western sources of financial and security assistance. On continued economic and political cooperation with the West, Foreign Minister Hennady Udovenko remarked, "Integration with the West is the main direction of our foreign policy."[102]

An increased sense of community with the West is evinced by Ukraine's engagement with the liberal commons. For example, Ukraine is a member of the Council of Europe and was a charter member of the Wassenaar Arrangement. In the area of nonproliferation, Ukraine is a member and/or adherent to nonproliferation supplier regimes, all of which necessitate a commitment to export controls. Furthermore, increased interaction continues to guarantee Ukraine's international commitments. For example, the U.S.-Ukrainian Binational Commission, or the Gore-Kuchma Commission, was created 19 September 1996. The commission explores economic, political, and security concerns shared by both governments. Specifically, the commission addresses nonproliferation and security issues.

The "Charter on a Distinctive Partnership between the North Atlantic Treaty Organization and Ukraine" was signed 8 July 1997. The agreement parallels the agreement signed between NATO and Russia in May. After the signing ceremony, President Kuchma explained that the most important item in the charter, in his opinion, is NATO's explicit recognition of Ukraine as a Central-Eastern European nation. "This is a key issue of the document," he said. The charter wording reads: "Noting NATO's positive role in maintaining peace . . . and its openness for cooperation with the new democracies of Central and Eastern Europe, an inseparable part of which is Ukraine." President Kuchma also expounded on what such recognition meant: "As President Jacques Chirac told me, 'We cannot allow anything to happen to Ukraine. We will defend it both by political and economic methods.'"[103] Although not a full NATO member, Ukraine has inched closer to the prospect. However, considerable parliamentary opposition—primarily Communist—exists to the agreement or to continued interaction with NATO to the exclusion of Russia.

Clearly, even at this early stage in Ukraine's political development, we can associate export control development with the formation of a liberal identity.[104] Increased interaction with the West and a growing sense of community with Europe and the United States are evident in Ukrainian foreign policy. For example, in addition to financial assistance, President Kuchma and the export control community are directly influenced by Western involvement in the export control field. Nonproliferation regime membership and export control assistance have both directly and indirectly influenced Ukraine's sense of interest and identity as the state-building process continues. Export controls, well-developed in the Western states, are part and parcel of the structure of liberal states. However, the political, regional, and cultural differences in Ukraine, combined with the lack of a coherent and uniform sense of political or national selfhood, suggest that Ukraine has yet to establish a universal foundation upon which to construct the overall political trajectory of its independence.[105] Despite peaceful transfers of power, universal suffrage, and a new, liberal-minded constitution, the emerging liberal order is, by and large, confined to sections of the government and to certain regions.[106]

The national government is still a mixture of Soviet-era and democratizing institutions and norms. Democracy and the rule of law are not universally practiced.[107] The emerging sense of community with the West does not reach beyond the elite level. In this respect, export controls may merely represent an attempt to conform to expectations thereby assuring continued material and financial assistance. Furthermore, Ukraine has indicated its willingness to trade in sensitive items with illiberal states. For example, the 1996 sale of 320 T-80 tanks to Pakistan suggests that Ukraine may be adopting a more pragmatic approach to export controls in practice.[108] Multimillion-dollar technology and trade agreements have been signed between Ukraine and Iran. Ukraine's largest non-CIS trading partner is China. In 1995, trade to China netted over $830 million. One economist notes: "A vast market exists in China for Ukraine's select scientific and technology exports."[109] Additionally, during Wassenaar negotiations, Ukraine hesitated to yield to the U.S. request to take an obligation proscribing armaments and dual-use exports to Iran, Iraq, Libya, and North Korea. Disputes centered primarily on exports to Iran. However, U.S.-Ukrainian negotiations resulted in compromise, the terms of which both countries agreed not to make public.[110]

Ukraine's present membership in the nonproliferation regime and other security communities and its proposed, albeit distant, intention to join the European Union (EU) will most likely further integrate the emerging political identity with that of Western, liberal states. Further political, economic, and security contacts ensure a long-term influence on the shape and scope of Ukrainian domestic and international policies generally, and export control policies specifically.

CONCLUSION

When considering the economic and political difficulties confronting a state in the midst of creating itself anew, the developments in the Ukrainian export control system are all the more remarkable. Since 1992, Ukraine has joined or adheres to all the treaties in the international nonproliferation regime and shown marked progress in developing the elements of an internationally compatible export control system. The theoretical examination accounting for these developments reveals interesting details about the Ukrainian case.

Upon examination of the approaches, we see that, apart from rational institutionalism, no one particular approach dominates. Instead, the results indicate a compounding effect, wherein parts of the approaches tend to buttress the others. For example, we see that the primary political actors in Ukraine, the elites, are leading the developments in export control. As such, they are realizing the benefits of steady interaction with the Western, liberal community through market access and direct financial material inducements. The evidence suggests that the liberalizing elites, primarily President Kuchma and his administration, have managed through constitutional and indirect political means to be the primary actors in governmental decision making regarding export control policy. However, the Kuchma administration is acting in, by and large, contradistinction to the political and economic preferences of the legislature, which is dominated by leftists steadfastly opposed to economic and social reforms.

Kuchma's strong relationship with the West has ensured continued financial and material support for his state-building efforts. Since independence, consistent interaction with Western governments, NGOs, and international financial and security organizations has fostered a decidedly liberal cadre of policy-makers in Kyiv. It is through these processes of interaction that identities and interests are formed:

> The mechanism here is reinforcements; interactions reward actors for holding certain ideas about each other and discourages them from holding others. If repeated long enough, these "reciprocal typifications" will create relatively stable concepts of self and other regarding the issue at stake in the interaction. It is through reciprocal interaction, in other words, that we create and instantiate the relatively enduring social structures in terms of which we define our identities and interests.[111]

Assistance is, in most instances, linked to issue areas of concern to donor countries and organizations. In this respect, export control developments are the direct and indisputable result of international financial and material assistance. Continued aid is contingent upon compliance and further cooperation. For example, the quick Ukrainian response on the Libya scandal, the decision not to supply power turbines to the Iranian Bushehr reactor, and Kuchma's recent avowal—prompted by working sessions of the Gore-Kuchma Commission—to decommission its stock of SS-24 missiles are all policy moves that suggest Kyiv is weighing its options. Nevertheless, despite convincing developments, proliferation is still an acute problem.

Structurally, the Ukrainian export control system has evolved to such a state that we can refer to it as technically competent. With U.S. assistance, a licensing automation system is being installed, complete with a component allowing the Gosexportcontrol, access to scientific research institutes for technical analyses. A draft comprehensive export control law is currently under parliamentary review. This law will establish the export control system on a permanent legal basis—the current system being based only on decrees. National control lists for sensitive and dual-use items have been harmonized with international standards. Furthermore, industry outreach efforts are under way through the Ministry of Foreign Economic Relations and the State Export Control Service. Nevertheless, owing to the lack of experience, low political priority status, and industries unversed in nonproliferation norms, the implementation of export controls may suffer from a lack of consistent and uniform understanding, sensitivity, and political will.

Having received inducements and having learned the international process by which states conform to prevailing norms for gain, export control practice in Ukraine may be an exercise in mollification and political survival. The rational institutional approach makes abundantly clear that states will cooperate when there are tangible gains at hand. However, the approach cannot account for neither sincerity, nor conviction. Faced with mounting economic difficulties and political tensions, Ukrainian officials frequently lack adequate resources for enforcement and outreach activities.[112] Furthermore, government corruption is rampant.[113] The uncertain economic and political environment makes monitoring and enforcing export activities extremely difficult. Furthermore, despite regime membership, Ukraine does not preclude future commercial interactions with "illiberal states," most notably Iran and China. Thus, despite export control developments, the proliferation threat emanating from Ukraine remains a weighty issue for the post–Cold War international security environment.

NOTES

1. Office of the Secretary of Defense, *Proliferation: Threat and Response* (Washington, D.C.: U.S. Government Printing Office, 1996).

2. William Potter, *Nuclear Profiles of the Soviet Successor States* (Monterey, CA: Monterey Institute of International Studies, 1993). One-third of the Soviet Union's military production is located in Ukraine, employing an estimated 2.7 million people.

3. *Nuclear Successor States of the Soviet Union: Nuclear Weapon and Sensitive Export Status Report*, the Monterey Institute of International Studies and the Carnegie Endowment for International Peace, no. 4, May 1996, p. 69.

4. See, for example, Graham Allison et al., *Avoiding Nuclear Anarchy: Containing the Threat of Loose Russian Nuclear Weapons and Fissile Material* (Cambridge: MIT Press, 1996); Gary K. Bertsch, ed., *Restraining the Spread of the Soviet Arsenal: NIS Nonproliferation Export Controls 1996 Status Report* (Athens: University of Georgia Press, 1997); and United States Congress, Office of Technology Assessment, *Proliferation and the Former Soviet Union*, OTA-ISS-605 (Washington, D.C.: U.S. Government Printing Office, September 1994).

5. For an assessment of U.S. MPC&A and export control assistance programs in the FSU, see National Research Council, *Proliferation Concerns: Assessing U.S. Efforts to Help Contain Nuclear and Other Dangerous Materials and Technologies in the Former Soviet Union* (Washington, D.C.: National Academy Press, 1997).

6. Interviews with Ministry of Foreign Affairs and other export control officials, Washington, D.C., September 1996.

7. Ukraine retained approximately 30 percent of the Soviet military-industrial complex (MIC), comprising 1,870 defense-related enterprises.

8. For an explanation of the scoring methodology and standard measure, see "Tools and Methods for Measuring and Comparing Nonproliferation Export Controls," by C. Craft and S. Grillot et al., occasional paper of the Center for International Trade and Security (Athens: University of Georgia Press, October 1996).

9. A description and history of the Ukrainian export control system is found in Jones and Zaborsky, "Ukraine," in Gary K. Bertsch, ed., *Restraining the Spread of the Soviet Arsenal: Export Controls 1996 Status Report*. (Athens, GA: University of Georgia, 1997), pp. 17–30.

10. Craft et al., pp. 1–17.

11. Ibid, pp. 13–15.

12. See Evan Maderios, "U.S. Warns Russia, Ukraine on Missile-Related Sales to China," *Arms Control Today*, May–June 1996, p. 24; Bill Gertz, "Ukraine and Libya Forge Strategic Alliance," *Washington Times*, 10 June 1996.

13. Taras Kuzio, *Ukrainian Security Policy* (Westport, CT: Praeger, 1995), p. 46.

14. Jones and Zaborsky, p. 27.

15. "Ukraine," *Economist Intelligence Unit: Country Report*, fourth quarter,

1996. The Ukrainian economy served, as did the other former republics, as a producer of semifinished goods. Consequently, Ukrainian industry is, by and large,
compromised by its lack of full-cycle production facilities, which makes the process
of economic transition especially difficult. An excellent study exploring the link between the Soviet-era economic system and the present economic challenges in
Ukraine is found in Raphael Shen, *Ukraine's Economic Reform: Obstacles, Errors,
Lessons* (Westport, CT: Praeger Press, 1996). See especially pp. 15–140.

16. John Baker, *Nonproliferation Incentives for Russia and Ukraine*, Adelphi
Paper 309 (Oxford: International Institute for Strategic Studies, 1997), pp. 14–15.

17. National Research Council, *op. cit.*, pp. 85–100.

18. Author's interviews with Expert and Technical Committee officials, Washington, D.C., October 1996.

19. Ustina Markus, "U.S. Daily Queries Ukraine's Entry into Missile Pact,"
OMRI Daily Digest, 24 September 1996; and Gary Bertsch and Victor Zaborsky,
"Bringing Ukraine into the MTCR: Can U.S. Policy Succeed?" *Arms Control Today*,
vol. 27, no. 2, April 1997, pp. 9–14.

20. The term *adaptive* is self-consciously fashioned on the "evolution" concept. Moreover, I wish to imply that institutional learning drives the present system's
shape. Current social science research on complex adaptive systems suggests that
collectivities, such as governments, learn as they evolve. Thus, as a new state,
Ukraine's state-building effort benefits from the considerable body of the political-
economic histories and developmental approaches of other countries. See Marcelo
Alonso, *Organization and Change in Complex Social Systems* (New York: Paragon
House, 1990); Warren Bennis, *Beyond Bureaucracy: Essays on the Development
and Evolution of Human Organization* (London: Jossey-Bass, 1993); and Douglas
Kiel and Euel Elliott, eds., *Chaos Theory in the Social Sciences: Foundations and
Applications* (Ann Arbor: University of Michigan Press, 1996).

21. Author's interview with Ukrainian government official, University of
Georgia, April 1997.

22. Ministries with export control departments are: the Ministry of Foreign
Affairs; Ministry of Machine Building; Military-Industrial Complex, and Conver-
sion; Ministry of Foreign Economic Relations and Trade; Security Service; State
Customs Committee; State Security Service; Ministry of Internal Affairs; State Border
Committee; Ministry of Environmental Protection and Nuclear Safety; Committee
on State Secrets and Technical Protection of Information; Ministry of Economics;
Center on Strategic Planning and Analysis (part of the National Security and De-
fense Committee of the Cabinet of Ministers); and National Space Commission of
Ukraine.

23. In its export control assistance to Ukraine, the United States has repeatedly stressed the importance of technical review in export control licensing, policy-
making and control list fabrication. Los Alamos and Argonne National Laboratories,
under the auspices of the U.S. Department of Energy (DOE), provide direct technical and financial assistance to this end.

24. Also, through the IAEA, limited financial and material assistance is provided by Australia, Finland, France, Hungary, Sweden, and the United Kingdom. See *IAEA Working Report: Progress Review on Technical Support to Newly Independent States in Non-proliferation Field*, PR 96/24 (Vienna, 1996).

25. National Research Council, *op. cit.*, p. 94.

26. Interview with U.S. Customs official, Washington, D.C., January 1997.

27. National Research Council, *op. cit.*, p. 95.

28. Sergey Svistil, "Ukraine," *Worldwide Guide to Export Controls*, 1994/1995 Edition (London: Deltac), p. 2.

29. Marget B. McClean and Deborah Palmieri, "Marketization through Defense Conversion: A Policy Prescriptive on the Ukrainian Case," in Deborah Palmieri, ed., *Russia and the NIS in the World Economy: East-West Investment, Financing, and Trade* (Westport, CT: Praeger, 1996), pp. 149–60.

30. See, C. Hummel, "Ukrainian Arms Makers Are Left on Their Own," *Radio Free Europe/Radio Liberty Research Report*, vol. 1, no. 32, 8 August 1992, pp. 33–41.

31. The costs involved in developing and maintaining export controls are considerable. For an examination of the costs, see Kathleen Bailey, "Nonproliferation Export Controls: Problems and Alternatives," in Kathleen Bailey and Robert Rudney, eds., *Nonproliferation and Export Controls* (Lanham: University Press of America, 1993), pp. 50–61. Bailey notes: "Export controls divert resources of governments—particularly in countries that do not have large bureaucracies or budgets—that might be more profitably diverted to other government activities" (p. 52).

32. See John Mroz and Oleksandr Pavliuk, "Ukraine: Europe's Linchpin," *Foreign Affairs*, vol. 75, no. 3, May/June 1996, pp. 52–63.

33. "Between East and West: Ukraine," *The Economist*, vol. 340, no. 7985, 28 September 1996, pp. 58–59.

34. It should be noted, however, that Russian-Ukrainian relations are complicated by a substantial ethnic Russian presence in the southern and eastern regions. The western region, traditionally nationalist and ultimately distrustful of Moscow, tends to see Russian regional activities as a threat to Ukrainian sovereignty. See John Morrison, "Pereiaslav and After: the Russian-Ukrainian Relationship," *International Affairs*, vol. 64, no. 9, October 1993, pp. 677–704.

35. Ukraine has generally good relations with its neighbors, as evidenced in the number of bilateral political and economic accords enacted among such states as Poland, Romania, Iran, Iraq, Turkey, and the Czech Republic. A scholar of Ukrainian security issues notes: "On the whole, external military threats from neighboring nations other than Russia are a distant security priority." N. S. Krawciw, "Ukrainian Security and Military Doctrine," in Bruce Parrott, ed., *State Building and Military Power in Russia and the New States of Eurasia* (New York: M. E. Sharpe, 1995), p. 138. See also, Leonid Kistersky "General Theory of Ukrainian Security," in Leonid Kistersky, ed., *Security in Eastern Europe: The Case of Ukraine* (Providence, RI: Brown University Press, 1994), pp. 7–17.

36. Ustina Markus, "Ukrainian Parliament Confirms Security Concept," *OMRI Daily Digest*, 25 May 1996.

37. Erik Whitlock, "Ukrainian-Russian Trade: the Economics of Dependency," *RFE/RL Research Report*, vol. 2, no. 43, 29 October 1993, pp. 38–42.

38. On 9 July 1993, the Russian Duma passed a resolution claiming that Sevastopol was a Russian city. Coupled with the Duma's attempt to pass legislation negating the dissolution of the Soviet Union, tensions between Moscow and Kyiv have been chronic; see "Kommjunike o Vstrece Prezidentov Rossii i Ukrainy," *Rossijskaja Gazeta*, 18 July 1995. However, the long-awaited *Basic Treaty on Friendship and Cooperation* between Russia and Ukraine, in which Ukrainian territorial integrity is observed, has been signed, as has a formal and final agreement on the division of the Black Sea Fleet.

39. "Russia's Bid to Stop Ukraine Arms to Pakistan," *The Hindu*, 3 December 1996. Increasing competition between Russian and Ukrainian arms manufacturers in the Middle Eastern and South Asian markets have served to exacerbate relations between the two. See also Paul Goble, "Arms Races and Cash Flows: Russian-Ukrainian Arms Competition Increases," *RFE/RL Research Report*, 4 April 1997.

40. A useful examination of Ukrainian-Russian strategic relations is Sherman W. Garnett, *Keystone in the Arch: Ukraine in the Emerging Security Environment of Central and Eastern Europe* (Washington, D.C.: Carnegie Endowment for International Peace, 1997). See especially pp. 41–82.

41. See Yevgenii Sharov, "Ukraine and the MTCR," *The Monitor*, vol. 1, no. 2, Spring 1995; and "Missiles to Get New Mission," *Asia Times*, 18 July 1997.

42. For example, the former Soviet missile and space infrastructure is now split between Ukraine and Russia. Consequently, commercial space launch activities engaged in by either necessitates involvement of the other. See, "Ukraine's Space Launch Industry: Interview with Yuzhnoye Plant Director," *Space News*, 29 November 1993, pp. 1, 20.

43. Author's interview with Ministry of Foreign Affairs official, Washington, D.C., January 1997.

44. Mroz and Pavliuk, p. 59.

45. See Vladimir Tsimbalyk, "The Ukrainian Export Control System." *The Monitor*, vol. 1, no. 4, Fall 1995, p. 1; and Victor Vaschilin, "State Export Controls in Ukraine," *The Monitor*, vol. 3, no. 3, Summer 1997, pp. 12–15.

46. Kuzio, pp. 25–30.

47. Interviews with Ministry of Foreign Affair and export control officials, July 1996, Los Alamos National Laboratory.

48. Kuzio (1995), *op. cit.*, p. 54.

49. Author interviews with Ukrainian government officials, June 1995, Kyiv.

50. Contingent upon enacting the Lisbon Protocol, the 1994 Trilateral Agreement, and the NPT, Ukraine predicated nuclear disarmament on Western Security guarantees as the primary means by which to address its security concerns. See Taras Kuzio, *Ukrainian Security Policy* (Westport, CT: Praeger, 1995). The resultant

guarantees were formally declared at a 1995 Budapest Organization for Security and Cooperation in Europe (OSCE) conference. For a succinct study on the Ukrainian effort to augment its military structure, see James Joung-Jun Na, "Non-Nuclear Military Security of Ukraine," in Leonid Kistersky, ed., *Security in Eastern Europe: The Case of Ukraine* (Providence, RI: Brown University, 1995), pp. 75–99. And for an analysis of how Ukrainian security concerns apply to state building, see Andrea Chandler, "Statebuilding and Political Priorities in Post-Soviet Ukraine: The Role of the Military," *Armed Forces and Society*, v. 22, no. 4, Summer 1996, pp. 573–97.

51. Ustina Markus, "Ukraine Seeks Investment," *OMRI Daily Digest*, 19 February 1996.

52. Ukrainian government officials and Western economists maintain that access to Western markets is necessary for successful economic transition. The dissolution of COCOM in March 1994 signaled a new era in East-West trade, thereby allowing for vital transfers of advanced technologies and goods to occur. Contingent, however, upon these changes were assurances that export controls would be implemented by FSU states.

53. Interview with Ukrainian export control official, Washington, D.C., February 1997.

54. For example, MTCR accession talks between the United States and Ukraine have resulted in the creation of cooperative space projects.

55. According to one Ministry of Foreign Affairs official, regime membership has "indicated to Ukraine that the U.S. is not using the supplier regimes as an economic tool against the less developed world, but that Washington has legitimate security concerns." Author's interview, Los Alamos National Laboratory, June 1996.

56. This issue is explored at greater length in the concluding section of this chapter.

57. Bill Getz, "Kyiv Imperils U.S. Aid with Libya Arms Deal," *Washington Times*, 9 December 1996, pp. A1, A12.

58. Jones and Zaborsky, in Bertsch, ed., p. 26; and Bill Getz, "Kyiv Imperils U.S. Aid with Libya Arms Deal," *The Washington Times*, 9 December 1996, A1, A12.

59. Author's interviews, Washington, D.C., January 1997.

60. Ustina Markus, "Ukraine to Set Up Commission on Libyan Arms Deal," *OMRI Daily Digest*, 13 December 1996. The release of 1996 U.S. aid for Ukraine was contingent upon the findings of a U.S. presidential investigatory committee.

61. Michael Sawkiw, "Senate Approved Foreign Aid Bill with Earmarks, Conditions for Ukraine," Ukrainian National Information Service (*Unian*), 20 July 1997.

62. Ukraine has received export control assistance from the U.S. Cooperative Threat Reduction Program (CTR)—from which $13.26 million is budgeted for export control development—and the Nonproliferation and Disarmament Fund (NDF). Export control assistance from Norway, Japan, and Germany and coordinated multilateral efforts from the International Atomic Energy Agency (IAEA) have

augmented Ukraine's export control system development activities. In addition, Ukraine is the third-largest recipient, behind Israel and Egypt, of U.S. direct aid. Receipt of aid is frequently contingent upon compliance with donor concerns.

63. See Anthony Gadzey, *The Political Economy of Power: Hegemony and Economic Liberalism* (New York: St. Martin's Press, 1994). U.S. nonproliferation activism can be seen, arguably, as part of its role as post–Cold War hegemon: "Hegemony rests on the subjective awareness by elites in secondary states that they are benefiting, as well as on the willingness of the hegemon itself to sacrifice tangible short-term benefits for long-term gains." In Robert Keohane, *After Hegemony: Cooperation and Discord in the World Political Economy* (Princeton, NJ: Princeton University Press, 1984), p. 88.

64. Under CTR and NDF funds, Ukraine received and continues to receive U.S. material assistance, thereby significantly reducing the costs incurred to Kyiv in constructing a system from scratch. European and Japanese material and financial assistance have also been significant. The latter contributions are coordinated through the European Union and the IAEA.

65. A Ministry of Foreign Affairs official noted that export controls were not high political priorities in Kyiv. He asserted that Western material and financial assistance were therefore crucial to export control development in Ukraine. Author's interview, Los Alamos National Laboratory, July 1996. Several export control agency officials later confirmed this assertion.

66. Michael Gordon, "Ukraine Decides Not to Supply Key Parts for Iranian Reactor," *New York Times*, 14 April 1997. More recently, however, Ukraine has expressed its intention of reviewing the earlier presidential decision against supplying the Iranian reactor. Speaking in the city of Kharkiv, home of the turbine plant, Foreign Minister Hennady Udovenko on 18 August said he would study a draft contract under which Turboatom would supply a 1,000-megawatt turbine for the plant in the Iranian city of Bushehr. Udovenko admitted that "fulfillment of the contract could complicate relations with our partners." The United States and Israel have argued that the plant could help Iran develop nuclear weapons. See, "Ukraine May Supply Turbine to Iran," *RFE/RL Daily Report*, 19 August 1997.

67. Author's interviews with U.S. government officials, Washington, D.C., fall 1996. See also Jeffrey Smith, "Iraq Buying Missile Parts Covertly," *Washington Post*, 16 October 1995.

68. An export control agency official likened export controls to nuclear divestiture: as a means of ensuring Western confidence in and support for the Ukrainian state building effort. Author's interview, Washington, D.C., January 1997.

69. An identification of the state actors leading export control developments is found in the subsequent section on the domestic politics approach.

70. See Khristina Lew, "Kuchma, Gore Convene First Session of U.S.-Ukraine Commission," *Ukrainian Weekly*, vol. 66, no. 21, 25 May 1997. During his May 1997 visit to Washington, President Kuchma assured U.S. officials that market-oriented economic and democratic political reforms would continue.

71. Potentially the most lucrative arms sale Kyiv has made to date (an estimated $500 million controversial tank deal with Pakistan) was recently canceled by Islamabad. After receiving 32 out of a proposed 320 T-80 UD tanks, Pakistan claimed the tanks were not built to specifications and suffered from manufacturing flaws. See Pavel Ivanov, "Ukraine Tries to Elbow Its Way into Global Arms Market," *Asia Times*, 2 July 1997.

72. The Ukrainian Ministry of Foreign Affairs continues to express concerns that the United States is attempting to limit Ukrainian access to the commercial space launch market. For an informative account of the complicated debate between the United States and Ukraine on MTCR compliance and membership, see Victor Zaborsky, "Ukraine's Missile Industry and National Space Program: MTCR Compliance or Proliferation Threat?" *The Monitor*, vol. 1, no. 3, Summer 1995; and Victor Zaborsky, "Ukraine's Niche in the U.S. Launch Market: Will Kyiv's Hopes Come True?" *World Affairs*, vol. 159, no. 2, Fall 1996, pp. 55–63.

73. This assertion is somewhat suspect. For example, in late 1993, Iran reportedly purchased eight SS-N-22 "Sunburn": supersonic anti-ship missiles from Ukraine for $600,000 each. See *Defense News*, 4 October 1993, pp. 25–26.

74. President Kuchma, through his association with the Kuchma-Gore Commission, acknowledged the necessity of an effective export control system to the future of the Ukrainian space and missile industry. See "Ukrainian President in U.S. Congress" *RFE/RL Daily Report*, 16 May 1997.

75. World Bank News Release no. 97/1369 ECA, "World Bank Supports International Aerospace Joint-Venture," 30 May 1997.

76. See G. Rozman and S. Sato, *Dismantling Communism: Common Causes and Regional Variations* (Washington, D.C.: Woodrow Wilson Center Press, 1994).

77. The post-Soviet constitution was ratified in June 1996. However, there is still considerable debate over the particulars of the division of political power as enumerated in the new constitution. The remaining friction continues between the Parliament and President Kuchma's reformist government. Furthermore, regional politics and players have complicated the national political landscape. Elite politicians and bureaucrats from economically and politically powerful regions, including Kyiv, the eastern city of Kharkiv, the Donetsk basin, and the port of Odessa, have challenged those from Dnepropetrovsk, a region heavy with military industry and President Kuchma's home district. See James Rupert, "Regional Tensions Trip Up Ukraine's Quest of Stability," *Washington Post*, 27 October 1996.

78. See Alexander J. Motyl, *Dilemmas of Independence: Ukraine After Totalitarianism* (New York: The Council on Foreign Relations, 1994).

79. Interviews with U.S. Embassy-Kyiv officials. See also United Nations Human Development Yearly Report: Ukraine 1995.

80. Motyl (1994), pp. 107–25.

81. Interview with Expert and Technical Committee official, University of Georgia, October 1995.

82. For details regarding the structure of the post-presidential December 1996

decree export control system, see Jones and Zaborsky, in Bertsch, ed., pp. 17–30.

83. Of the total occupied 414 seats in the Rada, 93 are held by the Communist Party of Ukraine. The Communist bloc holds a substantial amount of power in that there are no strong coalitions among the other parties to act as a counter. In practice, a Communist-agrarian bloc dominates the legislature; centrist-reformist parties, including the Interregional Reform Bloc of Kuchma, did very poorly in 1994 parliamentary elections. Opposition to Kuchma's economic reforms in parliament is led by Oleksander O. Morov, chairman of the Socialist Party, who threatens to overturn Kuchma's decrees and oppose economic reforms. Morov proclaimed the socialists as "opposition to the presidential course."

84. Mroz and Pavliuk, p. 60.

85. For brief biographical sketches on President Kuchma and former Prime Minister Pavel Lazarenko, see "Khto ie Khto v Ukrains'kiy Politytsi," *Vypusk 2* (Kyiv: KIS, 1995).

86. See Konstantin Parishkura, "President Kuchma Revamps Cabinet," *The Current Digest of the Post-Soviet Press*, 2 August 1995, vol. 47, no. 27, p. 21 (3). President Kuchma is leading the changes in government since adoption of the post-Soviet constitution. On the political front, his goal of paring down the swollen Soviet-era bureaucracy has met with, predictably, considerable parliamentary and bureaucratic resistance. For example, on 19 December 1996 President Kuchma signed a decree fixing the number of ministers in the cabinet as well as the total number of ministries. The decree also directly subordinates the interior, foreign, information, and defense ministers to the president. The decree has sparked controversy among deputies, some of whom say it is unconstitutional and accuse the president of taking over some of parliament's prerogatives. Rada Deputy Volodymyr Chemerys said parliament may turn to the Constitutional Court to have the decree revoked.

87. See Taras Kuzio, "A Friend in Need: Kyiv Woos Washington," *The World Today*, vol. 52, no. 61, April 1996, p. 96; and Ustina Markus, "Ukrainian President on CIS," *OMRI Daily Digest*, 27 March 1996.

88. For example, concerned over rampant official corruption and the pace and direction of economic reforms, the International Monetary Fund (IMF) decided not to extend a $2.5 billion credit until reforms are harmonized with IMF prerequisites. Shortly after the IMF decision, President Kuchma reshuffled his cabinet and upgraded the auditing powers of the newly created anti-corruption investigatory committee, the National Bureau of Investigation. See Pavel Polityuk, "Ukrainian Leader Shuffles Cabinet," *Washington Post*, 25 July 1997.

89. For example, although providing input into license reviews, the Ministry of Defense no longer makes export decisions on its own.

90. Ustina Markus, "Ukrainian President Increases Control over Arms Exports," *OMRI Daily Digest*, 3 January 1997.

91. Taras Kuzio, "Ukraine Arms Sales," *Jane's Intelligence Review*, March 1997, pp. 100–11.

92. Taras Kuzio (1995), *op. cit.*, pp. 45–47.

93. Interview with Gosexportcontrol official, Washington, D.C., January 1997.

94. Tor Bukkvoll, *Ukraine and European Security* (London: The Royal Institute of International Affairs, 1997), pp. 20–22.

95. For accounts of the history of nation-state building in Europe and Eurasia, see Charles Tilly, *The Formation of National States in Western Europe* (Princeton, NJ: Princeton University Press, 1975) and Fernand Braudel, *A History of Civilizations* (London: Penguin Books, 1987).

96. Orest Subtelny, "Imperial Disintegration and Nation State Formation: The Case of Ukraine," in John Blaney, ed., *The Successor States to the USSR* (Washington: Congressional Quarterly, Inc., 1996), pp. 184–96.

97. Braudel (1987), pp. 530–72. And R. Solchanyk, "Russia, Ukraine, and the Imperial Legacy," *Post-Soviet Affairs*, vol. 9, no. 4, Fall 1993, pp. 340–41.

98. Ukraine has always been somewhat of an international anomaly: posturing as state, but lacking the trappings thereof. For example, while in the Soviet Union, Ukraine occupied a nominal seat at the United Nations.

99. Bohdan Krawchenko, "Ukraine: the Politics of Independence," in Ian Bremmer and Ray Taras, eds., *Nationalism and Politics in the Soviet Successor States* (Cambridge: Cambridge University Press, 1993), pp. 99–115.

100. Speaking of the leftist Parliamentary opposition, President Kuchma observed: "The only problem with the Communists today is that they want to build a Soviet Socialist Republic, while I want to build a civilized, democratic, and lawful state" (The Ukrainian Information Agency, *Unian*, 5 May 1996).

101. Author's interview with Gosexportcontrol official, Washington, D.C., January 1997. Through CTR and NDF programs, the United States has taken an active role in export control initiatives in Ukraine.

102. Pavel Ivanov, "And What About Ukraine?" *Asia Times*, 5 May 1997.

103. Roman Woronowycz, "Ukraine and NATO Sign Partnership Charter," *Interfax-Ukraine*, 9 July 1997. On a visit to Kyiv shortly after the Madrid signing, U.S. Secretary of Defense William Cohen praised the Ukrainian president in his efforts to reform the Ukrainain state: "We appreciate the courageous stands that President Kuchma has taken in trying to develop a free market and a prosperous economy, the courageous steps that he has taken to get rid of nuclear weapons on Ukraine's soil, and that he intends to lead Ukraine into a very stable, democratic, and prosperous twenty-first century."

104. For more information on the subject of the emerging Ukrainian political identity see Taras Kuzio, *Ukraine: From Perestroika to Independence* (New York: St. Martin's Press, 1994) and Roman Szporluk, "Nation Building in Ukraine: Problems and Prospects," in John Blaney, ed., *The Successor States to the USSR* (Washington, D.C.: Congressional Quarterly, Inc., 1995), pp. 173–84.

105. Ukraine has a considerable political and economic distance to go before we can confidently refer to Ukraine as manifesting a "liberal identity." See *Human*

Development Report 1996: Ukraine, chapter 3: "Civil Society and Political Participation" (New York: United Nations, 1996). Some would argue that Ukraine, or Russia, is incapable of adopting a liberal identity. For example, see Samuel Huntington, *The Clash of Civilizations and the Remaking of World Order* (New York: Simon and Schuster, 1996).

106. For a comprehensive study of Ukraine's relative democratic development, see Roger Kaplan, ed., *Freedom in the World: The Annual Survey of Political Rights and Civil Liberties 1996–1997* (New York: Freedom House, 1997) and Adrian Karatnycky, Alexander Motyl, and Boris Shor, eds., *Nations in Transit: Civil Society, Democracy and Markets in Eastern and Central Europe and the Newly Independent States* (New York: Freedom House, 1997). Both works have lengthy sections exploring the Ukrainian case in terms of civil rights, political participation, and economic freedoms.

107. For example, the U.S. State Department Human Rights Report for Ukraine 1996 noted "the persistence of unreformed legal and prison systems, occasional government attempts to control the press, beatings by police and prison officials, limits on freedom of association, restrictions on foreign religious organizations, societal anti-Semitism, some discrimination against women, and ethnic tensions in Crimea."

108. "Ukraine Signs Tank Deal with Pakistan," *OMRI Daily Digest*, 1 August 1996. Pakistan is seen by many in the West as a nuclear proliferant and irresponsible exporter. The United States stopped all military supplies to Pakistan in 1990.

109. Shen, p. 145. See also, "Ukraine: Nuclear Agreement Signed with PRC," FBIS-SOV-96–064, *Interfax* (Moscow), 1 April 1996.

110. Jones and Zaborsky, in Bertsch, ed., pp. 27–28.

111. Alexander Wendt, "Anarchy Is What States Make of It: The Social Construction of Power Politics," *International Organization*, vol. 46, no. 2, pp. 391–425; quoted at pp. 405–06.

112. Author's interviews with Ukrainian government and scientific and nuclear community officials, June 1996, Los Alamos National Laboratory.

113. On 2 January, World Bank President James Wolfenson sent a letter to President Kuchma criticizing the extreme corruption within the Ukrainian government. In response, Deputy Prime Minister Viktor Pynzenyk admitted that the problem of government corruption exists, noting that international criticism has begun because of increased foreign investment in the country. On 11 July 1995, the Rada passed a corruption law that allows not only the recipients of bribes but their so-called intermediaries to be prosecuted. Those who give bribes to officials but report the offense to the authorities may be freed from prosecution. The parliament also ordered wage increases of 20–50 percent for Interior Ministry employees who specialize in investigating corruption and assisting Gosexportcontrol investigate export violations. Chrystyna Lapychak, "Ukrainian Parliament Passes Law on Corruption," *OMRI Daily Digest*, 12 July 1995.

FOUR

UNDERSTANDING EXPORT CONTROLS IN BELARUS
The Power of Inducements

SUZETTE R. GRILLOT

When Belarus declared its independence from the Soviet Union and established a sovereign state in the summer of 1991, it immediately inherited a substantial portion of the former Soviet nuclear arsenal, as well as materials, equipment, technologies, and expertise that contribute to nuclear programs.[1] Belarus relinquished its nuclear weapon inheritance, removing and returning to Russia its tactical nuclear weapons by May 1992 and its strategic nuclear weapons by November 1996. Nuclear research reactors, fuel storage facilities, and enterprises producing important dual-use technologies and materials, however, still operate in Belarus.[2] Moreover, a great number of former Soviet conventional weapons remain in Belarus.[3]

Despite its inheritance of dangerous nuclear and other weaponry, material, equipment, and technologies, Belarus did not equally inherit the means by which to control, monitor, and account for its deadly weapons and weapons-related items. Belarus was, however, the first of the former Soviet states to make a major attempt to create a national system of export control. In 1992, Belarusian officials signed Cooperative Threat Reduction (CTR) agreements with the United States that engaged the two countries in developing from scratch an export control system in Belarus.[4] By 1997 Belarus had developed its export control system to a level that was 74 percent compatible with Western common standards, compared to a system that was 31 percent compatible in 1992.[5] Throughout 1996 and 1997, however, Belarusian domestic political struggles relegated export control to a lower-level priority. Moreover, continued economic crisis in Belarus has heightened the importance of enhancing exports, perhaps to the detriment of nonproliferation export control efforts.[6]

Nonetheless, Belarus has made significant progress in establishing a national export control system that is compatible with Western standards, despite the serious political and economic crises it has experienced throughout its few years of independence. Additional development, implementation, and enforcement in the area of export control is, however, required for Belarus to truly contribute to international nonproliferation efforts. Why Belarusian leaders have sought, and would continue to seek, such a contribution remains puzzling given the country's political and economic instability. Understanding how and why Belarus has developed its export control system to this point, therefore, may be useful for those who seek to assist the country in its future export control efforts.

This chapter is organized in three sections. The first provides details of Belarusian export control development with particular attention given to the country's achievements as well as shortcomings. The second section offers an analysis of Belarusian export control behavior in light of the four theoretical approaches outlined in the introductory chapter. The goal of this section is to understand and explain Belarusian export control development. The final section of this chapter concludes with a discussion of the Belarusian study's findings and their implications.

THE BUILDING OF A BELARUSIAN SYSTEM OF EXPORT CONTROL
Decrees, Regulations, and Legislation

Beginning in 1992, the Belarusian president and Council of Ministers issued a number of decrees that provide the legal basis for the control of sensitive exports. The first export control–related act of the government of Belarus was to issue the Council of Ministers Resolution No. 516 on August 21, 1992, titled "On the Creation of Effective Controls for the Export of Specific Goods and Services in the Republic of Belarus." This decree identified the number of ministries and departments that were to play a role in export control processes, and defined those ministries' and departments' export control duties. The decree also introduced the term "specific goods and services" as those items which are to be subject to export control procedures. These goods and services included: nuclear, chemical, and biological weapons, and their means of delivery; conventional weapons, ammunition, and equipment; services, technologies, and expertise related to weapons and military items; radioactive materials, poisons, and drugs; and precious metals and rare-earth metals.[7]

On May 25, 1993, the Belarusian Council of Ministers issued Resolution No. 344, titled "On a Unified System for Establishing Quotas and Issuing Licenses for the Import and Export of Commodities (Goods and Services) on the Territory of the Republic of Belarus." Although this decree has since been replaced with another, it was the first to outline export licensing procedures for all Belarusian enterprises. The Council of Ministers

Resolution No. 213 of December 1, 1994, "On Measures to Improve Regulation of Exports and Imports of Goods," now serves as the primary decree describing all relevant procedures for export, import, and transit activity in Belarus.[8] A newer version of this decree, "On Improving Control Over the Export and Import of Specific Goods and Services in the Republic of Belarus," awaited approval in 1997 and would "broaden and internationalize" the Belarusian export control system even further.[9]

In addition to these and other related export control decrees, Belarusian officials drafted export control legislation in 1995, which would provide a sound legal basis for the Belarusian export control system. When adopted, the legislation will place export control principles, procedures, terms and bodies, as well as categories of controlled items, in Belarusian legal codes.[10] The Belarusian Security Council's Interdepartmental Commission on Control of Imports and Exports has approved the draft legislation, which is currently awaiting presidential approval before being submitted to the National Assembly. It is expected that the assembly will consider the draft before the end of 1997.[11]

Commodity Control Lists

Belarusian officials have developed seven lists of controlled commodities. They include the following items:

- nuclear weapons, materials, and equipment; and nuclear-related dual-use technologies;
- chemical weapons and equipment necessary for their production;
- biological weapons and equipment necessary for their production;
- delivery systems for nuclear, chemical, and biological weapons;
- conventional weapons;
- raw materials, equipment, technologies, and expertise related to the development of weapons and military hardware; and
- dual-use commodities.[12]

Belarusian officials have reported in the past that these lists corresponded to the control lists of international supplier regimes such as the Missile Technology Control Regime (MTCR), Nuclear Suppliers Group (NSG), Australia Group (AG), and Wassenaar Arrangement. Belarusian officials now admit that their lists correspond most closely with Russian control lists, and therefore differ "in small ways" from the lists of international regimes. Draft decrees and legislation currently under consideration, however, will reportedly bring Belarusian lists in compliance with internationally accepted control lists.[13]

Licensing Procedures

The Ministry of Foreign Economic Relations (MFER), which replaced in March 1994 the State Committee on Foreign Economic Relations, is the lead Belarusian agency responsible for export licensing. Specifically, the MFER (1) issues all export licenses for controlled goods and services; (2) determines licensing procedures, drafts lists of controlled items (in cooperation with other agencies), and outlines license application procedures; (3) maintains a database for licenses issued; (4) plays a role in determining export control policies; and (5) participates in determining Belarus's involvement in international nonproliferation regimes.[14]

The MFER's Department of Foreign Trade Regulation is the primary agency responsible for licensing controlled commodities. Three divisions within the department are responsible for various export control tasks. The Export Control Division oversees the licensing of dual-use and military exports; the Information and Technical Division handles the export of software; and the Non-Tariff Regulations Division manages the export of nonsensitive items. Together, these three divisions examine applications for export licenses, issue licenses in "routine cases," and offer recommendations in more difficult cases to the Interdepartmental Commission on Exports and Imports of the Security Council, which is the definitive judge for all decisions on export control matters (see discussion of Security Council below).[15]

Despite its expansive role in nonproliferation export control activities, the MFER does not have the authority, funds, or personnel to conduct sufficient pre- and post-license inspections nor to engage in undercover operations and other investigative actions. The ministry also does not have any enforcement authority and cannot, therefore, make arrests when export licensing procedures have been violated. Moreover, it is unlikely that the MFER will ever be granted such authority given that other agencies, such as the State Security Committee (still known in Belarus as the KGB) and Interior Ministry, have a monopoly on investigative and police activities.[16]

To aid its licensing process, Belarus installed in August 1995 an automated licensing system with the help of the United States. As part of its CTR aid, Belarus received computer equipment, software, and training needed to process its license requests electronically.[17] In 1996, Belarusian exporters applied for approximately 150 export licenses, including those requesting to export sensitive weaponry, goods, and services.[18] Nearly all licenses were granted. Approximately ten export licenses were denied in 1996 because (1) they either violated international sanctions or were considered controlled items; or (2) the Belarusian government was not pleased with the prices being charged for the exported items.[19] Officials expect that the numbers and types of license applications will remain consistent in the near future, and that the automated licensing system has and will contribute to more efficient licensing procedures.[20]

Regime Adherence

Belarus is not a member of, and allegedly not an adherent to, any international supplier regime (the NSG, MTCR, AG, or Wassenaar Arrangement).[21] Belarus did, however, accede in July 1993 to the NPT, which required that all recipients of nuclear-related exports be subject to International Atomic Energy Agency (IAEA) safeguards.[22] In addition, Belarus signed in April 1995 its own agreement with the IAEA subjecting its nuclear facilities, materials, equipment, and technologies to international safeguards.

Although not a member of the multilateral export control regimes, Belarus is reportedly favorably disposed to joining them.[23] In fact, Belarus signed in June 1992 the "Agreement on the Basic Principles of Cooperation in the Field of Peaceful Use of Nuclear Energy," which committed the country to adhere to the requirements of the NSG.[24] Belarus also submitted to the United Nations (UN) secretary general a note expressing its willingness to join the international export control regimes.[25] Moreover, recent (and as of yet unpublished) presidential decrees reportedly strengthen the Belarusian export control system in that they make the country's control lists more comprehensive to include all items currently controlled by multilateral supplier regimes.[26]

Bureaucratic Process

A number of ministries, agencies, departments, committees, and divisions are involved in and have responsibility for various aspects of export control practices in Belarus. At the top of the ministerial hierarchy is the Security Council, which the president of Belarus heads and includes the prime minister, ministers of Foreign Affairs and Defense, and other key officials. In December 1994, the Security Council created an Interdepartmental Commission on Control of Exports and Imports to coordinate the export control activities of all relevant ministries, and to cooperate with international export control organizations. This body is also the key authority in export control decision-making as it makes final judgments on export policies and controversial export licenses.[27]

The Ministry of Foreign Economic Relations plays a significant role in Belarusian export control procedures. As discussed above, the MFER is the primary agency responsible for export licensing. The ministry also coordinates activities with the Ministry of Foreign Affairs (MFA), Ministry of Justice (MOJ), the State Customs Committee (SCC), the KGB, and the Security Council related to the drafting of export control policies, regulations, decrees, and laws.[28]

The SCC, created shortly after Belarus's independence, oversees the country's customs checkpoints. Specifically, the SCC inspects goods that pass through Belarusian borders, provides information to the KGB about illicit exports that customs officials have confiscated, and maintains data on all exports and imports, including licensed exports, for the MFER and the Ministry of Statistics and Analysis.[29]

The Main Directorate of Border Guards (BG) monitors Belarusian borders at sixty-nine checkpoint locations. The BG is also responsible for monitoring cross-border activities where there are no checkpoints. When illegal shipments are apprehended, the BG is authorized to detain the individuals and goods until they are turned over to the State Security Committee for further action. The BG also assists the KGB in conducting preliminary investigations on illicit exports.[30]

The Disarmament and International Security Division of the MFA is the primary division within the Foreign Ministry responsible for export control issues. The division plays an active role in determining export control policies in coordination with many other agencies (mentioned above). It also contributes to the development of commodity control lists, and offers policy proposals regarding Belarus's participation in multilateral nonproliferation export control regimes. The MFA is not involved in granting export licenses, but is regularly consulted by the MFER on the export applications of certain enterprises.[31]

The role of the Ministry of Defense (MOD) in Belarusian export control procedures relates primarily to the direct and specific export of military items. Specifically, the MOD certifies companies that wish to develop and produce military goods. A company seeking to export such items must first obtain MOD certification before applying for an export license from the MFER. The MOD is then involved in assisting the MFER make decisions on export license applications for weapons, munitions, and military-specific equipment. Moreover, military-related industries that wish to export their goods must receive permission from the MOD to undertake such activities. Forty-seven enterprises that produce controlled goods have been granted such permission to export. Only two organizations (*Beltekheksport* and *Belspetsvenshtekhnika*), however, have permission to export military equipment.[32]

The State Security Committee or KGB is the primary agency responsible for export control investigations and enforcement. It is involved in all activities related to tracking and apprehending illegal exports. The KGB also assists the other agencies in drafting export control policies and lists of controlled items, participates in the review of export license applications, supplies intelligence information to export control officials regarding smuggling and other illegal export activities, and assists in the preparation of judicial cases for export violations.[33]

Together, these agencies work to control the export of sensitive goods from Belarus to undesirable end-users around the world. Approximately thirty individuals situated in these various ministries, departments, and committees are actively involved in export control matters on a daily basis. As one can see, there is no single agency that has a monopoly in export control practices in Belarus. Belarusian officials have established an interlinked, interagency process that requires the coordination and cooperation of many different individuals. According to one Belarusian official, the division of export control labor in Belarus provides for efficient and secure nonproliferation outcomes.[34]

Customs Authority and Border Control

The Council of Ministers Resolutions No. 82 ("On Measures to Limit the Transfer of Hazardous Items and Materials Across the Border of the Republic of Belarus," of February 19, 1993) and No. 213 (detailed above) provide the State Customs Committee and the Main Directorate of Border Guards the authority to inspect cargo moving across Belarusian borders to prevent illicit shipments of sensitive items.[35] Belarus shares borders with Russia, Latvia, Lithuania, Poland, and Ukraine. Of these, the Belarusian-Polish border is comparatively most secure.[36] Traffic congestion at this border, however, often prevents thorough inspections of cargo.[37] Moreover, there are reportedly only "periodic" checks of cargo being made at the Belarusian borders with Ukraine and the Baltic states.[38] Weak control of the Belarusian-Baltic borders perhaps creates the greatest concern as controlled goods may be shipped from Belarus (or through Belarus from Ukraine or Russia) to questionable destinations via Baltic Sea ports.[39]

Control of the Belarusian-Russian border also generates some concern. On February 21, 1995, Belarus and Russia signed the Agreement on Joint Management of the Customs Services of the Russian Federation and Belarus. Accordingly, the president of Belarus issued Decree No. 208, "On the Canceling of Customs Control on the Border of the Republic of Belarus with the Russian Federation," on May 30, 1995.[40] Checkpoints on the Belarusian-Russian border were then abolished, allowing materials, goods, services, labor, and capital to move freely and quickly between the two countries as the agreement intended. Since the creation of this "customs union," the Belarusian and Russian Customs committees have been working to harmonize the two countries' customs policies and procedures. A Joint Committee on Border Issues was created in December 1996 to oversee the unification of Belarusian and Russian customs systems.[41]

The Russian-Belarusian customs union has, however, been plagued by a number of misperceptions and misinterpretations on the part of both governments. After Russian officials became concerned that sensitive goods were being transported into Russia via Belarus, they reestablished check-points in March 1997 along their side of the border. For example, Russian officials allegedly believed that hazardous chemicals were being shipped into their country without the appropriate declaration.[42] Belarusian officials deny the Russian claims, and argue that the reinstallment of customs check-points on their common border violates the customs agreement between the two countries.[43] In addition, it remains unclear how and to what extent the customs union between Russia and Belarus will affect their respective criminal and customs laws, as well as law enforcement.[44] Some argue, for example, that the differences in such laws and procedures are not being addressed, and that the customs union is largely an agreement that exists only on paper.[45]

Although the numbers of border guards assigned to customs checkpoints along Belarusian borders have increased substantially since the country's independence (from 400 to 6,000), it is unclear whether they have made any real impact on the control of sensitive exports from and through Belarus to other countries. In fact, a 1997 report suggests that the increased numbers of guards on the borders is mainly indicative of the desire of the Soviet successor states to collect import and export fees, as well as to prevent the proliferation of dangerous weaponry and weapons-related goods.[46] Moreover, the personnel situated at borders in the FSU are often susceptible to corruption given that their salaries are low and paid irregularly. Bribing customs officials to overlook inspections of cargo is, therefore, a dangerous reality.[47]

Information Gathering and Sharing

Although Belarusian officials have been involved in gathering and sharing export control information with international parties, they have a mixed record of gathering and sharing information on export control procedures and activities domestically. Belarusian officials have attended numerous international workshops and conferences on the issue of export control where they shared information regarding their export control system with international participants, as well as learned about the export control policies, practices, and procedures of other countries—particularly the United States.[48] Thus far, few attempts have been made in Belarus to engage and educate the forty or so enterprises that produce controlled goods on Belarusian export control policies and procedures. The U.S. Department of Commerce has sponsored two workshops in Minsk for industry outreach, at which government and industry representatives discussed needs for regular consultations.[49]

Internally, the KGB is primarily responsible for gathering information on exporters. The KGB then shares its intelligence information with appropriate export control officials—especially information related to export violations and smuggling activities.[50] There are not, however, additional bodies tasked with gathering and distributing information on exporters or export procedures, allowing the KGB to remain as secretive as it wishes.

Training

The training of licensing, customs, and other export control officials in the practical and technical aspects of export control is an area in which Belarus requires much attention and assistance. The MFER is primarily responsible for conducting training sessions for export control personnel, but suffers itself from the lack of experienced officials and adequate resources to provide sufficient training programs.[51] The United States has assisted Belarus by offering export licensing and enforcement training seminars, and by attempting to establish the Nonproliferation and Export Control Training Center in the Belarusian National Security Institute.[52] It is unlikely, however, that this training center will ever become operational due to lack of funds.[53]

Despite the intentions of both Belarusian and U.S. officials, the training of export control personnel in Belarus is problematic. Licensing staff, customs officials, and border guards primarily receive their training on licensing processes, controlled items, and investigative techniques through trial and error while on the job. Arrangements are being made, however, for Belarusian border guards to be trained at the Russian Federal Border Guard Service beginning sometime in 1998.[54] And Belarusian officials continue to make repeated requests to the United States for more advanced and specialized export control training.[55]

Import Certification and Delivery Verification

To obtain an export license in Belarus, an exporter must first submit an import certificate with its export license application. An authoritative government agency in the recipient country must have issued this certificate to the Belarusian exporter agreeing not to (1) reexport the item(s) without obtaining written consent from Belarus; (2) use the item(s) to develop weapons of mass destruction; and (3) use the item(s) in any way that contributes to a nuclear-fuel cycle that does not operate under IAEA safeguards.[56] Verifying the end-use and delivery of an export is, however, more problematic for Belarus. While Western governments have tremendous access to computerized databases and in-country embassies and consulates that provide them with up-to-date information regarding end-uses, end-users, and the successful delivery of controlled goods to their appropriate destinations, Belarus does not have the resources to commit to such undertakings.[57]

Penalties

The Council of Ministers Resolution No. 733 of October 26, 1994, "On Responsibility for Violations of the Procedures for Following Quotas and Obtaining Licenses to Export and Import Goods and Services," outlines the penalties for violating Belarusian export licensing procedures. These monetary penalties range from 10 percent of the export contract's value for a minor offense to 100 percent of the contract's value for a major offense (e.g., failing to obtain an export license).[58] Criminal penalties for any kind of export violation, however, do not exist in Belarus. In the past, Belarusian officials were hesitant to amend the criminal code to account for export violations because (1) such violations were not considered "worthy of criminal prosecution"; and (2) there existed no export control law that required criminal prosecution if violated.[59] Nonetheless, according to official Belarusian sources, the country obligated itself to develop criminal procedures for export violations when it ratified the Chemical Weapons Convention in 1996. It remains unclear, however, whether Belarusian officials will actively enforce criminal penalties relating to export violations, once they have been established, as very few civil export violation procedures have been conducted.[60]

Catch-All Clause

Unlike the United States and other countries with well-developed export control systems, the Belarusian system of export control does not include any mechanism that triggers a review of any questionable export for proliferation purposes. It is possible, therefore, that sensitive exports may "fall between the cracks" of the Belarusian system and reach dangerous destinations around the world.

EXPLAINING BELARUSIAN EXPORT CONTROL DEVELOPMENT
Realism/Neorealism

The realist approach provides little assistance for understanding Belarusian efforts to develop a national system of export control. Belarusian leaders consistently suggest that their country suffers from no direct, external threat to its security.[61] In other words, Belarus is not concerned about conflict with any of its neighbors or any other potential adversary in particular. In fact, the lack of any perceived security threat led Belarus to adopt a policy of state neutrality and nonparticipation in military alliances upon its independence. Such a stance, however, quickly yielded to the notion of collective security as the Belarusian people became convinced that their existence was inextricably linked to that of Russia.[62]

Unlike most of its former Soviet counterparts, Belarus did not perceive Russia to be threatening to its sovereignty and security. Belarus engages in active, friendly relations with Russia, its larger and more powerful neighbor, and indeed, since its independence, has sought, and to some extent achieved, a greater degree of integration with Russia in many areas. Russia and Belarus have signed numerous agreements attempting to establish ties economically and politically. Agreements on monetary and customs unions, however, remain largely unimplemented. Serious doubts exist as to whether the Treaty on the Formation of a Russian-Belarusian Community, signed during an "elaborate ceremony" in April 1996 and intended to pool Belarusian and Russian material and intellectual resources to enhance living standards in both countries, will ever be implemented as well.[63]

Although Belarusian leaders have not expressed security concerns vis-à-vis any particular country, they have expressed concern about the security implications of NATO expansion.[64] Belarus argues that, in general, eastward expansion of NATO further divides the continent of Europe, rather than unites it. Specifically, NATO expansion leads to "a line of new confrontation passing along . . . [Belarus's] borders."[65] This heightens Belarus's awareness that it may again become a "front-line state" which may be "steamrollered from both East and West."[66] Moreover, becoming "locked" between an enlarged NATO and Russia would, in the Belarusian view, prevent their development as a European state due to the stagnating pressure of potential military confrontation. Accordingly, Belarus threatened to maintain the remaining strategic nuclear weapons on its territory to counter NATO expansion—especially if NATO expansion meant the deployment of Western nuclear weapons in East Europe.[67] The last of Belarus's nuclear weapons were, however, returned to Russia in November 1996.[68]

Despite such concerns, there do not appear to be any direct links between Belarusian national security perceptions and the country's efforts to control the trade of sensitive military-related items. Belarusian leaders do, however, suggest that the proliferation of weaponry threatens *international* security.[69] Moreover, Belarusian decision-makers argue that export controls are a necessary tool for preventing the spread of dangerous weaponry, equipment, material, and technology, thereby enhancing global security.[70] Internal security concerns also appear to motivate certain customs controls in Belarus. A 1993 ban on the transit of military equipment across the border and through Belarusian territory, for example, was the result of heightened concern for the health and security of its citizens.[71]

Although Belarusian decision-makers appear to be aware of the security implications of weapons proliferation and motivated somewhat, therefore, to control the export of sensitive military-related items, they do not appear to be controlling the flow of weapons and weapons-related exports in order to balance the power of any particular state or group of states, prevent the military gains of any particular state or group of states, or enhance their own national military security. In fact, Belarus has, in many cases, actively sought to sell certain military items. Recent reports, for example, suggest that Belarus has sold to China a vehicle that may be used as a mobile launcher for an ICBM.[72] Such sales may indicate that Belarus is not concerned about contributing to the military capability of other states. The realist approach to export control development, therefore, does not well explain Belarusian efforts to control sensitive trade.

Rational Institutionalism

The material nature of export control development, in terms of costs and benefits, is the most compelling explanation for Belarusian export control behavior. Belarusian officials regularly and consistently suggested that the bureaucratic, administrative, and opportunity (e.g., lost trade) costs associated with export control development were an impediment to effective export control practices in Belarus.[73] Belarusian decision-makers have not, however, regularly assessed and articulated the *specific* costs—presented in dollar or ruble figures—related to export control activities. In other words, they are aware that they are incurring costs by committing to and actively pursuing the development and implementation of export control procedures, but do not appear to be calculating explicitly what those costs entail. Similarly, Belarusian leaders are keenly aware of the benefits their country may gain through their efforts to develop and implement nonproliferation export control policies and institutions. They recognize, for example, that acceptable nonproliferation behavior will facilitate their access to Western markets for goods, services, and technologies, as well as Western financial aid and assistance.[74] Indeed, Belarus has received significant amounts of foreign aid for export control purposes. Of all the former Soviet republics, Belarus received the greatest amount of CTR aid specifically for the development of export controls.[75] By 1994, the United States had promised $16.26 million for Belarusian export control efforts. This amount included all activities related to U.S.-Belarusian relations on export control issues, such as policy and program development, information exchange, equipment procurement, and training. By August 1997, approximately $12.7 million had been obligated under contract.[76] Specifically, U.S. aid has assisted Belarusian export control practices by providing equipment, software and training for a national automated licensing network, vehicles for border authorities, and interdiction equipment such as X-ray machines and pedestrian and vehicle monitors.[77]

Other countries and organizations have provided aid to Belarus for nonproliferation activities as well. Germany, Japan, the European Union, and the IAEA have all donated millions of dollars to support the nonproliferation efforts of Belarus. In all of these agreements, export control development has been included as a key ingredient of responsible nonproliferation behavior.[78] Moreover, the United States has provided Belarus $59 million in non–export control related CTR aid. This assistance provided Belarus with nuclear emergency response equipment, defense conversion projects, and environmental restoration capabilities.[79]

The United States, key international organizations, and other key states have also provided aid and assistance to Belarus in a number of other areas such as democratic institution building, economic reform, environmental and nuclear safety, and humanitarian and social development. The

World Bank, for example, has committed nearly $200 million in loans to Belarus.[80] The United States has contributed $10 million to Belarus through the FREEDOM Support Act, which is meant to facilitate democratic reform in the former Soviet region, as well as an additional $140 million in humanitarian aid and $8 million in technical assistance.[81] Although this aid is not directly linked to Belarus's nonproliferation export control development, Belarusian leaders are aware that irresponsible proliferation policies may affect their country's receipt of aid in these other areas.[82]

Such outpouring of aid has not, however, been free of obstacles or miscommunication. Early on, for example, the flow of aid (particularly nonproliferation-related aid) from the United States was hampered by Belarusian misconceptions that they would be receiving the aid in cash rather than in the form of equipment, training, technical support, and business services.[83] Moreover, U.S. difficulties with bureaucratic hurdles, due to the lack of effective interagency coordination and the procurement problems associated with the higher-than-expected costs of equipment and materials Belarus needed, further delayed the flow of nonproliferation export control aid going to Belarus.[84]

In 1996 and 1997, Belarusian aid from the United States and other key governments and international organizations was suspended in response to unfavorable domestic political developments in Belarus. Specifically, the Belarusian president was accused of using his presidential power in dictatorial fashion by refusing to acknowledge the parliament's constitutional role in government operations, controlling the media, preventing peaceful demonstrations, arresting peaceful protestors, and seeking to eliminate any and all opposition to his activities in and out of the government (see details below in domestic politics section).[85] Given that Belarusian export control development corresponds closely to the amount of material aid and assistance provided to the country for that, related, and other purposes, the suspension of such aid may compromise past and future nonproliferation export control developments in Belarus.

From the beginning of their independent relationship with countries around the world, Belarusian leaders expressed expectations of reciprocity regarding their nonproliferation and export control behavior. In detailing the numerous impediments to arms control and reductions before the 1993 opening session of the UN General Assembly, Petr Kravchanka, the Belarusian minister of foreign affairs, stated that Belarus "is entitled to expect reciprocity from other states in overcoming these difficulties."[86] The Belarusian prime minster, Mikhail Chygir, reiterated before the 1994 UN General Assembly that nuclear and conventional weapons control "demands enormous additional expenses," and that Belarus "expect[s] the international community to support [its] actions in this field."[87] Ultimately, Belarusian leaders warned the international community that if it was not forthcoming in its willingness to support Belarus's nonproliferation efforts, such efforts could not and would not be accelerated.[88]

Internationally accepted nonproliferation rules and norms have motivated Belarusian leaders to support the responsible control of weapons and weapons-related items in Belarus. In general, Belarusian decision-makers suggest that their country's good standing in the international community of nations rests on its ability to implement reliably its many promises and commitments in compliance with international expectations and wishes.[89] Specifically, international treaties such as START and the NPT guide Belarusian nonproliferation and export control behavior, even when it comes to legitimate trade in weapons and military equipment. Despite the need to sell weapons and weapons-related items as a means to improve their dire economic situation, Belarusian leaders suggest that they do so only "in accordance with agreements achieved."[90]

Finally, although Belarusian officials have in the past highlighted the lack of certainty in, and the unpredictable nature of, relations among nations, they have not made specific links between interstate cooperation in the area of nonproliferation export control and potential increases in certain and predictable international interactions.[91] Moreover, Belarusian leaders have made no particular reference to a reduction in transaction costs for their country as a result of responsible export control behavior. Costs associated with conducting international relations in general do not appear to be a key factor influencing Belarusian decisions to develop, implement, and maintain a national system of export control.

Domestic Politics

Domestic political approaches provide little assistance for understanding Belarusian export control development. Few if any interest groups have formed and become outspoken in Belarus, and certainly none has taken an active interest in export control. Approximately 80 percent of Belarusian enterprises are still state-owned, which renders the potential role of private business in either supporting or discouraging the control of sensitive exports relatively meaningless.[92] Political groups such as the Belarusian National Front and the Belarusian Social Democratic Party have supported free market reforms, the necessary regulation of exports, and the creation of an effective national customs service, but the government's squelching of Belarusian political activity beginning in 1995 left such political parties powerless.[93] The military industrial complex (MIC) in Belarus has remained a relatively constant influence in Belarusian foreign policy decision-making, but members of the MIC have consistently advocated increases in Belarusian military sales rather than their control.[94] Such influence, therefore, should have led to a lower level of export control development in Belarus rather than the higher level (relative to its former Soviet counterparts) we have witnessed.

Elites have undoubtedly been most involved in establishing and maintaining a national system of export control in Belarus. Their interest in such activities, however, is seemingly tied strongly to the receipt of material aid and assistance (not to mention travel opportunities to the United States and other Western countries) than it is the result of independent perceptions of the national interest. An indicator of how Belarusian elites weigh the importance of export control activities in relation to the country's overall national interest is the small number of people in the government who are regularly involved in export control practices and the diverse issues with which they must deal. The thirty or so people involved in Belarusian export controls, in other words, are responsible for a number of other foreign and domestic policy issues as well. They are unable, therefore, to commit many resources (human and otherwise) solely to export control endeavors—activities which are considered in relative terms to be less significant.[95]

There is little question that Belarus is a centralized state, especially since July 1994 when Alexander Lukashenko became president. Since then, he has slowly consolidated his power, in the process suppressing all possible opposition and wrangling authority away from the parliament. Specifically, Lukashenko drafted a new constitution that would allow him to extend his term in office, annul the decisions of local councils, appoint all judges, restructure the parliament so that he could appoint one-third of its members, and dissolve parliament if he thought it necessary.[96] Because the parliament understandably opposed the president's constitution, Lukashenko held a referendum in November 1996 to determine the public's support. Eighty-four percent of the 7.5 million citizens who voted agreed with the president. Lukashenko then further centralized the Belarusian state and expanded his authoritarian control.[97]

The centralization of domestic-political processes in Belarus has not, however, had a positive effect on export control development as such domestic struggles have nearly sidelined all other issues—especially foreign policy issues outside of relations with Russia. Furthermore, the extreme authoritarian nature of Lukashenko's regime has alienated partner states that had been supporting and assisting Belarusian export control development. Key international organizations such as the International Monetary Fund and World Bank, as well as key counterpart states such as the United States, halted all financial and other support flowing to Belarus beginning in 1996, citing concerns over Lukashenko's undemocratic behavior.[98]

Within the executive branch, export control efforts of the numerous agencies that play a role in export control processes do not appear to suffer from a lack of cooperation or a heightened sense of rivalry as a result of power asymmetries. In fact, the main export control agency is also responsible for export promotion, which undoubtedly plays a more significant role. Moreover, export control duties are diffusely distributed among the many agencies involved so that there seems to be little competition among them. Seemingly, export control officials are committed to controlling sensitive exports (perhaps only one of their required duties), and appear to handle their often diverse responsibilities (as in the case of MFER officials responsible for both export promotion and export control) in terms of well-understood priorities.[99] There exists, therefore, no particularly powerful agency advocating export control practices and, thereby, positively affecting Belarus's relative level of export control development.

Liberal Identity

The liberal identity approach offers little support for understanding Belarusian export control development. Belarusian leaders certainly recognize the existence and importance of the international and Western communities of nations, but their vision has clearly been placed on Russia and the East in terms of foreign policy priorities.[100] In a statement before a meeting of trade unionists in 1994, for example, Lukashenko stressed that "the main partners of Belarus are in the East."[101] In the same speech he also criticized the media for wrongly characterizing Belarusian politics as "pro-Western."[102] Moreover, Belarusian officials also suggested that they were interested in close cooperative relations with countries, such as India and China, that are not considered liberal community members.[103]

Belarus's interaction with the Western liberal community, outside of that which has come as a result of material aid and assistance programs, has declined significantly since the first couple of years of its independence. Belarusian interaction with the United States, for example, was consistent throughout 1993 and 1994 when Belarusian President Stanislav Shushkevich visited Washington (July 1993) and U.S. President Bill Clinton visited Minsk (July 1994). During those visits, President Clinton recognized Belarus as a state making progress toward democracy, stating specifically that he was impressed with how far it had come in "building a strong and free nation."[104] Since Lukashenko became president in 1994, however, Western nations have slowly distanced themselves from Belarus and its authoritarian regime. In fact, Western leaders have openly condemned President Lukashenko's undemocratic activities, prompting the Belarusian president to acknowledge the lack of identification between his state and those in the West by saying that "these countries show no understanding of us."[105]

Although Belarus began its efforts to develop a national system of export control in its early years of independence while undergoing democratic reforms, its export control development continued while reverting back to an authoritarian form of government. From 1992 to 1996, the independent organization that monitors political and economic freedoms around the world, Freedom House, rated Belarus as "partly free." During these years, Belarus was recognized as making steady but cautious progress toward establishing a democratic state and market-oriented economy.[106] In 1997, however, Freedom House rated Belarus as "not free," citing the numerous undemocratic actions of President Lukashenko—from his crackdown on the media to his control of prices.[107]

A reversal of Belarusian democratic reform and the rise of Lukashenko's authoritarian control over Belarusian politics, economics, and society came as a result of, according to Lukashenko, the need for order. In particular, the insubordination of the media and certain government officials, he believed, was the root of Belarusian political and economic chaos. In a November 1994 address to the nation, for example, Lukashenko stated that he "demand[s] that the chairman of the National Broadcasting Company stop all broadcasting of nonconstructive speeches at the session of the Supreme Soviet. From today, the mass news media, both state and independent, must assume a constructive state position and carry out an appropriate policy."[108] He insisted that prices on "essential goods" be returned to an "appropriate place," and warned that "if instances of nonobservance of my order are revealed, the people who manage trading organizations and enterprises will be sacked and arrested."[109] Such threats and subsequent actions suggest that Belarus is moving further away from democratic and free market reforms. Given that Lukashenko's term does not expire until 1999 (the new constitution accepted via the November 1996 referendum extended his term by two years), it is unclear whether Belarus will again return to a process of democratization. Moreover, Lukashenko's preoccupations with order and stability suggest that issues of nonproliferation and export control are marginal at best.

Finally, Belarusian officials have not attempted specifically to target export controls toward illiberal states and away from liberal states. Belarusian military sales to China, for example, indicate that Belarus is not necessarily concerned about the democratic nature of the recipient state. Such cooperation may even increase as Chinese officials have reportedly suggested that they are open to "all-round and all-faceted friendship and cooperation with the Belarusian military."[110] Moreover, Belarus has developed cooperative relations with countries such as Syria and Cuba, both of which remain proscribed destinations for Western military (and other) items.[111] Belarus's non-liberal identification and lack of democratic reform, therefore, prevents us from explaining the country's motivation for developing a national system of export control based on the liberal identity approach.

CONCLUSION

Belarus has come a long way in its campaign to develop a national system of export control. With nothing to build upon (no policies, procedures, institutions, or personnel), Belarus developed from scratch an export control system that is nearly compatible with Western common standards. Despite many deficiencies and shortcomings, such as the lack of resources, adequate training, reasonable and enforceable penalties, and export control personnel without divergent interests and priorities, Belarusian officials seemingly remain (at least in the short term) committed to the continued development, implementation, and enforcement of nonproliferation export control policies, practices, and procedures.

The analysis provided in this chapter suggests that the rational institutional approach best explains the development of a Belarusian system of export control. Overwhelmingly, Belarusian export controls are the result of Western aid and assistance. Material inducements, in other words, clearly influenced, facilitated, and supported the development of an export control system in Belarus. The power of such inducements in the Belarusian case suggests that the halting of Western aid and assistance flowing to Belarus, given its unpopular domestic developments, may have dire consequences for export control practices there. Although a workable export control framework has been created in Belarus, it remains to be seen whether such a framework has been sufficiently entrenched so that the lack of Western incentives does not lead to its disintegration.

Despite Belarus's many export control accomplishments, many challenges lie before Belarusian leaders, and before Western nations that are particularly concerned about preventing the spread of dangerous weapons and weapons-related items. In general, domestic political unrest and economic crises in Belarus may continue to derail its export control efforts due to an increased emphasis on export promotion and a decreased commitment in human and material resources to export control. Unfortunately, unfavorable domestic developments in Belarus may further relegate export control activities to an even lower priority position, creating the possibility that such activities may become lost and irretrievable. Moreover, the nonproliferation export control culture that has slowly developed in Belarus may wane if export control policies are left unimplemented and institutions are left understaffed and underfunded. Given these realities, the West can ill afford to isolate Belarus and, in the process, turn a blind eye to an export control system that is not fully developed. Because international nonproliferation efforts depend on the consistent and comparable implementation of national export controls, Belarus cannot be ignored.

NOTES

1. Specifically, seventy-two strategic nuclear weapons (SS-25 ICBMs), a handful of tactical nuclear weapons, one power reactor (shut down), a few research reactors (with approximately 30–35 kilograms of highly enriched uranium), and a spent fuel storage facility remained on Belarusian territory. Moreover, Belarus inher-

ited an enormous amount of former Soviet conventional weaponry, as well as dozens of enterprises that produce critical dual-use (both civilian and military) technologies and equipment. See Robert S. Norris, "The Soviet Nuclear Archipelago," *Arms Control Today* 22 (January/February 1992), pp. 24–31; Leonard S. Spector, Mark G. McDonough, with Evan Medeiros, *Tracking Nuclear Proliferation: A Guide in Maps in Charts 1995* (Washington, D.C.: Carnegie Endowment for International Peace, 1995); and the Center for Nonproliferation Studies (CNS) Nuclear Database online (Monterey, CA: Monterey Institute for International Studies, 1997).

2. CNS Nuclear Databases (September 1997), online.

3. See Sergei Anisko, "Belarus: Problemy Reformirovaniya Armiyi I Eksport Vooruzheniyy," *Eksport Obychnykh Vooruzheniyy* 1–2 (1997), pp. 9–10, cited in Emily Ewell and John Parichini, "Belarusian Export Controls: A Status Report," (Monterey, CA: Monterey Institute of International Studies, May 1997), p. 18.

4. See the report of the National Academy of Science's National Research Council, *Proliferation Concerns: Assessing U.S. Efforts to Help Contain Nuclear and Other Dangerous Materials and Technologies in the Former Soviet Union* (Washington, D.C.: National Academy Press, 1997); and Ewell and Parachini, "Belarusian Export Controls."

5. See the introductory chapter of this volume for a brief, and Craft et al. for a detailed discussion of Western common standards and our method for measuring national export control development.

6. See "Belarusian Economy: Recent Developments and Long-Term Targets," Press Release, Embassy of the Republic of Belarus to the United States of America, October 25, 1996.

7. Ural Latypov, "The Belarusian Export Control System," *The Monitor: Nonproliferation, Demilitarization and Arms Control* 2, 1–2 (Winter-Spring 1996), p. 15; and Ural Latypov, "Export Control in Belarus: Trends in Evolution," (Minsk, Belarus: Development and Security Institute of Belarus and the Monterey Institute of International Studies, 1994), p. 8.

8. Latypov, "The Belarusian Export Control System," p. 15; and Ewell and Parichini, "Belarusian Export Controls," p. 23.

9. Personal communication with Belarusian official in the Ministry of Foreign Affairs, August 1997.

10. See draft of the Act of the Republic of Belarus on Export Controls, July 1996; Ivan Snitko, "Belarus's Export Controls Policy," *The Vector* 1, 1 (Spring 1996), pp. 12–13; and Ewell and Parichini, "Belarusian Export Controls," p. 10.

11. Ewell and Parachini, "Belarusian Export Controls," p. 10; and personal communication with Belarusian official in the Ministry of Foreign Affairs, August 1997.

12. Latypov, "The Belarusian Export Control System," p. 16.

13. Personal communication with Belarusian export control officials, November 1995 and August 1997.

14. Latypov, "The Belarusian Export Control System," p. 13; and Ewell and

Parachini, "Belarusian Export Controls," pp. 3–4.

15. Ewell and Parachini, "Belarusian Export Controls," p. 4.

16. Latypov, "The Belarusian Export Control System," p. 13; Latypov, "Export Control in Belarus," pp. 12–13; and Latypov, "Belarus," *Worldwide Guide to Export Controls* (London: Deltec, May 1996), p. 8.

17. National Research Council, *Proliferation Concerns*, p. 103.

18. Personal communication with Belarusian export control official, August 1997. The numbers of license applications have been approximately the same for 1993, 1994, and 1995.

19. Ibid.

20. Ibid.

21. Leonard S. Spector, Mark G. McDonough, with Evan S. Medeiros, *Tracking Nuclear Proliferation* (Washington, D.C.: Carnegie Endowment for International Peace, 1995).

22. "Belarus," *Nuclear Successor States of the Soviet Union* 4 (Monterey, CA and Washington, D.C.: Monterey Institute of International Studies and Carnegie Endowment for International Peace, May 1996), p. 61.

23. National Research Council, *Proliferation Concerns*, p. 4.

24. *Nuclear Successor States of the Former Soviet Union*, p. 63.

25. Latypov, "Export Control in Belarus," p. 4.

26. Personal communication with Belarusian official in the Ministry of Foreign Affairs, August 1997.

27. Snitko, "Belarus's Export Controls Policy," p. 12; and Ewell and Parachini, "Belarusian Export Controls," p. 3.

28. Ewell and Parachini, "Belarusian Export Controls," p. 4; and Latypov, "The Belarusian Export Control System," p. 13.

29. Ewell and Parachini, p. 8, and Latypov, p. 14.

30. Ewell and Parachini, p. 9, and Latypov, p. 14.

31. Ewell and Parachini, "Belarusian Export Controls," p. 5. Also see personal communication with Belarusian export control officials, August 1997.

32. Ewell and Parachini, "Belarusian Export Controls," p. 6.

33. Ibid., p. 7; and Latypov, "The Belarusian Export Control System," p. 14.

34. Personal communication with Belarusian official in the Ministry of Foreign Affairs, August 1997.

35. On March 18, 1997, the Council of Ministers issued Resolution No. 218, "On Establishing Prohibitions and Limitations on the Transference of Commodities across the Customs Border of the Republic of Belarus," which addresses the authority of customs officials to control the export of sensitive goods. The author has been unable, however, to obtain as of yet the complete text of the decree to determine its specific impact on Belarusian customs. Others are also in the process of seeking the text of this decree. See Ewell and Parachini, "Belarusian Export Controls," p. 24.

36. Personal communication with Belarusian officials, October 1995, October 1996. Also see Ewell and Parachini, "Belarusian Export Controls," p. 8.

37. Personal communication with Belarusian officials, October 1995, October 1996, August 1997.

38. *Nuclear Successor States of the Soviet Union*, p. 62.

39. Personal communication with Belarusian officials, October 1995, October 1996, August 1997.

40. Ewell and Parachini, "Belarusian Export Controls," p. 24. Also see Derek Nowek, "CIS Customs Union Develops," *BISNIS Bulletin* (Washington, D.C.: Department of Commerce, October 1996), pp. 1, 5.

41. Viktor Khamrayev, "Rossiya I Belorussiya Obedinyayut Svoyi Pogransluzhby," *Segodnya* online edition, no. 236 (December 19, 1996), as cited in Ewell and Parachini, "Belarusian Export Controls," p. 19.

42. Ewell and Parachini, "Belarusian Export Controls," p. 19.

43. *OMRI Daily Digest* (March 6, 1997).

44. Igor Khripunov and Sergei Pushkarev, "CIS Reintegration: Implications for Export Controls," *The Monitor: Nonproliferation, Demilitarization and Arms Control* 1, 3 (Summer 1995), pp. 8–10.

45. See Jeremy Bransten, "Russia and Belarus: The Politics of 'Integration,'" *RFE/RL News Report* (February 29, 1996).

46. National Research Council, *Proliferation Concerns*, p. 94.

47. Ibid.

48. National Research Council, *Proliferation Concerns*, p. 103. Also see, Lawyers Alliance for World Security, "Protecting Trade and Strengthening Export Controls in Belarus," Trip Report from Minsk, Belarus, February-March 1996.

49. Personal interview with U.S. Department of Commerce official, June 1997; and with Belarusian export control official, August 1997.

50. Latypov, "The Belarusian Export Control System," p. 14.

51. Personal interview with Belarusian export control official, August 1997.

52. About the training seminars, see National Research Council, *Proliferation Concerns*, p. 103. Concerning the Training Center, see the testimony of Connie J. Fenchel before the Permanent Subcommittee on Investigations, Committee on Government Affairs, U.S. Senate, March 22, 1996; and Anatoli Rozanov, "U.S.-Belarusian Cooperation on Nonproliferation Export Controls," *The Monitor: Nonproliferation, Demilitarization and Arms Control* (Summer 1995), p. 11.

53. Personal communication with Belarusian export control official, August 1997. According to a U.S. official in the Department of Defense, the funds for the Training Center have not been obligated and approved. See personal communication with U.S. official, August 1997.

54. Larisa Klyuchnikova, "Russia, Belarussia Agree on Status of Border Guard Committee," *TASS* (July 14, 1997), in Lexis.

55. Connie J. Fenchel, testimony before the Permanent Subcommittee on Investigations, U.S. Senate, March 22, 1996; and interview with Belarusian export control official, August 1997.

56. Ewell and Parichini, "Belarusian Export Controls," p. 13.

57. National Research Council, *Proliferation Concerns*, p. 95; Snitko, "Belarus's Export Controls Policy," p. 12; and personal interviews with U.S. and Belarusian export control officials, June 1997 and August 1997.

58. Ewell and Parichini, "Belarusian Export Controls," p. 23.

59. Latypov, "The Belarusian Export Control System," p. 17.

60. Interview with Belarusian official in the Ministry of Foreign Affairs, August 1997.

61. See Belarusian statements before the 47th through 51st opening sessions of the U.N. General Assembly, 1992–1996.

62. Kathleen Mihalisko, "Belarus: Neutrality Gives Way to 'Collective Security,'" *RFE/RL Research Report* 2, 17 (April 1993), pp. 24–31.

63. See Ustina Markus, "Russia and Belarus: Elusive Integration," *Problems of Post-Communism* 44, 5 (September/October 1997), pp. 55–61; "Yeltsin, Lukashenko Sign Revised Union Charter," *Current Digest of the Post-Soviet Press* (June 25, 1997), in Lexis; Martin Sieff, "Treaty of Union with Belarus Could Divide Russia," *Washington Times* (April 6, 1997), in Lexis; and "Highlights on the Belarus-Russia Community," Press Release of the Embassy of the Republic of Belarus to the United States of America, April 30, 1996.

64. See Andrei Sannikov, deputy minister of foreign affairs of the Republic of Belarus, "Enlargement of NATO: Apple of Discord or Fruit of Wisdom?" *Belarus in the World* 1, 1 (June 1996), pp. 57–59.

65. "President Lukashenko Addresses Belarusian Parliament," *Belarusian Radio* (April 11, 1997), from *The British Broadcasting Corporation* (April 14, 1997), in Lexis.

66. Ibid.

67. "Belarus Set to Transfer All Nuclear Materials to Russia," *Agence France Press* (October 30, 1996), in Lexis; and "Eighteen Nuclear Missiles Still in Belarus," *The Washington Times* (September 15, 1996), in Lexis.

68. "Belarus Removes Last Nuclear Missiles," *Reuter Information Service* (November 22, 1996), online; and "Belarus Holds Ceremony Marking Removal of Nuclear Weaponry," *Associated Press* (November 27, 1996), online.

69. Belarusian statements before the 47th and 48th opening sessions of the UN General Assembly, 1992 and 1993.

70. Snitko, "Belarus's Export Controls Policy," p. 13; and personal communication with Belarusian export control officials, June 1994, February 1995, October 1996, June 1997, and August 1997.

71. Aleksandr Lyushkevich, "Decision Bans Weapons, Harmful Substances Traffic," *ITAR-TASS* (February 22, 1993), in *FBIS*-SOV-93–034 (February 23, 1993), p. 42.

72. Bill Gertz, "Missile-Related Technology Sold to Beijing by Belarus," *Washington Times* (June 12, 1997), in Lexis. Concerning other Belarusian military sales, see "Belarus is Again Selling Russian S-300 SAMs," *Aerospace Daily* (December 23, 1996), in Lexis.

73. See statement of Belarusian representative at the 1993 international conference, "U.S.-NIS Dialogue on Nonproliferation Export Controls," as reported in Mike Beck and Suzette Grillot, "U.S.-NIS Dialogue on Nonproliferation Export Controls," *The Nonproliferation Review* 1, 1 (Fall 1993), pp. 67–68; "Belarus's Shushkevich on Currency, Nuclear Disarmament," *Minsk Radio* (February 1, 1993), in *FBIS*-SOV-93–021 (February 3, 1993), p. 1; Snitko, "Belarus's Export Controls Policy," pp. 12–13; and personal communication with Belarusian export control officials, June 1993, June 1994, February 1995, October 1996, June 1997, and August 1997.

74. Belarusian statements before the 47th, 48th, and 49th opening sessions of the U.N. General Assembly, 1992, 1993, and 1994; "Belarus Nuclear Ideas Cause 'Surprise,'" *PostFactum* (April 17, 1992), in *FBIS*-SOV-92–076 (April 20, 1992), p. 2; Vladimir Senko, minister of foreign affairs of the Republic of Belarus, "Foreign Policy of the Republic of Belarus: Directions and Prospects," *Belarus in the World* 1, 1 (June 1996), pp. 45–46; and personal interviews with Belarusian officials, June 1993 to August 1997.

75. For specifics on CTR aid, see the "Cooperative Threat Reduction Act of 1993, Title XII of Public Law 103–160;" and Theodor Galdi, "The Nunn-Lugar Cooperative Threat Reduction Program for Soviet Weapons Dismantlement," *CRS Report for Congress* 94–985F (December 6, 1994).

76. Personal communication with representatives of the CTR office in the U.S. Department of Defense, August 1997.

77. Ibid; and personal interviews with Belarusian export control officials, August 1997.

78. CNS Nuclear Databases (September 1997), online. Also see "Technical Support to Newly Independent States in Non-Proliferation Field," *IAEA Newsbriefs* (November/December 1996), p. 3; and "Japan's Denuclearization Programs Take Off in Ex-USSR," *Nucleonics Week* (November 11, 1993), p. 12.

79. U.S. Department of State, "Fact Sheet: Belarus," *Department of State Dispatch* (May 1997), in Lexis.

80. "Belarus and the World Bank," *World Bank online* (September 1997).

81. U.S. Department of State, "Fact Sheet: Belarus," in Lexis.

82. Statements before the 47th and 48th opening sessions of the UN General Assembly, 1992 and 1993; and personal interviews with Belarusian officials, June 1993 to August 1997.

83. Harold J. Johnson, "Cooperative Threat Reduction—Status of Defense Conversion Efforts in the Former Soviet Union," *GAO Report* GAO/NSIAD-97–101 (April 11, 1997), in Lexis.

84. "Former Soviet Union: U.S. Bilateral Program Lacks Effective Coordination," *GAO Report* GAO NSIAD-95-10 (February 1995), pp. 26-45; and personal communication with U.S. officials in the CTR office of the U.S. Department of Defense, August 1997.

85. James Rupert, "Opposition Grows to Belarus Leader," *International Her-

ald Tribune (July 31, 1996), in Lexis; "USIA Report on State Department Briefing," *M2 Communications Ltd.* (March 24, 1997), in Lexis; and "Poor Human Rights Limits U.S. Investment in Belarus," *Agence France Presse* (July 7, 1997), in Lexis.

86. Statement before the opening session of the 48th UN General Assembly, September 1993.

87. Statement before the opening session of the 49th UN General Assembly, September 1994.

88. "Nuclear Conversion Poses Problems for Staff," *Izvestiya* (April 15, 1992), p. 3, in *FBIS*-SOV-92–075 (April 17, 1992), pp. 3–4; "Shushkevich on Currency, Borders, Democracy, Arms," *Rossiya* (September 15, 1992), p. 7, in *FBIS*-SOV-92–183 (September 21, 1992), pp. 46–47; "Officials Sign Agreements With U.S. on Nonproliferation," *Interfax* (October 2, 1992), in *FBIS*-SOV-92–192 (October 2, 1992), p. 27; "Talks With Belarus Hasten Accords on Arms, Payments," *Interfax* (October 28, 1992), in *FBIS*-SOV-92–210 (October 29, 1992), pp. 12–13; and Frank Umbach, "Back to the Future? The Security Policy of Belarus," *Jane's Intelligence Review* 5, 9 (September 1993), pp. 410–14.

89. See statements before the 47th to 50th opening sessions of the UN General Assembly, 1992–1995.

90. "Government to Sell 'Surpluses of Its Weapons,'" *Interfax* (July 27, 1992), in *FBIS*- SOV-92–145 (July 28, 1992), p. 53. Also see "Belarus Begins Dismantling Strategic Arms," *ITAR-TASS* (June 30, 1992), in *FBIS*-SOV-92–127 (July 1, 1992), p. 2; "Defense Minister Cited," *ITAR-TASS* (February 4, 1993), in *FBIS*-SOV-93–023 (February 5, 1993), p. 50; and personal interviews with Belarusian officials, June 1993 to August 1997.

91. See statements before the 47th and 48th opening sessions of the UN General Assembly, 1992 and 1993.

92. "Belarus," *Economist Intelligence Unit: Country Report* (Second Quarter 1997), p. 14.

93. Stanislav Bogdankiewicz, "Belarus," in John Williamson, ed., *Economic Consequences of Soviet Disintegration* (Washington, D.C.: Institute for International Economics, 1993), pp. 349–50.

94. Mihalisko, "Belarus: Neutrality Gives Way to 'Collective Security,'" p. 30.

95. Personal interviews with Belarusian export control officials and experts, June 1993 to August 1997.

96. Larisa Sayenko, "Belarus Leader Accused of Seeking to Set Up Dictatorship," *Reuters* (August 30, 1996), in Lexis; "Belarusian President Unveils New Constitution," *OMRI Daily Digest* (September 3, 1996), in Lexis; and James Rupert, "Belarus Slides Toward Political Collision as President and Parliament Square Off," *Washington Post* (September 17, 1996), in Lexis.

97. "Belarus's President Wins Referendum," *Associated Press* (November 25, 1996), in Lexis; Kiryll Verandin, "Regime Tightens Grip," *Minsk Economic News* (September 15, 1997), in Lexis; and "Belarus President Blocks Access to Old Parliament," *Reuters* (November 28, 1996), in Lexis.

98. Rupert, "Opposition Grows to Belarus Leader," in Lexis; "World Frowns on Result of Belarus Referendum: Country Could Face Isolation Should Vote Hold," *Reuters* (November 25, 1996), in Lexis; and "Poor Human Rights Limits U.S. Investment in Belarus," in Lexis.

99. Personal interviews with Belarusian officials and experts, October 1996, June 1997, and August 1997.

100. See Belarusian statements before the 47th to 51st opening sessions of the UN General Assembly, 1992–1996.

101. "Lukashenko Addresses Trade Union," *Reuters* (November 26, 1994), in Lexis.

102. Ibid.

103. Senko, "Foreign Policy of the Republic of Belarus: Directions and Prospects," p. 45.

104. William J. Clinton, "Remarks to Future Leaders of Belarus in Minsk," *Public Papers of the Presidents of the United States* (Washington, D.C.: United States Government Printing Office, 1994), p. 78. Also see William J. Clinton, "Message to Congress Reporting on the Continuation of Export Control Regulations," *Public Papers* (1993), pp. 524–26; and William J. Clinton, "Statement by the Press Secretary on the President's Meeting with Chairman Stanislav Shushkevich of Belarus," *Public Papers* (1993), p. 1165.

105. "Belarus President Lashes at Western 'Interference,'" *Agence France Presse* (October 16, 1996), in Lexis. Also see "CFSP Statement on Belarus," *The Reuter European Community Report* (May 5, 1997), in Lexis.

106. *Freedom in the World: The Annual Survey of Political Rights and Civil Liberties* (New York: Freedom House, 1992/3–1995/6), pp. 122–25; 143–46; 130–33; and 137–39 respectively.

107. *Freedom in the World: The Annual Survey of Political Rights and Civil Liberties* (1996/7), online.

108. "Belarus: President Lukashenko Addresses the Nation," *BBC Monitoring Service* (November 14, 1994), in Lexis.

109. Ibid.

110. "U.S. Demands Explanation from Belarus," *OMRI Daily Digest* (September 24, 1996), online.

111. Victor Zhilyakov, "Krasnodar Territory and Belarus Sign Cooperation Accord," *TASS* (June 27, 1997), in Lexis; and Igor Varlamov, "Belarus Strengthens Relations With Cuba," (July 2, 1997), in Lexis.

FIVE

A WORK IN PROGRESS
The Development of Export Controls in Kazakhstan

KEITH D. WOLFE

The rapidity with which the Soviet Union was dismantled at the end of 1991 came as a great surprise to most observers of the Soviet political scene. Many leaders of the former Soviet republics were equally surprised. Some new countries, such as those in the Baltics, were quick to capitalize on the chaos and claimed their independence in the fall of 1991. Others such as Russia, Ukraine, and Georgia happily grabbed independence as it became obvious that Gorbachev had lost authority. However, Central Asian countries waited until the last moment at the very end of the year to accept the inevitability of independence.[1] One of the greatest concerns after these unprecedented developments was the fate of the enormous Soviet military-industrial complex.[2]

This concern rose out of the massive amounts of technologies and equipment which were an inherent part of the military-industrial complex widely dispersed throughout the territory of the former Soviet Union. With disarray from top to bottom in a now de-unifying state structure, the central system used in the past to control these items for internal or external distribution collapsed. Along with this collapse, both analytical observers and foreign policy-makers began to question not merely ownership, but also who was responsible for controlling and limiting the trade and sale of these items.[3] The resulting disarray of both centralized government practices and within the military-industrial complex led to heightened worries about the potential for a newly independent state (NIS) selling newly found arms and technologies without proper consideration of control.[4]

The states in Central Asia were particularly unprepared for the challenges of independence. The management of autonomous governments and the expectations that came along with them, such as controlling the technologies and materials on their territories, would prove to be daunting. Probably the most important among Central Asian states in terms of inheritance of military technologies and critical military items was Kazakhstan.[5] Kazakhstan inherited a tremendous estate of nuclear technologies and materials primarily, but also significant amounts of biological and chemical technologies as well as conventional arms.[6] Included in the nuclear complex of controlled goods were a nuclear weapons test facility and related equipment in Semipalatinsk, and significant amounts of lowly enriched uranium, beryllium, and weapon-grade fissile material.[7] The military and chemical production capabilities included research and design institutes, factories, and personnel who have advanced knowledge of the related technologies and commodities in their fields of expertise.[8] These holdings warranted enough concern to garner attention from the outside world specifically focused on control over these goods and technologies.

Kazakhstan began as a state without any internal government processes or procedures, and, for the most part, had no bureaucracy capable of developing and implementing new policies.[9] Like all other levels of government, the new Kazakhstani bureaucracy was merely the old Soviet system which had been subordinate to the central authorities in Moscow. Despite these circumstances, Kazakhstan had to take on the responsibilities of an independent state while at the same time undergoing a state-building process. This condition of independence, without a cleansing revolution or careful preparation, provides a unique opportunity to see what drives policy choices and development in conditions of uncertainty.

EXPORT CONTROL DEVELOPMENTS

Constructing a system to control the export of sensitive technologies and materials is a natural part of constructing a self-sustaining government, and much progress has been made in Kazakhstan toward the goal of building a viable, solid system of export control.[10] Considering the handicaps present in Kazakhstan, its system of export control has developed quite well over the past five years. This chapter demonstrates the driving forces that led to the level of export control development witnessed in Kazakhstan.

Kazakhstan is still in the middle of a long process of building a functional export control system consistent with Western standards. Largely due to the considerable amount of inherited technologies and materials on its soil, Kazakhstan's internal policy processes became a focus of the Western community. Experts and policy-makers in the West understood that a new and immature state would struggle on its own to build the structures needed to sufficiently protect the sensitive materials and technologies that would be of interest to would-be proliferants. Most of this focus was on Kazakhstan's nuclear policy. Not only did Kazakhstan inherit a significant nuclear arsenal, which it rather quickly agreed to transfer back to Russian soil, but it also inherited a significant nuclear complex including enrichment facilities, a BN350 fast breeder reactor on the Caspian Sea, and one of the largest uranium mining facilities in the world.[11] With all of these capabilities, the West, including the International Atomic Energy Agency (IAEA), wanted to ensure that proper controls were placed over these materials and technologies. In the beginning, much of the focus was steadfastly on the types of safeguards placed on Kazakhstani nuclear installations including the existing material protection, control, and accounting (MPC&A) procedures. As time progressed, however, some attention also began to be paid to the state's export control processes as well. Western partners—e.g., the U.S. government—demonstrated to the Kazakhstanis repeatedly in the early 1990s that export control should be on their policy agenda, but any development would need to come from within Kazakhstan's policy circles and bureaucracies.

Elements

When breaking down the Kazakhstani system of export control element by element as this book does, interesting and important differentiations can be drawn.[12] By August 1997, Kazakhstan had a system that was 64 percent complementary with Western standards of export control development.[13] While this is far from what would be considered a system without faults, for a country that began from scratch some five years before, such a record represents tremendous strides. In 1992, for example, Kazakhstani controls were at a level only 27 percent consistent with Western standards. Thus, in a five-year period, Kazakhstan more than doubled its level of development. When considering that in 1994, Kazakhstan's level of export control development was only 32 percent compatible, one sees that most of this development took place in a two-year period, which is very encouraging.

The most fully developed aspect of the Kazakhstani system is the licensing process. There exists a full legal basis for the licensing system, although it was created by decree in only a rudimentary fashion, and has since been enhanced through bureaucratic standard operating procedures in cooperation with the Cabinet of Ministers.[14] The commonly accepted reviewing agencies for an export control system are included such as the Ministry of Economics and Trade, the Ministry of Defense, the Ministry of Finance, along with specialty reviewing agencies such as the Atomic Energy Agency and the Ministry of Science.[15] All of these bodies have the right to deny the issuance of a license, and without full consent a license is not granted to an exporting firm. One surprising omission is that there is no significant role played by the Ministry of Foreign Affairs, except in receiving appropriate guarantees from foreign governments when called for by international agreement.[16] Such a situation where the major foreign policy arm of the government is excluded leads one to question the policy underpinnings of the review process in Kazakhstan, but the full functioning of the system cannot be denied. It clearly controls both sensitive exports and reexports, although some question remains on how well the system is designed for the tracking of reexports since a great deal of the trade involves states with which Kazakhstan is in a customs union.[17]

A group of other elements which can be considered highly developed relatively for Kazakhstan, but not up to Western standards, are those governing control lists, training, and bureaucratic process. Kazakhstan's control lists do exist, but there are questions remaining on how well maintained they are. Furthermore, the development of these lists is also not consistent with Western standards.[18] Because Kazakhstan is not a member of any of the international export control regimes, its control lists need not coincide with international lists, and currently they do not. Rather, Kazakhstan tends to control items based on what technologies and items the state possesses, and leans toward not controlling those items which cannot be found in Kazakhstan.[19] For Kazakhstan to receive a score indicating consistency with Western standards, the control lists will need to be brought up to international standards.

The training and bureaucratic processes elements are probably the most encouraging for those hoping to see improved development in export controls in Kazakhstan. This is because these two elements require good cooperation as well as forethought given to export control processes. Training is scored as high as it is primarily because of the efforts made by the West to train customs and border guards on these matters.[20] The training of these groups does occur although not as often as would be desired. Moreover, it is also difficult to reach officers on Kazakhstan's more distant borders.[21] Unlike customs officers and border guards, licensing officials receive no real training. Provisions and procedures do exist allowing for the training of licensing officers, and even some very limited training has taken place, but such activities remain too minimal to consider the training up to Western standards.[22]

One of the more surprising of the elements in terms of its level of development was that of bureaucratic process. Considering that the bureaucracies now involved in the processes have been ever-changing and are very underdeveloped, it is striking how well they have been cooperating on issues of license review and decision-making.[23] Most relevant ministries and departments are involved in the licensing process as mentioned earlier, although questions remain as to the inclusion of all relevant agencies at all stages in the process.[24] Because, as mentioned above, the system has been constructed primarily through decree and standard operating procedure through the direction of the Cabinet of Ministers, there are times when licenses may slip through the cracks. This has been a concern for Kazakhstani licensing officers who recognize the shortcomings of an untraceable paper system which can lead to secrecy and withholding of information.[25]

For a young and immature export control system, one of the more important elements is the customs authority, which, being situated at a country's points of entry and exit, is the last stage of protection for a control system. In Kazakhstan, the customs authority has developed at a moderate pace. Quite clearly, customs is still considered a revenue-producing body for the state. Accordingly, it concentrates its authority not on upholding export control procedures, but on collection of tariffs. While customs certainly is a functioning body in Kazakhstan, the amount of available interdiction equipment and the ability of officers to conduct cargo checks when they suspect export control violations make it difficult to proclaim Kazakhstani customs up to Western standards.[26] The lack of any type of radiation detection equipment at most border posts as well as the lack of officers to recognize illegally shipped equipment, or even possibly falsified licenses for export, are examples of some of the shortcomings present in the customs system.[27]

The penalties element is also not very well developed. This element is damaged particularly by the lack of export control regulations supporting the law on export control. Provisions for punishing violators of export control restrictions do exist. They are prosecuted, however, based on violations of procedures, and this carries a lesser penalty. The criminal laws are such that violations bring only administrative penalties, which do not carry jail time. This is because the falsification of licenses is considered internal violations of procedures, and thus, is punished as such.[28] Another weakness in the penalties element comes in smuggling attempts, which must be prosecuted for offenses related to export control, but not specifically covered in any of the relevant regulations or decrees. Thus, the system still is lacking, and no examples exist where prosecution was carried out on direct export control violations.[29]

A very important element for an immature system is that which speaks to information gathering and sharing because with entirely new organizations and people involved in export control processes, information distribution and sharing is required to build and maintain a well-functioning system. It is also an element that requires a very different bureaucratic mind set than what is the norm for most former-Soviet states. In the Soviet system, for example, information was usually protected and not shared. Such a background hampers former-Soviet information sharing. Progress made on this element in Kazakhstan is, therefore, both surprising and commendable. Strides have been made in sharing information with potential exporters as well as between licensing authorities.[30] Much remains to be done to fully inform industry of the purposes of export control and its procedures, as well as within licensing bodies to share information on exporters and procedures.

Finally, several export control elements show few signs of development including regime adherence, catch-all clause, and verification. Currently, Kazakhstan is not a member or adherent to any of the four international export control supplier regimes.[31] This is not likely to change in the near future, although Kazakhstani authorities have inquired into membership in the Nuclear Suppliers Group (NSG) and Wassenaar Arrangement (WA).[32] NSG membership is at the top of Kazakhstan's agenda due to its large amount of nuclear possessions. There still exists, however, some discord within the Kazakhstani government on the issue of NSG membership.[33] Thus, until internal discrepancies are resolved and the system as a whole becomes much more developed, it is unlikely that Kazakhstan will make much headway in the area of regime membership.

The catch-all element is the least developed element in the Kazakhstani system. This level of export control sophistication is simply not present in Kazakhstan, and thus a catch-all clause would far outreach the capabilities of the system. Even with a catch-all clause on the books, it is unlikely that the system could guarantee its enforcement. At present, however, there are no plans to include a catch-all clause in current export control provisions.

Finally, Kazakhstan is far from fully implementing, or even providing and checking, verification procedures. While provisions exist to certify and verify exports, the procedures are rarely, if ever, used. The problem is primarily one of lack of resources. Kazakhstan does not possess the financial or personnel resources to perform realistically anything but rudimentary pre-license and post-license checks, does not in practice require import certificates or delivery verification (IC/DVs), and the end-use and end-user checks are made primarily by intelligence bodies, which remain very secretive.[34] The conduct of end-user checks is especially damaged by lack of information sharing and lack of resources—a direct result of few personnel available at foreign consulates and embassies in countries where Kazakhstan does happen to have some type of representation. As export control gains importance among policy circles, it is possible that verification activities will continue to see modest levels of development. Without such an elevation in stature, verification is likely to remain underdeveloped.

DRIVING FORCES

While Kazakhstan has made advances in its efforts to develop an export control system since its independence, there have been factors pushing them both toward and away from further development. This section attempts to assess those factors that have both supported and hindered the development of nonproliferation export controls in Kazakhstan using the insight of international relations theory. Some factors contributing to export control development may be encouragement and support from foreign governments, internal bureaucratic support for stronger controls, and security concerns, which lead to strengthened controls in order to restrict the military capabilities of other states in the region. Likewise, there are many factors that may lead a state to not aggressively establish an export control system. Some of these factors include industrial opposition to any sort of control structure, bureaucratic opposition to controls due to their constraints on trade and the expansion of markets, and the lack of resources to implement an effective overall policy.

As the above discussion of Kazakhstani export control development demonstrates, the analysis of such development must touch on a number of issues that a state faces. Accordingly, the four theoretical approaches outlined in the opening chapter highlight the various factors that may affect export control development. Therefore, to understand Kazakhstan's development of export controls, this section examines the issue based on these approaches. The behavioral expectations set forth in the opening chapter are applied to the Kazakhstani case to better understand which approach best explains its nonproliferation export control development.

Realism/Neorealism

The realist/neorealist approach does not well explain Kazakhstani export control development. Security concerns, in other words, do not particularly motivate export control development in Kazakhstan. Several states immediately come to mind when thinking about Kazakhstani security concerns. The first two would be Russia and China, both of which have voiced territorial claims on Kazakhstan. Russian nationalists have repeatedly stated that northern Kazakhstan, which is primarily Russian in nationality, should be repatriated to Russian soil.[35] Likewise, China has historical claims to some sections of eastern Kazakhstan, which has a large Uighur ethnic Chinese population.[36] Another state that could conceivably pose a security threat to Kazakhstan is its chief rival for dominance in the Central Asian region, Uzbekistan. While Uzbekistan has never voiced any type of threat toward Kazakhstan itself, there is a continual struggle for influence in the region.[37]

In the case of China especially, one can certainly see Kazakhstani perceptions of threat. The move of the capitol of Kazakhstan from Almaty, which sits some mere 200 miles from the Chinese border, to Akmola, which is far to the north approximately 700 miles away from China, is one example of Kazakhstani security concerns.[38] There is also a widespread mistrust of the Chinese among public officials, as well as the population as a whole in Kazakhstan, especially in towns near the Chinese border.[39] Yet, such a direct correlation cannot be drawn to perceived security threats from either Russia or Uzbekistan like in the case of China. While Russia certainly attempts to bully Kazakhstan in many of the states' interactions, Kazakhstan views Russia as more of a critical ally than an adversary. Concerns do remain, however, as to Russian intentions in the future. While a healthy rivalry exists between Uzbekistan and Kazakhstan, the utter lack of any military component to their rivalry leaves realism with little to explain. This is exacerbated by the fact that none of the above security threats appears to be the result of proliferation concerns.

Given that Kazakhstan does apparently fear China, and possibly Russia, realism would expect that Kazakhstan would develop nonproliferation export controls with the express purpose to limit the military power of China and Russia, thus using export controls to enhance state security. It does not appear, however, that any perceived security threat led to export controls aimed specifically at any of these states, or that export controls were developed as a way to enhance security.[40] Kazakhstan understands very well that it would not have much to gain by limiting technology transfers to states such as Russia and China, which are already much better armed with high-tech weaponry, including nuclear arms.

Kazakhstani export control development therefore does not appear to be the result of military security related factors. While Kazakhstan does perceive certain states to be potential security threats, these perceptions are not specifically linked to the proliferation of weapons, equipment, and technology to those threatening states. Moreover, there is little evidence that Kazakhstan believes it could balance its power against states such as China and Russia; and it certainly understands that export controls would not be a viable means to that end. There exists little evidence to suggest that Kazakhstan purposefully attempts to limit the military capability of Russia, China, or any other state. Finally, no real evidence exists to demonstrate that Kazakhstan views export control as a mechanism to enhance state security.

Rational Institutionalism

The approach that better explains export control development in Kazakhstan is rational institutionalism. Rational institutionalism attempts to understand state behavior through an assessment of the costs and benefits associated with such behavior. If a policy is perceived to be more beneficial that costly, then the state is likely to pursue the policy. For export control, costs and benefits can be understood in the following way. An associated cost with export control, for example, is the amount of lost trade due to controls over trade for security reasons. Associated benefits include side payments such as assistance from abroad and the greater sense of security the state has because it did not transfer critical materials and technologies to states that present a military threat. In a most simple fashion, policy-makers would merely subtract the cost of lost trade from the benefit of possible economic gains and increased security and, if positive, support export control development, and if negative, eschew it.

In practice, of course, analyzing costs and benefits is much more complicated and comprehensive. Another critical factor for understanding costs and benefits associated with export control development is the "payments" a state may receive. In Kazakhstan, incentives other than those which are security relevant seem to have the greatest impact on the development of nonproliferation export controls. Kazakhstani officials and industrialists undoubtedly calculated explicitly the costs and benefits associated with the development of nonproliferation export controls.[41] Perhaps most revealing are statements made by officials in the Ministry of Industry and Trade that specifically referred to such calculations.[42] When asked why Kazakhstan would choose to promote export control development despite its pressing need to expand economic markets, officials responded that they considered export controls to be in the long-term interest of the state because they made Kazakhstan a more attractive trading partner to the world.[43] Individuals at the Ministry of Foreign Affairs, the Atomic Energy Agency, and even within President Nazarbaev's governing apparatus made similar statements, leaving little doubt as to whether or not the policy was carefully chosen based on costs and benefits.[44]

Rational institutionalism leads us to expect that a state would acknowledge and accept the constraints on behavior set by the international nonproliferation regime. As mentioned earlier, one of the least developed export control elements in Kazakhstan is that concerning international regime membership. At present, Kazakhstan is not an adherent or member in any of the nonproliferation regimes, and future membership or adherence does not seem imminent. There have been indications, however, that Kazakhstan's interest in regime membership has increased as the Kazakhstani system has become more developed. The Kazakhstani government, for example, has expressed interest in NSG membership. The NSG is at the forefront of the Kazakhstani wish list in terms of regime membership due to its desire to become a player in the international nuclear market.[45] The question over membership is still hotly debated within the government as there is some disagreement whether joining the NSG will in the long run help nuclear sales, or hinder them due to excessive international limitations on exports.

Considering the rational institutionalist expectation that a state may develop a export control system as a way to reduce transaction costs and uncertainty in international relations, Kazakhstani officials certainly perceived such reductions to be in their interest. Without a doubt, the Kazakhstanis see export controls as a way to do what is expected of them. In other words, Kazakhstan largely sees that other states have shown export control development to be important, and thus, export control has been placed on the Kazakhstani agenda. If other states had not made export control an issue, the subject may never have been broached. In dealing with the United States, or Western Europe, or even Russia, Kazakhstan often hears about the importance of nonproliferation export control development. The Kazakhstanis, therefore, calculated that because their government's potential partners of the future consider export control to be important, it is worth the effort to develop such a system to help ensure future stability. Kazakhstani officials determined that their support for a policy wanted by its major partners would serve to reduce future transaction costs and uncertainty in dealing with those partners.

Rational institutionalism also expects that states would be interested in future interaction and reciprocity. In the case of Kazakhstan, evidence exists to support such an expectation. The importance given to future interaction with desirable partners transformed export control policy, which would normally be perceived as unimportant and be unlikely to be placed on the agenda, into a prominent one. This is the case despite the fact that Kazakhstan suffers from serious political, economic, and social problems that are not being given the same attention as export control.[46]

Finally, rational institutionalism leads us to expect that material incentives would be offered and received for the promotion of export control development. Such material incentives may be in the form of direct export control aid, but also may be in the form of side payments made for other general purposes. On both counts, Kazakhstan fits the expectations of rational institutionalism well. Under the Nunn-Lugar, or CTR program, Kazakhstan has received just over $2 million in export control aid. Most of this money has been spent on visits and exchanges of leading officials and businessmen. Some equipment, however, has also been delivered, such as various radiation detection equipment for domestic customs activities, patrol boats for the Caspian Sea, and a computer licensing system with a server and computers for all relevant agencies and licensers.[47] Such equipment, and even the exchanges and meetings, have greatly enhanced support within the Kazakhstani government for export control development.[48]

Similarly, overall nonproliferation efforts have also served to promote export control development. U.S. FREEDOM Support Act funding and other non-export-control-related Cooperative Threat Reduction spending, largely being disbursed through money guaranteed to Kazakhstan through Project Sapphire, has helped to assist any and all nonproliferation policies in Kazakhstan.[49] While not explicitly linked, funding provided to upgrade the security at the BN350 fast breeder reactor in Aktau also serves to strengthen the goals of export control development. For the most part, the Kazakhstanis see issues of nonproliferation, such as MPC&A and export control, as much more linked than do officials within the United States.[50] This is critical in being able to tie developments in MPC&A to other nonproliferation activities such as export control. While Western policy may be to separate the issues, within the Kazakhstani system they are inextricably linked.

Another linkage can be made with the FREEDOM Support Act aid aimed at democratic development. While this aid, which primarily is tied to efforts of the Agency for International Development working within Kazakhstan, does not specifically target nonproliferation efforts in any way, it does reinforce the nature of the Western message to Kazakhstani policy-makers that liberalization, democratic development, and general foreign policy cooperation with the United States and the West is seen as critical for continued efforts to assist in the large tasks which lay ahead of Kazakhstan in efforts to further develop the state economically.

Clearly, rational institutionalism best explains export control development in Kazakhstan. Four of the five behavioral expectations are met in the Kazakhstani case. Kazakhstani policy-makers appear to have explicitly calculated both the pros and cons of export control development. There seems to have been an interest in reducing transaction costs and future uncertainty in international relations thus leading to further development. Also, future interactions were apparently valued enough to push for some level of development. Finally, significant payments have been made to Kazakhstan to foster nonproliferation policy as a whole and export control policy specifically. Little evidence exists, however, to support the expectation concerning the nonproliferation regime's rules and norms as constraints on behaviors, but the other expectations clearly demonstrate the validity of the rational institutionalist approach.

Domestic Politics

Probably the most difficult theoretical approach to analyze is the domestic politics approach. This is because it is also the most diverse of the approaches, drawing its foundations from some disparate analyses of policy-making. However, oftentimes it is exactly this element which is missing in the analysis of policy-making in foreign countries, and, therefore, such an analysis can be very productive for our understanding of both export control development as well as the policy-making environment in new states. The disparate literature on the impact of domestic factors on policy makes it clear that there exists no clear agreement on which factors are the most prevalent. This is the case even more clearly in states such as Kazakhstan, which to this point cannot be well understood within an institutional framework. In a young state such as Kazakhstan, however, the analysis of micro-level factors should help establish if indeed domestic forces are influencing state policies.

Part of the difficulty in analyzing the effect of domestic politics on export control development is the diversity of domestic political theories which abound in the international relations literature. A diverse literature leads to an eclectic analysis, and may therefore be regarded as inconclusive. However, a composition of these theories can serve well to provide indications of the viability of domestic political theory in assessing export control development.

The first domestic expectation concerns the activities of interest groups and their efforts to pressure the government to develop or avoid export control policies and procedures that are consistent with international standards. For several reasons, this expectation does not apply in the Kazakhstani case. The concept of democracy is still very immature in Kazakhstan, and most would argue it is very foreign to Kazakhstani citizens. Thus, active interest groups participating in pluralist politics are basically non-existent in Kazakhstan. Reports of 100-person marches demonstrating against the president are stunning enough to those in the capitol, much less the systematic formation of interest groups pressuring public policy. Kazakhstan remains, therefore, a long way from this type of activity focusing on export control development.

The next expectation, that elite decision-makers perceive and believe export control policies to be in the "national interest," seems to be more viable. Elite decision-makers in Kazakhstan are indeed making nearly all policy decisions on export control, and in the end are responsible for either the relative development or lack thereof of the export control system in Kazakhstan. Specific elite perceptions of export control as in the "national interest," however, are weak. In fact, elite decision-makers have largely been apathetic toward export control from the beginning. In the Kazakhstani system, broad policies are made by central authorities and then further developed and implemented at the ministerial level. It is at this ministerial level where much of the development has taken place, rather than at the insistence of the central, or elite, authorities. Little attention has been paid to the issue at the higher levels. The existing legal structure governing export control in Kazakhstan is an example of the lack of attention elites pay to the issue. While Kazakhstan is the only state of the NIS to possess a law on export control, the law is only thirteen brief articles in length and provides nothing regarding regulatory structures or processes.[51] Furthermore, the president delayed signing the law for many months after the parliament approved it.[52] Such apathy can also be seen in the decree structure, which leaves almost all details and export control structures to be created by the "licensing authority" rather than outlining any type of structure within the governing decree.[53]

The next expectation suggests that highly centralized states will be better able to develop and coordinate export control activities. Without a doubt, Kazakhstan can be considered a highly centralized state with the entire government structure falling under the president and his apparatus. The ministries report directly to presidential bodies on any and all policy issues, including export control, and the central authority is, in the end, responsible for policy decisions. Thus, in theory, export control processes are highly coordinated and centralized. In practice, however, other factors are prevalent. As mentioned above, export controls have largely been delegated to the ministerial level, and only scant attention is paid to the issue within the central administrative body.[54]

The State Committee on Export Controls, which was created in 1993, is an example of ministerial domination in export control issues. This committee was to bring together all relevant state agencies and bodies into a committee at the level of the Cabinet of Ministers, which would coordinate and run all export control functions. Since its inception, the committee has met only twice, and has had no impact on export control processes.[55] While the government is highly centralized, at least concerning the issue of export control, it is at the ministerial level where developments have been made.

The final domestic political expectation concerns bureaucratic politics, and, in many cases, is the most applicable (within the domestic approach) to the case of Kazakhstan. This expectation suggests that for export control development to be prevalent, those agencies with export control functions will be more powerful and influential than agencies with trade promotion functions. In Kazakhstan, an analysis of the agencies and bureaucracies involved in export control shows that they are fairly typical bureaucratic organizations. In other words, they lack significant resources and are continually struggling with other organizations for legitimacy and prestige. Thus, it is indeed important for them to promote the cause of export control development. In comparison to enterprises and the groups that represent them within government, however, it would be improper to assert that one has power over the other. In most instances, due to limited resources and opportunities, these two groups work together very closely. Enterprises have been successful in keeping the central authorities wary of setting up too stringent a system of control such as in making commitments to international nonproliferation regimes, and the export control authorities have been successful in further developing certain aspects of the system. Thus, the results concerning the bureaucratic approach to export control development appear to be significant, but mixed.

Domestic political forces are often difficult to analyze when looking at policy decisions of the state. In this case, domestic political expectations do not well explain the level of export control development in Kazakhstan. The one exception is the somewhat contradictory evidence regarding the bureaucratic approach. The bureaucratic authorities have a serious impact on export control, but since there are factions in both support and against export control, they have tended to balance one another out. Interest groups have not pressured for or against export control developments in Kazakhstan. Similarly, elite decision-makers have not pushed for export control policy to the extent that they have driven export control development. Finally, while Kazakhstan is indeed a centralized state, in the area of export control, there appears to be a more decentralized and bottom-up approach to development.

Liberal Identity

In applying the earlier approaches to export control development in Kazakhstan, the results have been rather clear. In assessing their explanatory capability, the results for both realism and domestic politics are relatively negative, and for rational institutionalism, positive. The liberal identity approach, however, provides much more of an unclear outlook. First, Kazakhstan is far from being a liberal state, and has had problems with international organizations and Western states disapproving of its domestic political maneuverings.[56] In the policy area being addressed here, however, it is fair to say that the officials responsible for export control activities do acknowledge a "sense of community" in export control matters. On these issues, Kazakhstan is dealing closely with Russia, the United States, Western Europe, and Japan, and would view these states as the "export control community."[57] It is important for Kazakhstan to do its best to belong to this community.[58] The goal may not strictly be one of liberalization, but more a sense of belonging.

Quite clearly, Kazakhstan values highly its regular interaction with the liberal community on matters of export control. There is little doubt that without such interaction Kazakhstan would not have made the advances in export controls it has. If interactions with the West and Russia on export control matters were to cease, it is highly unlikely that export control would continue to be given the priority it currently holds within the Kazakhstani government. When one official was asked about the relative importance of U.S. attention given to export controls for Kazakhstan, his response was blunt. He answered quickly, "my job," implying that without the attention paid by the United States to the issue, he would not be working in this issue area. This clearly shows how important a value is placed on such interaction for export control development. The export control bureaucracy is already quite pressed for financial resources and personnel, and without the attention of the Western community, even less would be available for export control. It is difficult, however, to further tie this feeling of belonging to an export control "community" to a broader sense of community with liberal states and policies. This indicates that liberal identity is not particularly applicable to Kazakhstan in a broader sense of community building.

Also according to the liberal identity approach, development of export control would occur in tandem with the development of the normative and institutional bases of a liberal, democratic government. This, however, is not the case in Kazakhstan. While there has been significant export control development, it would be difficult to argue that Kazakhstan has made advances toward democracy or liberalization. The state is still controlled by the highly popular and powerful president, Nursultan Nazarbaev, who has become quite adept at keeping protests and opposition to a minimum.[59] Thus, export control development cannot be tied to liberalization of the state.

Finally, little evidence exists to support the final expectation that there will be greater interest in targeting the control of materials toward illiberal states. Some of Kazakhstan's largest trading partners are states which the Western, liberal community considers "illiberal," such as India, Pakistan, and Iran. While trade is still heavily dependent on CIS partners, especially Russia, the expansion of markets to states such as the above is deemed critical for economic growth in Kazakhstan. In fact, Kazakhstan has heightened interests in furthering trade and exchanges with India on the very sensitive matter of nuclear technologies.[60]

Liberal identity, therefore, provides mixed support for export control development in Kazakhstan. Clearly, Kazakhstan is a state that wishes to identify itself with the liberal community on matters of export control and nonproliferation, but does not show this same desire in a broader political sense. Such identification, however, appears largely to be motivating future interactions more than to provide a genuine sense of community building. Kazakhstan does view regular interaction with the liberal community as critical to its efforts to develop in the manner it prefers, and without such interactions it is likely that no export control development would have taken place.[61] Kazakhstan is not making great strides toward liberalization or democracy, and such a move cannot explain export control development in Kazakhstan. Finally, Kazakhstan also does not target illiberal states with its export controls as three illberal states—India, Pakistan and Iran—are considered vital trading partners for Kazakhstan. Moreover, evidence suggests that nuclear exchanges have taken place, and continue to occur, with India.

CONCLUSION

From the evidence collected in this study, the rational institutional approach appears to provide the strongest explanation for the development of export controls in Kazakhstan. Kazakhstan apparently calculated the relative importance of export controls to its Western partners and Russia, and developed its policy accordingly. Many important questions remain, however. If a state develops export controls largely in response to the wishes of its partners, can we expect such development to be sustained? Will Kazakhstan continue to develop its export control policies in accordance with how it perceives the wishes of Russia or the United States? It is also important to note that such policy-making may lead to "paper policies," where the policy is very weak and not likely to withstand the test of time. For export controls to become a more concrete and solid policy for Kazakhstan, there must be valid and important domestic foundations for the policy, rather than that based only on the calculation of costs and benefits associated with external factors. It seems likely that Western policy has led to an opportunity for Kazakhstan to discover for itself what those positives are, and indications are that the Kazakhstanis are learning. For the first time, one can see Kazakhstani officials making arguments independently for export controls, rather than merely supporting export control development in order to gain carrots and rewards from the West. This is the process that must take place for continued development.

Although not as strong a factor, liberal identity seems to assist somewhat in explaining Kazakhstani export control development. Interactions with the West have been very important to export control development in Kazakhstan and will continue to be critical in the future. Although Kazakhstan wants to be associated with the United States and other liberal states on export control matters, the markings of a liberal state are not present there today. Finally, realist and domestic political approaches do not provide much insight concerning export control development in Kazakhstan.

Continued analysis of export control development over the next couple of years in Kazakhstan will be critical. Kazakhstan in the late 1990s is somewhere between being a success and a failure in developing a thorough system of nonproliferation export controls. Given more time and more interactions with states (especially Western states) advocating meaningful export control, Kazakhstan could well continue its export control development.

NOTES

1. For a full discussion of how independence was viewed within Central Asia, see Martha Brill Olcott, "Central Asia's Catapult to Independence," *Foreign Affairs*, vol. 71, no. 3, (1992), 108–40.

2. Office of the Secretary of Defense, *Proliferation: Threat and Response*, (Washington, D.C.: U.S. Government Printing Office, 1996).

3. For examples of independent analysis calling into question the stability of control in these states, see National Research Council, *Proliferation Concerns: Assessing U.S. Efforts to Help Contain Nuclear and Other Dangerous Materials and Technologies in the Former Soviet Union* (Washington, D.C.: National Academy Press, 1997); and Graham T. Allison, Owen W. Cote, Jr., Richard A. Falkenrath, and Steven E. Miller, *Avoiding Nuclear Anarchy: Containing the Threat of Loose Russian Nuclear Weapons and Fissile Material* (Cambridge, MA: MIT Press, 1996). For examples of policy concern refer to *Report on Nonproliferation and Counterproliferation Activities and Programs*, (Washington, D.C.: Office of the Deputy Secretary of Defense, May 1994); or United States Congress, Office of Technology Assessment, *Proliferation and the Former Soviet Union*, OTA-ISS-605 (Washington, D.C.: U.S.

Government Printing Office, September 1994).

4. To see a related discussion on how the collapse of Soviet military-industrial complex processes may lead to proliferation, see National Research Council, 32–51.

5. Its importance can be drawn from the fact that the international community, led by the United States, focused more attention on Kazakhstan than any of the other NIS with the exception of Russia, Ukraine, and Belarus.

6. For examples of Kazakhstan's capabilities, see William Potter, *Nuclear Profiles of the Soviet Successor States* (Monterey, CA: Center for Nonproliferation Studies, Monterey Institute for International Studies, 1993), and Shirin Akiner, "Soviet Military Legacy in Kazakhhstan," *Jane's Intelligence Review*, December 1994, 552.

7. Potter, *Nuclear Profiles of the Soviet Successor States*.

8. Peter Almquist and Edwin Bacon, "Arms Exports in a Post-Soviet Market," *Arms Control Today*, vol. 22 (July/August 1992), 12–17.

9. For a more thorough discussion of the state of Kazakhstani bureaucracy at the time of independence, and subsequently, see Keith D. Wolfe, "Nonproliferation Policy in Kazakhstan: Development and Implementation," prepared for presentation at the 1997 International Studies Association Annual Meetings, 19–22 March 1997, Toronto, Ontario, Canada. Available upon request.

10. For a more detailed overview on the state of export controls in Kazakhstan, see Gary K. Bertsch, ed., *Restraining the Spread of the Soviet Arsenal: NIS Nonproliferation Export Controls Status Report—1996*; Keith Wolfe, "Kazakhstan," 36–52, (Athens: University of Georgia Center for International Trade and Security, 1997).

11. Potter, *Nuclear Profiles of the Soviet Successor States*.

12. The elemental breakdown of export controls was originally put forth in Cassady Craft and Suzette Grillot with Liam Anderson, Michael Beck, Chris Behan, Scott Jones, and Keith Wolfe, "Tools and Methods for Measuring and Comparing Nonproliferation Export Control Development," Occasional Paper of the Center for International Trade and Security (Athens: University of Georgia Press, 1996).

13. For scoring methods, see Craft and Grillot, "Tools and Methods."

14. The latest decree governing the export control system is Decree No. 298, "On the issuing of export and import licenses for goods and services," dated 12 March 1996. The decrees are general and do not set up the system in detail, and thus bureaucracies, in conjunction with the Cabinet of Ministers have come up with procedures over time. Field work in Kazakhstan by the author.

15. Paper prepared by Dastan Eleukenov, chief of Division of International Arms Control, Ministry of Foreign Affairs, Republic of Kazakhstan, "The Responsibilities of the Ministries and Departments Involved in Export Control in the Republic of Kazakhstan."

16. Interviews with Ministry of Foreign Affairs officials, September 1996.

17. The existing customs union is between Russia, Belarus, Kyrgyzstan, and Kazakhstan, although Kyrgyzstan has expressed dissatisfaction with the conditions of the union and has threatened to withdraw.

18. The maintenance of control lists is an ad hoc and irregular process, and changes occurred only twice through the summer of 1997, although a more rigorous review process including technical experts in the field is being developed. The previous changes took place without significant scientific input. Interview with technical experts responsible to the Ministry of Science, January 1996.

19. Ibid.

20. U.S. programs such as Project Amber have successfully trained customs officers in Kazakhstan on issues of export control, and further training programs are being coordinated by both the U.S. Customs Service and the Nonproliferation and Disarmament Fund (NDF) program. It should be noted that in Kazakhstan, the border guards perform a very minimal role when it comes to export control. Their role is more akin to that played by the INS in the U.S. However, the border guards are instructed to report any detection of export control violations and are trained side by side with customs officers. Interviews with both Kazakhstani customs officers and border guard officials, October 1996.

21. Personal interview with customs official in Almaty October 1996. It is especially difficult to reach officers at the border due to Kazakhstan's size and the number of active border posts.

22. Interviews with licensers within different licensing arms including the Atomic Energy Agency and the Ministry of Industry and Trade (now defunct and renamed the Ministry of Economics and Trade), September 1996–March 1997.

23. An example of the changing bureaucratic environment can be seen in the change of chief licensing authorities. In 1993, the central authority was the Ministry of Foreign Economic Relations, but once this ministry was disbanded, the Ministry of Industry and Trade took over until 1997 when it also was reorganized. Currently, the Ministry of Economics and Trade serves this role.

24. Eleukenov, "The Responsibilities of the Ministries and Departments Involved in Export Control in the Republic of Kazakhstan."

25. The concern comes in that a licenser really cannot confirm that each stage in the process is being followed consistently. Both licensers and exporters expressed concern for this issue in interviews, January 1996. The hope is that the new electronic licensing system will further institutionalize the process and lead to greater transparency of the process. This being said, the author knows of no confirmed licenses which did not go through all proper channels.

26. Interviews with Kazakhstani customs officials in Almaty 1996 and 1997.

27. Ibid.

28. It should be noted that it is considered an "internal" violation because all exporting enterprises are government owned and operated. Regulations will need to be developed to account for privatization. Even so, no known examples exist of even administrative penalties, typified by restrictions on exports or fines, ever being enforced for violations of export control regulations.

29. A good example of this can be seen in the prosecution of a group of guards at the Ulbinsky Metallurgical Plant who were convicted for stealing uranium fuel

pellets with intent to export. The group was prosecuted for failing to follow proper security procedures at the facility because no laws existed to prosecute them for attempting to trade without a license.

30. Such an example can be seen with the holding of a three-day seminar entitled "Nonproliferation and Export Control in Kazakhstan," in January 1997, run jointly by the Atomic Energy Agency of the Republic of Kazakhstan and the Institute of Atomic Energy, National Nuclear Center of Semipalatinsk, Kazakhstan, sponsored by Los Alamos National Laboratory and the U.S. Department of Energy. The seminar was attended by all relevant governmental agencies as well as by representatives from industry and was fully Kazakhstani run and developed. This type of event portrays the type of information exchange taking place today which did not in the beginning.

31. The international export control regime is generally accepted to be made up of the Nuclear Suppliers Group, the Wassenaar Arrangement, the Australia Group, and the Missile Technology Control Regime.

32. Interview with Ministry of Foreign Affairs official, February 1997.

33. This issue is further discussed in the subsequent rational institutionalism section.

34. Import delivery and verification is, however, carried out as called for under IAEA guidelines on nuclear items of import. Guarantees are also given foreign governments regarding reexport provisions through the Ministry of Foreign Affairs.

35. For some background on the Russian-Kazakhstani relationship, see "Russian Rumblings," in *The Economist*, Volume 330 (March 12, 1994), 42; Andrei Kortunov, Yuri Kulchik, and Andrei Shoumikhin, "Military Structures in Kazakhstan: Aims, Parameters, and Some Implications for Russia (View From Russia)," in *Comparative Strategy*, Volume 14 (July/Sept. 1995), 301–09; Robert Kaiser and Jeff Chinn, "Russian-Kazakh Relations in Kazakhstan," in *Post-Soviet Geography*, Volume 36 (May 1995), 257–73; Graham E. Fuller, "Russia and Central Asia," in Michael Mandelbaum, ed., *Central Asia and the World: Kazakhstan, Kyrgyzstan, Tajikistan, Turkmenistan, and Uzbekistan*. (New York: Council on Foreign Relations, May 1994); and Maxim Shashenkov, "Russia in Central Asia: Emerging Security Links," in Anoushiravan Ehteshami, ed., *From the Gulf to Central Asia: Players in the New Great Game* (Exeter: University of Exeter Press, 1994).

36. For some background on the China-Kazakhstan relationship, see Ross Munro, "Central Asia and China." in Mandelbaum, ed., *Central Asia and the World: Kazakhstan, Kyrgyzstan, Tajikistan, Turkmenistan, and Uzbekistan*; Peter Ferdinand, "The New Central Asia and China," in Peter Ferdinand, ed., *The New Central Asia and Its Neighbours*, (London: Royal Institute of International Affairs, Pinter Publishers Ltd., 1994); and Yuriy Kulchik, Andrey Fadin, and Victor Sergeev, *Central Asia After the Empire* (Chicago: Pluto Press, 1996).

37. For some background on the Uzbekistan-Kazakhstan relationship, see Marth Brill Olcott, "Ceremony and Substance: The Illusion of Unity in Central Asia," in Mandelbaum, ed., *Central Asia and the World: Kazakhstan, Kyrgyzstan,*

Tajikistan, Turkmenistan, and Uzbekistan; "Awkward Friends," in *The Economist*, Volume 335 (8 April 1995), 37; and Shirin Akiner, "Post-Soviet Central Asia," in Ferdinand, ed. *The New Central Asia and Its Neighbours*.

38. This was cited as one reason for the move according to numerous interviews with Kazakhstani officials September 1996-January 1997. Other reasons included nationality issues, trade issues with Russia, and the most publicized being the potential for earthquakes in Almaty. See "High Stepping," in *The Economist*, Voume 338 (16 March 1996), 41–42.

39. Author's field work. This information was gathered in talking to officials and citizens living in Almaty, as well as in towns and villages farther toward the Chinese border.

40. Interviews with various Kazakhstani officials, January 1997.

41. These findings are based on field interviews by the author during his residency in Kazakhstan September 1996–March 1997.

42. When the interviews were conducted (September 1996–March 1997), the main agency responsible for export control was the Ministry of Industry and Trade. Since then, however, this ministry was merged into the Ministry of Economics and Trade, which performs the same export control functions.

43. Interview with officials at the Ministry of Industry and Trade, January 1997.

44. Interviews with officials within the Ministry of Foreign Affairs, the Atomic Energy Agency, and the offices of the Cabinet of Ministers, December 1996–January 1997.

45. This desire is echoed from all involved, including both enterprise representatives from KazAtomProm and other smaller manufacturers, as well as from governmental and policy bodies such as the Kazakhstani Atomic Energy Agency and the Ministry of Foreign Affairs. These interests were expressed again and again in numerous interviews with representatives from varied backgrounds (January-February 1997).

46. A good example of this can be seen from the status of the Committee for Crisis Situations in Kazakhstan, which is regularly given essentially no budget and huge policies to implement. In an interview with a highly placed official in this state committee in December 1996, specific attention was brought to export controls when I was asked how did the export control authorities "catch the attention of the United States"? The point was that the Committee on Crisis Situations hoped to do the same type of "marketing" so that their policies were given more attention within policy-making bodies in Kazakhstan.

47. Interviews with American officials from the Departments of Commerce and Energy, April 1997.

48. A good example of the building of relationships and fostering support within the Kazakhstani government for strong export control policy can be seen with the Graduate Student Facilitator Program run by Los Alamos National Laboratory for the Department of Energy. Under this program, the author had the opportunity

to work for eight months within the Kazakhstani export control structure at the Atomic Energy Agency on issues specifically related to nuclear export control. This type of effort underscores the importance placed by the U.S. government in gaining support within the Kazakhstani government for the development of export controls.

49. Under Project Sapphire, the United States purchased 600 kilograms of HEU from Kazakhstan in 1994. Payment for the uranium has been made through the implementation of various MPC&A programs and upgrades, rather than as a direct payment. This issue is still very sensitive within both the United States and Kazakhstani governments because of the secrecy of the U.S. military mission in taking the material as well as due to the ongoing disagreement over how the funds for the HEU were to be distributed. Kazakhstani officials, and some in the United States, assumed the payment would be in the form of direct funds instead of in the form of goods and services.

50. In discussing the difference between the programs, the Kazakhstanis never understand why there is such a differentiation in the bureaucracies which handle these issues in the United States. This is very telling for a number of reasons, but in this instance explains the logic of tying side payments to export control development.

51. See Law No. 9–1, "On the export control of arms, military hardware, and dual-use goods," signed into law by President Nazarbaev 18 June 1996.

52. The officials who were involved in the drafting of the law claimed that it had been prepared for one year before being taken up by parliament, and once passed sat on President Nazarbaev's desk for months before it was signed into law. Being that it was signed as it had been passed by the parliament, some took President Nazarbaev's reluctance as a direct sign of disinterest in the issue of the central government.

53. See Decree No. 66, "On the order of export and import of goods (work and services) on the territory of the Republic of Kazakhstan," dated 19 January 1995, Decree No. 338, "On the further development of the export control system in the Republic of Kazakhstan," dated 24 March 1995, and Decree No. 298, "On the issuing of export and import licenses for goods and services," dated 12 March 1996.

54. Interviews with individuals located within both the ministerial and departmental level as well as within the presidential apparatus and the Cabinet of Ministers (January 1997).

55. Interviews with several officials who took part in one of the meetings, as well as with individuals who were on the commission which created the committee. They stated that the idea of the committee would be to coordinate all export control activities, similar to the roles played by similar committees in the Russian Federation and Ukraine. September-December 1996.

56. Groups such as Amnesty International have constantly complained about the lack of political freedom in Kazakhstan. Freedom House scores suggest that Kazakhstan is an "illiberal" state with a scoring of "not free" under their system. In the 1996 scores on political rights, Kazakhstan was given a score of 6 where 7 is the

"least free," while on civil liberties Kazakhstan scored a 5 with 7 again being the "least free." Also, the last time Nazarbaev dissolved parliament in 1995 to hold new elections, many states and organizations, including the United States and the Organization for Security and Cooperation in Europe, questioned the legitimacy of such a move. This was covered up with a new set of parliamentary elections in 1995, which had large irregularities according to outside assessments. See Freedom House 1996 "Overview of Political Rights and Civil Liberties in Kazakhstan," Reuters World Service, 30 January 1996, "Kazakh Leader Calls on Parliament to Back Reforms," by Douglas Busvine, in Lexis, and Xinhua News Agency, 20 December 1995, "House Election Results Published in Kazakhstan," item no. 1220219, in Lexis.

57. In discussing issues of export control with Kazakhstani officials, inevitably issues of foreign cooperation and other states' expectations arise. The state with the most explicit expectations is Russia, and the highest levels of cooperation on this issue come from the United States, although several states in Western Europe, especially Sweden, also have interactions with Kazakhstan.

58. Interviews with officials from various ministries and departments responsible for export control, August 1996–March 1997.

59. The Kazakhstani constitution states that it is illegal to "defame without justification the President of the Republic," making organized political opposition difficult to legitimately operate.

60. "India to Get Nuclear Fuel From Kazakhstan." 22 September 1996, from the Delhi All India Radio Network. Also, several technical exchanges have taken place between Kazakhstani scientists and officials and Indian scientists and officials on the matter of nuclear fuel and technology, primarily in the way of Kazakhstani visits to nuclear sites in India, but also including Indian visits to Kazakhstani nuclear facilities such as the reactor complex in Aktau. Personal interviews, February 1997.

61. While somewhat speculative in nature, the response of officials to this was overwhelming and convinced the author that there is little doubt that the issue is a part of the domestic policy agenda not due to internal policy choices, but external expectations.

SIX

ESTONIA, LATVIA, AND LITHUANIA
Western Countries Eyeing More Western Integration

CHRIS BEHAN

History plays a particularly important role in understanding the contemporary politics of the three Baltic countries Estonia, Latvia, and Lithuania. Unlike the other states of the FSU, the Baltic countries were already European, independent nations before their occupation and incorporation into the USSR in 1940. Many of the issues they face today, therefore, relate to continuing what they started in the interwar period between 1920 and 1940 when they were developing democratic governments and market-oriented economies. Characteristics of their development as independent countries at that time included: obtaining recognition from Bolshevik Russia and concluding peace treaties with that country in 1920; developing constitutions that had provisions for universal and equal adult franchise; forming governments with directly elected single-chamber parliaments; and becoming members of the League of Nations.[1]

After the emotional (and successful) drive for independence during the late 1980s and early 1990s, the Baltic countries resumed the process of developing into independent nations. Indeed, this concept of continuity—that these countries are simply continuing what they started earlier in the century—is an important one in the eyes of today's Estonians, Latvians, and Lithuanians. For example, on October 7, 1992, the Riigikogu (the Estonian parliament) declared legal continuity between the 1920–1940 republic and the current state. The Latvian and Lithuanian parliaments declared similar acts. The concept of continuity also arose during recent border negotiations between Estonia and Russia. Estonia is willing to concede land it lost to Soviet Russia in 1945 to present-day Russia if the Russian Federation would recognize the 1920 Estonian treaty of independence, the Treaty of Tartu. In recognizing Tartu, Russia would be admitting that the Soviet incorporation of Estonia was in fact an "occupation," and thus was a violation of Estonia's sovereignty and international law.[2] (At the time of this writing, negotiations between Estonia and Russia on a border settlement had ended, but an agreement had not been signed.)

Whether or not Russia recognizes the Soviet incorporation of the Baltics as an "occupation" is not that important in terms of continued development for these three countries today. The fact is, since regaining independence, Estonia, Latvia, and Lithuania have all outperformed their former Soviet contemporaries in becoming developed nations. All of the Baltic states now possess established proportional representation, multiparty parliamentary systems, national militaries, environmental programs directed at cleaning up the ecological damage that the Soviets left behind, successful privatization programs, stable national currencies, and GDPs per capita that place all three countries in the top four of the Newly Independent States (NIS).[3] Moreover, the Baltic nations' policies toward minorities, particularly in Lithuania, have been more successful in cooling ethnic tensions than in many other former Soviet states. By maintaining democratic governments in ethnically diverse societies, these countries have established themselves as responsible, advanced nations and have gained important international support.

CURRENT NONPROLIFERATION SITUATION

In their continued drive toward developing as advanced industrialized countries, Estonia, Latvia, and Lithuania are actively pursuing foreign and domestic policies that, not surprisingly, are similar to those of most Western democracies. One example of this is their rather quick start at introducing nonproliferation export control systems. Soon after becoming independent nations, each of the three initiated programs or governmental decrees that acknowledged the worldwide importance of strong nonproliferation policies. In real terms, the Baltic states quickly understood the importance of stopping the transshipment of illicit strategic weapon commodities and dual-use goods that were crossing their relatively weak borders and onto the Baltic sea. In fact, Estonia can claim one of the first convictions in the NIS for the illegal possession of radioactive materials. On 24 January 1995, a man in Estonia was convicted to one year of imprisonment for possessing almost 3 kilograms of uranium oxide.[4]

As former republics of a country that possessed an enormous arsenal of weapons of mass destruction, Estonia, Latvia, and Lithuania also recognized the important need to control and safeguard the massive arsenal that still existed in the region, as well as the related technologies and the know-how possessed by many weapons scientists and engineers throughout the NIS. Though the Baltic countries themselves were never home to former

Soviet nuclear weapons or design or testing facilities, they were (and still are) home to several facilities that have become a proliferation concern in the past few years. The large Ignalina model RBMK 1500 civilian power reactor (two units), which supplies up to 90 percent of Lithuania's electricity, and its spent fuel storage facility, for example, have already experienced an alleged number of cases of attempted theft and smuggling.[5] In fact in 1993, an entire fuel assembly containing 100 kilos of uranium was reported missing from the Ignalina plant.[6] The uranium refinement facility at the Silmet Metal and Chemical Production Plant in Estonia is a source of proliferation concern as well given that it provided the uranium for the first Soviet atomic bomb. Other nuclear entities in the Baltic states include the nuclear waste repository site at Saku, Estonia, and the relatively small research reactor at the Academy of Sciences in Riga, Latvia.[7]

Though the number of nuclear facilities in these countries is small, their existence requires the development of nonproliferation export control systems. Export control policies in the Baltics, however, are not just directed at controlling nuclear commodities and nuclear-related dual-use goods but target all strategic weapons-related commodities. Thus, Latvia's relatively large chemical and pharmaceutical industry, which is capable of producing important precursors for chemical weapons, should also be taken into account as a possible source of proliferation, and are a target of Latvian and regional export controls.

More important for nonproliferation concerns, however, is the geography of these three countries, which makes them an easy target for criminal groups trying to smuggle sensitive commodities through the extremely porous borders of the NIS and into Europe or onto the Baltic sea. Though most cases of theft and smuggling of strategic commodities have emanated from Russia, reports of the illegal transshipment of sensitive materials in the Baltics have been quite numerous as well. For example, according to press reports in early 1996, more than one ton of unlicensed beryllium, a dual-use material used in nuclear warheads, was believed to be in Sweden after arriving in Stockholm by boat from Estonia.[8] Transshipment issues, therefore, should be of particular concern to the governments of Estonia, Latvia, and Lithuania.[9] To prevent illicit transshipment from the NIS region and to fight the proliferation of weapons of mass destruction, the Baltic governments have indeed made serious progress since regaining independence in establishing systems for controlling the import and export of sensitive commodities.

EXPORT CONTROL DEVELOPMENTS

Unlike Russia, the beneficiary of many of the Soviet bureaucratic structures, the Baltic countries have had to start from scratch in building state ministries, agencies, and regulating bodies for almost every type of domestic and foreign policy imaginable.[10] Such was the case regarding nonproliferation export controls. Nonetheless, as of mid-1997, all three Baltic nations' export control systems were developed to the point that each have in place export licensing systems (which are soon to be supplemented by U.S. Department of Commerce–developed automated licensing systems), laws or decrees delineating the ministerial roles in export controls and licensing, and mechanisms for training officials in the government and out in the field at border posts and ports of entry.

Other developments in their export control systems include the introduction of strict export control lists. These three countries have developed commodity control lists that correspond to many of the international export control regimes and the European Union (EU). Latvia, in fact, is a member of the chemical suppliers control regime, the Australia Group (AG), and also ratified the Chemical Weapons Convention (CWC) in 1996. Regarding control lists, Latvia's contains three parts: The first is the former COCOM International Munitions List, which covers munitions, weapons, equipment, and parts that are designed for military use; the second, which controls dual-use goods, is based on the EU's list of dual-use goods; and, the third controls chemical commodities as enumerated in the CWC.[11] Estonia's lists are also based on those of the international export control regimes and were developed with the help of Finnish, Swedish, and EU expertise.[12] Like her Baltic neighbors, Lithuania currently has lists that mirror those of the export control regimes and of the EU.

Concerning Lithuanian export control developments, this country experienced bureaucratic problems that delayed the implementation of a *comprehensive* export control system until July 1997.[13] As of that date, Lithuania has a complete regulatory basis for export controls. A working group within the Ministry of Economics reviews licenses in Lithuania. This group, with representatives from twelve ministries and agencies whose activity covers controlled items (including the important Nuclear Power Safety Inspectorate which oversees the Ignalina nuclear power reactors), is responsible for approving or denying license applications.[14] The license will be reviewed only once the applicant meets all requirements for such, including an end-use statement and an import license signed by the importer.[15] Once the working group approves the license application, it is the responsibility of the Ministry of Economics to actually issue the license.

Interministerial cooperation on licensing also occurs in Estonia and Latvia. Both of these countries have an independent interagency commission on export controls (or "control committee," as it is called in Latvia) with representatives from between five and ten different ministries. These commissions coordinate the export control policies of each country and help make decisions concerning the approval of licenses.[16] In both Estonia and

Latvia the commission is chaired by the Ministry of Foreign Affairs (MFA). In Estonia the MFA is the actual body that issues the export license, whereas in Latvia the agency responsible for issuing licenses is an executive nongovernmental body called the Export and Import Control Department.[17] Though this department is not a governmental agency, it is fully funded and supported by the Latvian government much like a contractor. The government created this arrangement partly to facilitate interaction with industry.[18]

When comparing the systems in these countries, it is clear that Estonia and Latvia are further ahead in their export control development than Lithuania. Small, but interesting, developments that typify the progress made in these two countries include Estonia's Internet Web site on export controls (which lists all regulations and current procedures for exporting and importing), and Latvia's yearly publication of updated lists and customs regulations, which is readily available at all customs sites and ports of entry free of charge.[19] Access to control lists and regulations available to prospective exporters is but one example of how earnest Latvia, in particular, is in developing a thorough system for controlling strategic trade. Latvia's seriousness in observing international nonproliferation guidelines on export controls is perhaps best exemplified by the fact that this country applied for membership to the Nuclear Suppliers Group and the Wassenaar Arrangement (the nuclear dual-use and conventional arms export control regime) even though it is not a producer or supplier of nuclear, nuclear-related, or conventional arms commodities.[20]

Most of the export control problems that *do* exist in these countries do not center on the development of bureaucratic structures. As one can see from the above descriptions, aside from the rather slow progress Lithuania has made, these countries are moving along well in building the different agencies and regulations needed for controlling exports. Latvia, with its "nongovernmental body responsible to the government" and control committee arrangement, has done a particularly good job of developing a process that allows for licenses to be properly reviewed and expedited. This is not to say, however, that these countries are not experiencing bureaucratic problems or difficulties. Because these countries are small, weak, developing nations, their difficulties associated with committing financial resources to their nonproliferation bureaucracies constitute a serious problem. This is evident in government positions where often an export control official must also be responsible for many other issues. In Latvia, for example, officials who work for the Export and Import Control Department are at the same time working for the Latvian Development Agency, which promotes foreign investment and business in Latvia. This creates a situation that could lead to serious conflicts of interest, and is an example of where problems occur due to limited financial means from within the Latvian government.

Other significant problems with these countries' export control systems center around the very crucial elements of customs authority, border enforcement, and information gathering and intelligence. As is the case in all of the NIS, government agencies in the Baltics simply do not have the resources to pay their customs and enforcement staff reasonable salaries. The turnover rate therefore is dangerously high, especially within the lower ranks of these agencies. [21] Without steady competitive incomes for border guards and customs officials, the Baltic governments run the risk of increased bribery at border sites in exchange for allowing illicit commodities (including narcotics) through the border.

Information gathering and intelligence also pose real problems for these countries' export control activities. Again, one can point to the lack of financial resources as the source of the problem. Simply put, these countries cannot afford the intelligence capabilities on which most other developed nations rely to identify which end-users are "good" and which are "bad." Consequently, even though Estonia, for example, is trying hard not to proliferate strategic commodities, because of a lack of intelligence and adequate information gathering capabilities, Estonian officials may not know the difference between an acceptable end-user and an unacceptable one with the intentions of building a nuclear bomb. On the other hand, these countries may often have intelligence on a particular end-user, but because cooperation between customs authorities and government export control officials is a problem in Estonia, Latvia, and Lithuania, the intelligence may not be properly utilized.[22] This results from a working environment within these governments that suffers from a lack of communication. In fact, the lack of communication between government agencies is quite possibly the most significant problem overall. During one particular meeting in Latvia, for example, it was obvious that the customs official responsible for export controls present at the meeting had never before been at the Export and Import Control Department. The official was visibly amazed at the sophistication of the licensing and computer system this department operates, and expressed his deep interest in obtaining the same type of hardware. This is clearly an example of agencies who share the same issues not communicating and, therefore, not cooperating, on any level.

Despite the many export control problems these countries face, and despite the fact that they began their export control development from scratch after gaining independence in 1991, the Baltic nations' systems of export controls are now 65–74 percent compatible with Western standards. Lithuania is the least developed, scoring a 65 percent on the export control development scale. In comparison, Estonia scores 70 percent, and Latvia scores 74 percent.[23] Ultimately all three of these countries have made significant progress in the past few years and are well on their way to developing systems comparable to those in Western Europe. Although problems exist, and the transshipment problem is far from being solved, time will only improve these systems.

ASSESSING ALTERNATIVE EXPLANATIONS

As discussed in the introduction to this volume, we find at least four theoretical approaches that offer explanations as to why states such as the Baltic republics would develop export control systems despite numerous costs (both tangible and intangible). It should be noted, however, that the cost of developing and implementing export controls in the Baltics is not as severe as those faced in countries like Russia, Ukraine, and Kazakhstan. All three of these countries are rich in strategic commodities or know-how and, thus, by adhering to international nonproliferation norms and building systems of export control, may be forgoing enormous financial trade opportunities. The Baltic states, on the other hand, are economically more stable than the other NIS (due largely to Scandinavian and European investment), and therefore are not facing the economic pressures to export "anything and everything" in order to earn needed hard currency. Nonetheless, that Estonia, Latvia, Lithuania are committing their limited financial and human resources toward the development of export control policies, practices, and procedures remains puzzling.

The behavioral expectations outlined earlier in this volume rely on realist, rational institutionalist, domestic politics, and liberal identification explanations of export control behavior. This chapter suggests that of the four, liberal identity and rational institutionalism best explain export control development in the Baltic states. The material and nonmaterial incentives they have received and are receiving from the United States and the Scandinavian countries to develop such systems, however, may become less crucial, and indeed may begin to wane. Liberal, Western identity may then emerge as the dominant approach for explaining the continued export control behavior.

Realism

Estonia, Latvia, and Lithuania share the same single security threat: the Russian Federation. Though other countries have dominated or occupied the Baltic states in the past, the three countries were forcefully incorporated into the Russian empire three times, during 1795–1914, 1940–1941, and 1944–1991.[24] As if this history were not enough to instill a horrific fear of their eastern neighbor, in 1996 Russian armored combat vehicles increased from 200 to 600 in the Pskov region, along the border of Latvia and Estonia, under the Conventional Forces in Europe Treaty (CFE). The Estonian Foreign Ministry described this as "a question of national survival . . . Russian airborne and *Spetsnatz* forces in Kaliningrad, Pskov, and in other areas of the Leningrad Military District pose a direct threat to Estonia and the other two Baltic states."[25]

Moreover, campaign rhetoric from the 1996 Russian presidential elections included many statements from all contenders, including Boris Yeltsin, on the feasibility of annexing the Baltics in the hopes of restoring the power and prestige of the former Soviet Union. Regarding NATO enlargement issues, many presidential hopefuls also commented on what would happen if the Baltics were ever admitted into the military alliance. Communist leader Gennady Zyuganov declared, "Eastern expansion of NATO [to the Russian border] would mean the division of Estonia."[26] In April 1996, Anatoly Surikov, the individual considered to be the author of the Russian defense concept, told a newspaper in the Baltic states, "If a real attempt is made to admit the Baltic states into NATO, we will introduce our troops into the Baltic states. This is an inevitability."[27] The most important policy statement issued from the Kremlin regarding Baltic membership in NATO and other Western organizations came in February 1997. This document, titled "Russia's Long Term Guidelines in Its Relations with the Baltic States," is perhaps the strongest indication of Russia's intentions to keep the Baltics within Moscow's orbit. It stated that the only basis for Baltic security is "the preservation of their status outside blocs."[28]

Based on these types of statements and policies from the Russian Federation, one can understand the fear the Baltics have of possible reabsorption by their most hated enemy. Unfortunately there is not much the Baltic states can do about Russia's threats or intentions other than plea for security guarantees from Europe or hope for NATO membership. The development of nonproliferation export controls will not aid in enhancing Baltic security given that their large, powerful neighbor already possesses a tremendous arsenal of nuclear, chemical, biological, and advanced conventional weapons. As non-nuclear weapon states who have pledged not to develop weapons of mass destruction and who are having severe difficulties building their own conventional militaries, the Baltics collectively have nothing worth controlling in order to keep from falling into the hands of Russia therefore adding to the military capability of that country.

Along the same line, the Baltics are small, weak states in the international community that rely on military cooperation to improve their physical security and thus are more dependent on absolute gains in security than on relative gains, hence their stated desire to join NATO. All three countries see full integration into Western Europe, including membership in the Western European Union (WEU, the military arm of the EU) and NATO, as the only realistic way to secure their defenses against Russia. Some examples of their cooperation with these organizations include their "associate partners" status with the WEU and their willingness to work with NATO as Partnership for Peace countries.[29] Both of these are seen as stepping-stones to full

NATO membership, which undoubtedly would increase their security and help balance the power of Russia. More directly, the Baltics are collaborating with each other to help increase their military capability. In April 1997, for example, the Baltic defense ministers agreed on several defense projects to help build a common defense structure. Latvia will preside over the formation of the joint Baltic peacekeeping battalion BALTBAT. Estonia will be home to the staff headquarters of the BALTRON mine-sweeper squadron, while Lithuania's air control center in Karmelava will become the major air control headquarters of the Baltic states.

In sum, the realist approach maintains that states with security threats will develop export controls to help counter those threats. These three nations can undoubtedly identify a large, potentially predatory country that threatens their existence. Export control development in the Baltics, however, will not enhance their security vis-à-vis Russia because the Baltics themselves are not in any position to balance the military strength of Russia. Realism, therefore, offers no expected behavior that would help explain the development of export controls in these three countries.

Rational Institutionalism

As small states interested in and dependent on foreign investment to strengthen their economies, the Baltic countries know very well the value of cooperation with other nations. Significant cooperation with the United States, with their European neighbors, and with each other on everything from trade agreements to establishing stock exchanges and banking networks has occurred since regaining independence. Regarding nonproliferation policies, evidence shows that much cooperation has also taken place between the Baltics and the Western community in developing export controls. The Baltics have received material aid (equipment) and nonmaterial aid (technical and policy advice) from countries like the United States to strengthen their licensing systems and stabilize their borders so as to limit the number of illegal transshipments. Baltic states' export control development has also been effected by their interest in *future* cooperation, interaction, and reciprocity with the United States and the Western community. Accordingly, the Baltic countries have calculated that the benefits of developing solid nonproliferation policies are apparent—such as increasing their chances of EU membership—and outweigh the costs of building nonproliferation bureaucracies.

Many states of the former Soviet Union have received direct assistance (material aid) from the Western community linked to export control development. Through the Cooperative Threat Reduction program (more popularly known as Nunn-Lugar) Belarus, Kazakhstan, and Ukraine have all received direct financial, material aid to help develop policies for controlling sensitive exports. The Baltics, though not part of the Nunn-Lugar program, have also received help from the United States (through programs such as Project Amber and the Nonproliferation Disarmament Fund) and Europe to strengthen their export controls.[30] In late 1997 through 1998, for example, Estonia, Latvia, and Lithuania will all be receiving an automated system from the U.S. Department of Commerce to increase the efficiency of their licensing procedures.[31] In 1996, Estonian customs was provided a $250,000 mobile unit by the U.S. Customs Service to detect radioactive materials, nuclear weapons, and other types of explosives to curb cross-border smuggling.[32] Estonian customs has also been the beneficiary of nonmaterial aid in the form of advice and consultations from EU customs organizations.[33] The Scandinavian countries in the past have also provided material and nonmaterial aid to the Baltics to develop export controls. Such nonmaterial aid includes advice from Finnish and Norwegian specialists on developing control lists and drafting export regulations.[34]

While material and nonmaterial aid from the West has certainly affected the development of important nonproliferation export control policies in the Baltic countries, the possibility of future cooperation, interaction, and integration with Europe has, undoubtedly, also played a role in the development of export controls. For example, EU membership and integration into transatlantic structures is the most important strategic goal of the Baltic countries. To be considered as serious candidates, the Baltics must raise their export control levels to standards compatible with Western nations. Though NATO membership in the near future appears improbable, the Baltics are still being considered for EU membership, with Estonia most likely being in the next round of new EU countries.[35] The Baltic states' affiliation with the EU dates back to June 1993, when the EU announced at the Copenhagen meeting of the European Council of Ministers that the associated Central and East European countries would eventually be invited to become full-fledged members of the European Union. But membership in the EU brings costs, such as the implementation of domestic and foreign policies that must correspond to EU policies. Nonetheless, membership would provide the Baltics access to trade in one of the largest, most competitive markets in the world.

In this regard, the benefits of possible EU membership and trade and interaction within the European community are substantial. Effective export controls are expected before EU membership will be permitted. The benefits of developing export controls, therefore, far outweigh the costs. The statements of export control officials in the Baltics have confirmed this. In fact, Baltic officials conveyed to the author on a number of occasions that the reason why they are developing such policies was to increase their chances of EU membership. [36] Official statements by policy leaders in these countries would confirm this as well, though in a more general sense. For example, Lithuanian President Algirdas Brazauskas at a WEU Permanent

Council meeting in 1996 was quoted as saying, "in pursuit of integration into Western and transatlantic structures, Lithuania has resolved to further coordinate its interior and foreign policy with Western partners."

The Baltic governments are also willing to maximize the amount of cooperation amongst each other to increase their chances of one day becoming members of the EU. Despite what one might think, however, the Baltic states often are at serious odds over each other's foreign and domestic policies. All three countries, for example, have had problems settling border disputes with their Baltic neighbors. Latvia and Lithuania, in particular, have heatedly debated their respective sea borders since independence. On the other hand, the policy leaders of the Baltic states acknowledge the many statements from Europe which call for cooperation between them, as well as normalized relations with Poland and Russia, if they want to strengthen their chances of integration into European organizations.[37] European Parliament President Klaus Haensch, for example, told the Estonian parliament in May 1996 that the Baltic states have a better chance of EU membership if they act *together*. Baltic policy leaders seem to know this very well. In October 1996 at a NATO meeting in Brussels the presidents of Estonia and Latvia stated they understand that "*close cooperation and mutual integration of the Baltic states* is an important factor for their successful integration into European and transatlantic structures" (emphasis added). They then stated that in order to achieve these strategic goals, their countries "underline the importance of cooperation in external border control" and will continue "to coordinate efforts against organized crime, illegal migration, smuggling of weapons and drugs, and international money laundering."[38]

With EU expansion coming in the near future, Estonia, Latvia, and Lithuania have undertaken many cooperative initiatives to show the extent of their ability to work together on issues. For example, cooperation between the Baltic countries on nonproliferation policies, export controls, and border control since the beginning of 1996 has intensified. An agreement on cooperating on strategic export controls between Estonia, Latvia, and Lithuania was drafted in 1996 and is pending approval by each of the three governments.[39]

In sum, rational institutionalism best explains the development of export controls in these three countries. The Baltic states have been induced to develop controls on strategic commodities through two means. First, they have been recipients of both material and nonmaterial aid from countries like the United States. This aid has certainly benefited their systems. Second, Estonia, Latvia, and Lithuania, all three of which are very interested in future cooperation and interaction with the Western community, have calculated that the benefits of developing nonproliferation systems and complying with multilateral export control regimes outweigh the costs. The benefits of EU membership, in other words, outweigh the costs of developing nonproliferation bureaucracies.

Domestic Politics

The analysis of export control development in the Baltics has thus far been presented collectively, rather than individually. This has been possible because all three states face much the same security threat, all three are applying for EU membership and are having to meet the same requirements for such.[40] Furthermore, in terms of U.S./foreign government assistance, all are approached, generally speaking, in a collective, regional manner. However, in the spirit of Lithuanian Prime Minister Vyatuatas Landsbergis's recent statement, "*Baltic* is not a country," it is more appropriate to analyze Estonia, Latvia, and Lithuania individually in order to determine the likelihood of whether or not domestic influences help explain export control development in these countries. One general statement that should be made about their domestic situations is that all three are democratizing more quickly than the other NIS. Evidence such as decreasing Support for East European Democracy (SEED) Act funds supports this finding. SEED programs, which are coordinated by the U.S. Department of State, are divided into three categories: economic restructuring, democracy building, and quality of life. SEED funding has been winding down for the past two years in the Baltic countries because of the speed with which Western political and economic standards have taken hold. For example, fiscal year 1997 requests from the U.S. Congress for SEED programs was zero for Estonia and Latvia, and only $7 million for Lithuania, down from $12.4 million two years ago.[41]

Another general observation concerning these countries' domestic political environments concerns the role of nongovernmental organizations (NGOs). Though democracy seems to have taken hold, that does not necessarily mean there is yet a climate in Estonia, Latvia, or Lithuania conducive to all facets of modern democracies, such as interest groups and nongovernmental organizations that play important roles in influencing government policies. Interest groups are beginning to appear, more or less, but it is impossible to speak of nonproliferation interest groups in these countries similar to those in the West, such as the Arms Control Association in the United States or the Peace Research Institute of Frankfurt, Germany. At the same time, private businesses and industries are not yet pressuring governments to the extent they do in other Western countries. Moreover, because the volume of strategic imports and exports in these countries is relatively small, it is unlikely that NGOs or private firms are going to emerge demanding increased or decreased controls on sensitive commodities. The influence of domestic interest groups and private companies, therefore, is not an important factor to consider when analyzing reasons for export control development in Estonia, Latvia, and Lithuania.

The influence of just a few key bureaucrats in these countries, on the other hand, does affect export control development. Despite the success of democratic institutions in Estonia, Latvia, and Lithuania, these countries (as mentioned above) are developing nations with limited budgets that inevitably restrict the number of officials working on export control issues. We should understand that the limited number of export control officials is due partly to the fact that the Baltic economies are not heavily dependent on sensitive exports, and thus export control issues are not as important as they are in major supplier countries like the United States and Russia. Nonetheless, export control agencies in the Baltics have only a small percentage of the staff that their Western counterparts have. This aspect of their domestic political situations—small budgets and small bureaucracies—does affect export control development. Because only a few officials within these governments work on these issues, those who are charged with export controls have wide-ranging responsibilities. Export control developments therefore are based on the work of these few individuals. Take for example the situation in Estonia. Though Estonia's system is solid, it relies heavily on the shoulders of just a few officials within the Ministry of Foreign Affairs (MFA). For instance, if the commission that reviews licenses in Estonia cannot come to a consensus, the chairman, who is located within the MFA, makes the final decision. Clearly, this individual and the other export control officials within the ministry are in rather powerful positions to influence the export control policies of Estonia consistent with their *own* preferences and opinions. The same can be said for Lithuania, whose export control bureaucracy basically consists of four individuals within the Ministry of Economics. Latvia, as mentioned above, has developed a contractor agency independent of the government that is responsible for many export control functions and acts as an intermediary between the Latvian government and industry. Again, however, it was the preferences of only a few elites (perhaps only one very influential official within the Export and Import Control Department) that decided this arrangement.

It appears that all export control individuals in Estonia, Latvia, and Lithuania are committed to developing stringent systems of control for their countries. The problem lies in the future. If any one of the handful of these officials decides to leave his post, it will take much time for a replacement to learn the ropes of export controls. Such are the consequences of small government budgets and small bureaucracies.

As for the other expected behaviors outlined in the domestic politics approach, neither state centralization nor power asymmetries between export promotion and export control agencies have affected the development of strategic trade controls in these three countries. Unlike many of the other FSU states, the Baltic countries do not suffer from a lack of openness within their political environments. In fact the Baltic countries are all rated in the top two categories for political rights and civil liberties on the Freedom House scale.[42] This is reflective in their government structures. State centralization would not affect export control development in these countries any more than it would in any other Western nation.

Trade and exporting are extremely important to the economic livelihood of these three developing countries. It would, therefore, be naive to claim that the Baltic governments are not more interested in promoting exports than controlling them. But these governments at the same time know the importance of adhering strictly to the nonproliferation regime and controlling sensitive trade. Thus, there does not seem to be any significant competition between agencies responsible for nonproliferation policies and those responsible for promoting increased trade. In fact in Latvia, as already stated, the main export control agency is also responsible for export promotion, yet it seems it is able to balance the two interests in a responsible manner.

Liberal Identity

Without falling too far into the pitfalls of ethnocentrist comparison, it is possible to state that the Baltics are more "developed" than the other NIS, as their respective per-capita GDPs indicate. Indeed, because the Baltics are of the industrialized West with traditions in capitalism, this is to be expected. Even as Soviet republics, the popular designation for the Baltic republics in the U.S.S.R. had been *nash zapad* ("our West"), whereas in official circles they were referred to collectively as "Pri*baltika*," in reference to their geographic location. This distinction between popular and official Soviet language is evidence that among the Soviet masses the three Baltic countries were always seen as different from the rest of the Soviet Union.[43] The Baltics were in fact different from the other Soviet republics in the sense that before their incorporation into the U.S.S.R. they were already rather liberal states with Western traditions, Western religions (Lutheran and Catholic heritage as opposed to Russian Orthodox), and strong influences from European cultures (Germanic, Polish, and Scandinavian). Unlike many of the other former Soviet states, these countries also had experiences with democratic governance *and* in international organizations, such as the League of Nations, before they became republics of the Soviet Union. Baltic states' identification today with Western, liberal norms and values continues to play a significant role in the development of their foreign policies, in general, and in the development of strict nonproliferation and export control procedures, in particular.

The Baltics return to and reintegration with Europe is their first foreign policy priority. As already stated, there are many political and economic gains to be made by closer interaction with Europe and with the rest of the Western community. However, their pursuit of membership in these economic and security organizations is also based on their identification with the values represented by these institutions and not just on a calculation of costs and benefits. Estonian, Latvian, and Lithuanian leaders often stress the role of values when speaking about EU or NATO membership. For example, in an op-ed published in a major American newspaper in 1996 on the need of Baltic membership in NATO, Mecislovas Laurikus, chairman of the Foreign Affairs Committee of the Lithuanian parliament, wrote, "We want to be recognized as an inseparable part of the Western community sharing common values."[44] In March 1996, the then Estonian minister of foreign affairs, Siim Kallas, when speaking about Estonian relations with Europe, stated, "In the last five years of our independence, Estonia has emerged as the frontier of Western values and principles in Europe."[45] Because of these common values with Europe, Baltic policy leaders often also stress the "right" of Estonia, Latvia, and Lithuania to membership in the major European and transatlantic structures. For example, in 1993 the then Lithuanian chief negotiator with Russia stated, "Despite fifty years of suppression, the Lithuanian, Latvian, and Estonian nations have managed to preserve their affinity to Western European civilization and they are basing their development on the model of Western democracy. The integration of Lithuania and the other two Baltic states into the community of Western nations means a return to their natural places in the international community."[46]

These statements of Baltic officials are evidence of the importance of Western values in shaping their general foreign policies, but they do not directly link nonproliferation export controls with Western identification. At a 1997 conference on export controls in Washington, D.C., however, an official from Estonia did just that when he acknowledged a "sense of community" in export control matters and when he mentioned the importance of the objectives of nonproliferation in his country's development of strategic trade controls. He stated, "Estonia's prime consideration for the pursuance of export control[s] are the objectives of nonproliferation and we are in a position that adherence to *a club of like-minded countries* has many more political advantages in the long run than have illegal exports in the short run" (emphasis added).[47]

Baltic states' day-to-day interaction with Europe since regaining independence has also affected their nonproliferation export control policies. This is particularly evident in Latvia's list of "sensitive destinations," which prohibits export licenses to states that support international terrorism and to states developing weapons of mass destruction.[48] Countries that are building clandestine nuclear bombs or that support terrorism are referred to in the West as "rogue" nations. Latvia's recognition of the importance of not cooperating with these "rogue" countries is certainly due in part to this countries' interaction with the Western community and its refusal to cooperate with illiberal states.

Western identification drives the development of foreign policies and, in particular, export control policies, in these countries probably more than in any of the other NIS. Though there are still significant internal, domestic problems in the Baltics, such as those surrounding Russian minorities' rights in Estonia, the Baltic countries no doubt view themselves as different from the other NIS and take pride in their adherence to the norms and values of most, if not all, of the international organizations of the Western community and of Europe, including the nonproliferation regime. For example, despite Estonia's tenuous relationship with Russia, which is characterized by nagging border issues and double taxation of Estonian goods on the Russian border, Estonia nonetheless has behaved admirably within European institutions regarding these issues. In fact, the Council of Europe (CE), of which Estonia was the president in 1995, recently decided to close its monitoring procedure citing that Estonia had honored and fulfilled its most important commitments to Russian minorities. As well, in late 1995, an Organization for Security and Cooperation in Europe (OSCE) report concluded that "one could not speak of a consistent pattern of human rights violations in Estonia."[49] Though the Russian minority problem has not yet been totally eliminated, Estonia's ability to meet the criteria of the CE and OSCE is an example of the importance this country puts on liberal values such as human rights and adherence to international standards. In fact, Estonia scores the highest of the three Baltics on the Freedom House scale with a score of 1 (the highest score) for political rights and a score of 2 for civil liberties. Again, statements from Baltic leaders are evidence of the shared values and norms these nations have with the Western community. Lithuanian President Algirdas Brazaukas stated in 1996, "Membership [in the EU and NATO] is the only way for us to return to the community of Western nations which share the common values of democracy, individual liberty, and the rule of law."[50]

In sum, it is evident from Baltic leaders' statements on nonproliferation, from the states' participation in the nonproliferation regime, from their development of control lists that target illiberal, "rogue" states, and from the types and numbers of international organizations of which they are members and adherents to that they do indeed hold the values of the Western alliance. Considering their affinity for European integration, or, more importantly, considering the fact that the Baltics are of the historical, traditional West, it would be difficult to deny the importance of their identification with Western norms in shaping their foreign policies. Indeed, the evidence shows that identification does in fact play a role in their foreign policies. Baltic states' identification with Western norms, values, and standards plays a significant role in their development of nonproliferation export control systems.

CONCLUSION

Baltic states' calculations of the costs and benefits of export controls, along with Baltic states' interests in future interaction with and reciprocity from Europe, have helped motivate the development of strategic export control policies in this part of the world. In this regard, the policy leaders of Estonia, Latvia, and Lithuania believe that in order to increase their chances of future membership in the European Union they must develop important foreign policies, such as stringent nonproliferation export controls, that correspond to those of the EU.

Another important factor influencing the development of such policies include Baltic states' identification with Western and European nonproliferation norms and values. Being that the Baltics are European countries that hold the same values as the Western, liberal community regarding political and economic freedoms, and given their past and present experiences in Western democracy and in European organizations and institutions, their identification with the practice of controlling strategic trade should not be surprising.

Security concerns, on the other hand, have little to do with the recent development of nonproliferation export controls in Estonia, Latvia, and Lithuania. The Baltic states collectively possess nothing worth controlling in terms of preventing the military gains of their chief adversary, Russia. Domestic influences have influenced export control development only in the sense that the key individuals who are responsible for these issues clearly perceive and believe export control policies to be in the "national interest," and thus are using their positions to shape such policies.

Cooperation with other nations and the Baltic states' sense of community and identification with Europe and the Western community, therefore, are the driving forces behind their development of nonproliferation export controls. It is difficult, however, to determine which of these two is more influential in the Baltics. This study suggests that neither set of influences is playing a dominating role and that instead it is a combination that drives export control development in Estonia, Latvia, and Lithuania. This can be best supported by the remarks of the Estonian official (quoted earlier) at the export control conference in Washington in 1997 who, in mentioning the importance of nonproliferation norms and objectives, also stressed the benefits to be gained by adhering to the nonproliferation regime.

As for the future of nonproliferation policies in these countries, it seems that both rational, material factors, and value-oriented factors will continue to drive export control development, at least until the material and nonmaterial aid is no longer available from the United States, Europe, or the Scandinavian countries. Estonia, Latvia, and Lithuania are likely, however, to continue to abide by the rules of the international nonproliferation regime, and continue to update and maintain their export control policies because these countries identify with the norms and values of the Western nonproliferation community and understand the importance behind such adherence. Keeping in mind their experiences with Western democracy and market-oriented capitalism prior to their incorporation into the USSR, such behavior as new democracies in the post-Soviet world is not all that surprising. As they pursue their goals of becoming advanced, Western countries, they hold the same values and standards today as they did earlier in the century.

NOTES

1. For more on the twentieth-century histories of these nations see Kristian Gerner and Stefan Hedlund, *The Baltic States and the End of the Soviet Empire* (New York: Routledge, 1993); David Crowe, *The Baltic States and the Great Powers* (Boulder, CO: Westview, 1993); D. G. Kirby, *The Baltic World 1772–1993* (New York: Longman Group, 1995); and Georg Von Rauch, *The Baltic States; The Years of Independence (Estonia, Latvia, Lithuania): 1917–1940* (Berkeley and Los Angeles: University of California Press, 1974).

2. Graham Smith et al., "Statehood, Ethnic Relations and Citizenship," in Graham Smith, ed., *The Baltic States* (New York: St. Martin's Press, 1994), p. 186.

3. Top four NIS GDP per-capita rankings in 1997 are: Estonia, $4,354; Lithuania, $4,270; Russia, $4,167; and Latvia, $3,462 (The EIU, First Quarter 1997).

4. Center for Nonproliferation Studies (CNS) Nuclear Database online (Monterey, CA: Monterey Institute for International Studies, 1997).

5. Ibid.

6. "Nuclear Developments," *The Nonproliferation Review* 4, 1 (Fall 1996), p. 133.

7. Material, protection, control, and accounting improvements at the Latvian Academy of Sciences Nuclear Research Center demonstrate the strategy of the U.S. Department of Energy's Russia/NIS Nuclear Materials Security Task Force.

8. "Swedes Lost a Tonne of Nuclear Material," *The Herald* (Glasgow, Scotland), 23 November 1996, in Lexis.

9. During July 1997 discussions with Baltic export control officials, all conveyed that transshipment is the most important nonproliferation issue.

10. This section is based on research conducted during the author's visit to the Baltic states in July 1997, on other personal communications with export control officials in Estonia, Latvia, and Lithuania, and on official government policy papers and articles from these countries.

11. "System of Control of Export, Import and Transit of Strategic Goods, Services and Technologies in the Republic of Latvia," Ministry of Foreign Affairs,

Control Committee of Strategic Export and Import, Republic of Latvia, 1997.

12. Personal discussions with Estonian official in the Ministry of Foreign Affairs, July 1997. See also Inderek Tarand, "Estonia," in *Nuclear Export Controls in Europe*, ed. Harald Müller (Brussels: European InterUniversity Press, 1995), p. 267.

13. Personal discussions with Lithuanian officials in the Ministry of Economy, July 1997, confirmed the introduction of their new system. This system is based on a more sophisticated regulatory foundation.

14. Ibid.

15. Ibid.

16. For more details on the systems of these two countries, see the following: "Memo of Legal Base on the Export and Transit of Strategic Goods," Ministry of Foreign Affairs, Republic of Estonia; and "System of Control of Export, Import and Transit of Strategic Goods, Services and Technologies in the Republic of Latvia," Ministry of Foreign Affairs, Control Committee of Strategic Export and Import, Republic of Latvia, 1997.

17. Ibid.

18. Personal discussions with Latvian official, July 1997.

19. Personal discussions with Estonian official in the Ministry of Foreign Affairs, July 1997. (Note: the Web site is currently in Estonian, but is being translated into English with the help of the Stockholm International Peace Research Institute (SIPRI). Information on Latvia's yearly publication of updated lists and publications was conveyed to the author by a Latvian export control official, July 1997.)

20. For more details on the systems of these two countries, see the following: "Memo of Legal Base on the Export and Transit of Strategic Goods," Ministry of Foreign Affairs, Republic of Estonia; and "System of Control of Export, Import and Transit of Strategic Goods, Services and Technologies in the Republic of Latvia," Ministry of Foreign Affairs, Control Committee of Strategic Export and Import, Republic of Latvia, 1997.

21. This particular problem was iterated to the author on several occasions by Baltic export control officials during the author's July 1997 visit. For more on this topic, please see "Project Amber," *Customs Today* 31, 1 (Winter 1996). J. Terry Conway, the U.S. Customs Department official in charge of Project Amber, describes Latvian border enforcement as "a figment of somebody's imagination."

22. Personal discussions with Latvian official, July 1997.

23. See the introductory chapter of this volume for a brief, and Craft et al., for a detailed discussion of Western common standards and our method for measuring national export control development.

24. Ceslovas V. Stankevicius, "NATO Enlargement and the Indivisibility of Security in Europe: A View from Lithuania," *NATO Review*, September 1996, p. 23.

25. Felix Corely, "Estonia: Facing Up to Independence," *Jane's Intelligence Review*, March 1996, p. 110.

26. All quotes in Republic of Estonia Ministry of Foreign Affairs Press Release No. 12, *Reflections of Estonia*.

27. FIBS-SOV-96–084, 30 April 1996; Baltic States: Estonia.

28. "Russia's Long Term Guidelines in Its Relations With the Baltic States," Presidential Press Office of the Russian Federation, 11 February 1997.

29. On 9 May 1994, in Luxembourg, the Baltic states became associate partners of the WEU. Regarding their cooperation with NATO's Partnership for Peace, Lithuania, for example, joined the Partnership Planning and Review process in 1995, and since then Lithuania's troops have participated in over twenty-five joint military exercises and in over a hundred events within the PFP framework. Four Lithuanian peacekeeping platoons took part in the peacekeeping and peace implementation missions in Croatia and Bosnia-Herzegovina.

30. Personal communications with export control officials in the Baltic nations, August 1996–July 1997.

31. Ibid.

32. Center for Nonproliferation Studies (CNS) Nuclear Database online (Monterey, CA: Monterey Institute for International Studies, 1997).

33. Discussions with Estonian officials, July 1997.

34. During the very early stages of developing their export control system, Estonian officials took advantage of Finnish and Norwegian expertise in developing control lists. The result was a list "basically identical to the Norwegian list of strategic goods," wrote Deputy Foreign Minister Inderek Tarand in 1995. See Tarand, "Estonia," in Müller, p. 267.

35. At the NATO Madrid Summit in July 1997, it was decided that the first round of new members would include Poland, Czech Republic, and Hungary. Baltic states' membership in the short term is unlikely due to vehement opposition from the Russian Federation.

36. Personal communications with export control officials in the Baltic nations, August 1996–July 1997.

37. Though relations between the Baltic countries and Russia are tenuous at best, relations between Poland and the Baltics, despite Poland's history of vying for control of the region for centuries, could not be better. Polish support for Baltic integration into NATO was dramatically expressed by Polish President Kwasniewski's attendance at a Baltic presidential summit in Tallinn on 27 May 1997, the very day Russia was signing its historical charter with NATO.

38. Joint Declaration by the President of the Republic of Estonia and the President of the Republic of Latvia at NATO Headquarters, Brussels, 25 October 1996.

39. "System of Control of Export, Import and Transit of Strategic Goods, Services and Technologies in the Republic of Latvia," Ministry of Foreign Affairs, Control Committee of Strategic Export and Import, Republic of Latvia, 1997.

40. In fact, regarding EU membership, the Baltic countries until 1996 were applying based on the policy that all three *must* be admitted at the same time.

41. The U.S. Department of State Report to Congress for Foreign Operations, 1996.

42. *Freedom In the World: The Annual Survey of Political Rights and Civil Liberties* (New York: Freedom House, 1996/97, online).

43. Gerner and Hedlund, *The Baltic States and the End of the Soviet Empire*, p. 50.

44. Mecislovas Laurinkus, "The Baltics and a Growing NATO," *Washington Times*, 2 July 1997.

45. FBIS-SOV-96–062, 29 March 1996, "Estonia: Foreign Minister on Relations with U.S., Europe."

46. Stankevicius, "NATO Enlargement," p. 21.

47. Personal communication with Estonian official in the Ministry of Foreign Affairs, July 1997.

48. "System of Control of Export, Import and Transit of Strategic Goods, Services and Technologies in the Republic of Latvia," Ministry of Foreign Affairs, Control Committee of Strategic Export and Import, Republic of Latvia, 1997.

49. "OSCE Brass Reviews Treatment of National Minorities," *The Baltic Observer*, 16 November 1995, p. 5.

50. President of the Republic of Lithuania at the North Atlantic Council, Brussels, 16 October 1996.

SEVEN

CENTRAL ASIA
The Absence of Incentives

LIAM ANDERSON

Relative to most of the other states addressed in this book, the development of nonproliferation export control in the four Central Asian states of Turkmenistan, Uzbekistan, Tajikistan, and Kyrgyzstan has been a slow process. Using the export control measure described earlier in this volume, Kyrgyzstan ranks highest with a score of 15, followed by Uzbekistan with 7, and both Turkmenistan and Tajikistan with scores of 4. Based on these figures, the system in Kyrgyzstan is approximately 35 percent compatible with Western standards, that in Uzbekistan, 17 percent, and those in Turkmenistan and Tajikistan, 10 percent.

EXPORT CONTROL DEVELOPMENT

The higher score registered by Kyrgyzstan is due primarily to the existence of a rudimentary legal framework specifically targeted toward nonproliferation export controls. The legal basis of the Kyrgyz system is provided by two decrees in March 1993 and February 1996. The former outlines the basic bureaucratic structure of the system, creating a Commission for Export Controls to be composed of representatives from the President's Office, the Committees of Science and New Technologies and National Security, and the Ministries of Foreign Affairs, Industry, Internal Affairs, Trade, Agriculture, and Health. In addition, this document provides instructions for the drawing up of lists of products, materials, equipment, technologies, and services that could be of use in the production of weapons of mass destruction.[1] According to officials in the Kyrgyz Ministry of Foreign Affairs, however, the commission was never actually convened, and hence no formal structure existed to evaluate license applications.[2] Moreover, while several agencies were charged with the responsibility of drawing up lists of dual-use items (Ministry of Trade, Department of Science and New Technologies), such lists were never coordinated into a single document, and were deemed inadequate for the purposes of controlling dual-use exports.[3]

The lack of success achieved by the decree of February 1996 led to its modification via the passage of the subsequent one. This document provides a more detailed description of the goods for which export licenses are required, including weaponry, military technology, and specifically designed items for their production; explosives, nuclear materials, technology and equipment, machine tools, and radioactive isotopes; and materials, equipment, and technologies which have peaceful uses but which can also be used in the production of missiles, and nuclear, biological, and chemical weapons. The specifics of this latter category of dual-use items are currently being determined by the Department on Science and New Technologies of the Ministry of Education.[4] The latter decree provides no detailed information on the bureaucratic agencies involved in the licensing process, assigning responsibility for the signing of licenses to the Ministry of External Trade and Industry with the cooperation of "relevant ministries." Theoretically, prior to license approval, input is sought from a combination of six sources—the State Customs Inspectorate, the Department on Science and New Technologies, and the Ministries of Foreign Affairs, Internal Affairs, Defense, and Health. In practice, however, this degree of coordination has yet to be achieved.[5]

While both Uzbekistan and Turkmenistan have enacted legislation to assert general control over exports, neither possesses a legal framework specifically related to nonproliferation export controls. In Turkmenistan, all exports and imports are monitored by the State Commodity and Raw Materials Exchange (CRME), while the Ministry of Foreign Economic Relations issues export licenses.[6] A presidential decree of November 1994 provides a list of goods for which licenses must be acquired prior to export.[7] However, these lists do not contain reference to sensitive nuclear goods or technologies. Instead, these appear to be controlled by a government enactment of July 1992 which simply prohibits the import or export of certain goods including arms and ammunition, military hardware, explosives, nuclear materials, ionizing sources, and machinery and equipment for producing armaments.[8] To date, however, Turkmenistan has yet to produce any lists which provide further details as to the items covered by these categories.[9]

Similar to Turkmenistan, Uzbekistan possesses a legal framework for the control of exports, but only in the most general sense. Three decrees—of April 1994, July 1995, and March 1996—form the legal basis for the control of exports in Uzbekistan. Only the second of these, Cabinet of Ministers Decree 287, is of direct relevance to the control of sensitive items.[10] Annex 4 of this document outlines goods whose import and export require licenses from the Ministry of Foreign Economic Relations, subject to the approval of the Cabinet of Ministers. These include weapons, military equipment, and uranium and other radioactive materials. Annex 8 contains a list of products which cannot transit the territory of Uzbekistan without the permission of the Cabinet of Ministers. Included here are flying apparatuses, weapons, machine tools, and machines designed for the manufacture of weapons. Annex 6, added in January 1997, assigns responsibility for the licensing of technology and scientific know-how to the State Committee for Science and Technology. As is the case with Turkmenistan, what the Uzbek system critically lacks are dual-use control lists. Moreover, the very concept of a dual-use item does not appear to be widely understood in government circles.[11]

In Tajikistan, attempts to exert control over exports have been ad hoc, and generally unsuccessful.[12] Regarding targeted nonproliferation export control measures, Tajikistan recently drafted a law on controlling dual-use chemical items. Titled "On Procedures for Controlling the Export from the Republic of Tajikistan of Chemical Substances and Technologies Which are Intended for Peaceful Purposes but Can Be Used for Developing Chemical Weapons," the law outlines responsibilities for the evaluation and approval of export license applications. The Ministry of Foreign Economic Relations is responsible for issuing licenses after consideration by the Tajik government. It also specifies criteria for the granting or refusal of licenses and outlines end-user verification procedures. As of the end of 1997, however, the law remains in draft form and has yet to be enacted.[13]

For Turkmenistan, Uzbekistan, and Tajikistan, therefore, while some degree of control is exercised over exports, none can be said to possess a legal basis for a system of nonproliferation export controls.[14] The levels of export control development in these three countries are primarily a reflection of the fact that some degree of control is exercised over borders. Similarly, all three have established customs control over major entry and exit points, although the quality of control varies considerably.

In general, control over "external" (non-FSU) borders throughout Central Asia is significantly tighter than that exercised over "internal" (FSU) borders.[15] Russia continues to assist in the guarding of external borders in all states except Uzbekistan. In Kyrgyzstan, control over the Kyrgyz/Chinese border was delegated by the government of Kyrgyzstan to the border troops of the Russian Federation under a series of bilateral agreements signed in late 1992 and 1993.[16] Approximately 2,000 Russian border troops are currently serving in Kyrgyzstan, concentrated mainly on the Chinese and Tajik borders.[17] Most experts consider indigenous border troops to be highly unreliable.[18] The Kyrgyz State Customs Inspectorate was established in 1992 and currently comprises approximately 1,100 officers, concentrated mainly at Manas Airport in Bishkek and the two official crossing points along the border with China. A nominal customs presence is

maintained at crossing points along the borders with Kazakhstan, Uzbekistan, and Tajikistan.[19] There is currently no program in operation for the
training of customs officials, nor is equipment available for detecting radioactive materials.[20] Ultimately therefore, there is very little prospect of
Kyrgyz customs officials intercepting sensitive materials at border cross-
ings. Further undermining the effectiveness of customs controls in Kyrgyzstan is the widespread corruption of officials.[21] The head of the Kyrgyz
Customs Inspectorate suggested that this was likely to remain the case as
long as customs officers continued to be paid at the rate of $20 a month.[22]

Control over Turkmenistan's 900–1,000 kilometer border with Iran
and its 750–850 kilometer border with Afghanistan is governed by the provisions of three bilateral agreements concluded with Russia in 1992, 1993,
and early 1994.[23] Under these agreements, border control has become a
dual responsibility, and a binational command structure has been established, with a Turkmen commander and a Russian chief of staff. Approximately 5,000 Turkmen and up to 1,000 Russian border guards are currently
responsible for controlling Turkmenistan's external borders.[24] The status of
Russian troops in Turkmenistan was reaffirmed in January 1996 under the
terms of a bilateral protocol. The accord confirmed the number of Russians
serving in Turkmenistan at 1,000, and made provisions for the establishment of a staff of border troops' advisers to assist in the training of Turkmen border guards.[25] Turkmenistan has a long history of involvement in the
guarding of its own borders, and the Turkmen Border Command is considered among the most effective of all the FSU states.[26] Reportedly, the Turkmen Customs Service was formed in November 1991.[27] However, the decree
providing legal authority for the Turkmen State Customs Service to assume
control over all customs operations in the country was not issued until July
1992.[28] Moreover, it seems that by mid-July 1993, very little in the way of
customs control was actually operating in Turkmenistan, forcing President
Niyazov to issue a second decree to implement that of July 1992.[29] Customs
posts now exist on external borders and at Ashkhabad Airport. By January
1995, there were reportedly three functioning customs posts on the border
with Iran.[30] According to U.S. customs experts, the control exercised by customs officers and border guards stationed at Turkmenistan's external borders is among the tightest in the region.[31]

Tajikistan established its own border guard force in December 1992,
but this contingent—numbering approximately 2,000—soon proved entirely inadequate to deal with the constant incursions by armed opposition
groups from across the Afghan border.[32] Hence, in August 1992, Russian
border troops assumed responsibility for the control of Tajik borders.[33] Currently there are about 18,000 border guards serving under Russian command stationed in Tajikistan.[34] Twelve thousand of these are Tajik
conscripts, supported by the Russian contingent and approximately 2,000

troops from Kyrgyzstan, Kazakhstan, and Uzbekistan.[35] Unlike the Russian border guards stationed in other parts of the FSU, those posted to serve in Tajikistan are almost exclusively professional soldiers rather than conscripts.[36]

Customs control in Tajikistan consists of 56 customs units, distributed primarily along internal borders with Kyrgyzstan and Uzbekistan.[37] Border troops control the small number of border-crossing points at the external borders with Afghanistan and China. Customs officials are also stationed at Dushanbe Airport, where all outgoing flights are inspected. Only those incoming flights originating from outside the CIS states, however, are subject to the same procedure.[38]

Uzbekistan remains the only Central Asian state capable of exercising control over its own borders. This task is rendered substantially easier by the fact that Uzbekistan's only non-FSU border, with Afghanistan, is only 110 kilometers long. A presidential decree of March 1992 placed all border troops in Uzbekistan under Uzbek jurisdiction as part of a broader attempt to emphasize military independence from Russia.[39] The strength of the Uzbek Border Troop Command is estimated at between 900 and 1,000 guards.[40]

A presidential decree issued in August 1992 established the Uzbek State Committee on Customs with a special emphasis being placed on the role of customs in the fight against illegal drug trafficking and arms smuggling.[41] There are currently approximately 200 customs posts dispersed along borders and at internal transit points (airports, railway stations). Uzbekistan also possesses facilities for the training of officers (though not in the recognition and interdiction of proliferation-related items), and a customs laboratory. However, both the laboratory and customs officials in the field possess only the most basic of equipment, which would be of little use in the detection or evaluation of suspected nuclear materials.[42] Most experts consider Uzbek border guards and customs officials to be competent and well organized.[43]

While some degree of control continues to be exercised over the region's external borders, both in terms of border protection and customs control, control over Central Asia's internal borders is tenuous at best.[44] The only tightly guarded internal border is that between Uzbekistan and Tajikistan where a consistent Uzbek military presence has been maintained in order to prevent the Tajik civil war from seeping across the border. Borders over which control is very limited include those of Turkmenistan, Uzbekistan, and with Kazakhstan; that between Turkmenistan and Uzbekistan; and that between Kyrgyzstan and Tajikistan. While all four states have established functioning customs services, and customs posts exist at least nominally on all borders throughout the region, in many cases these posts remain either unmanned or operate only on a part-time basis.[45] Relating this back to the measure of export control development, all four states score relatively high on the "customs authority" element (66 percent), though in each case, this reflects the existence of policy rather than consequent institutions or effective implementation. In terms of the "training" element, all four states record very low scores. This reflects the fact that policies and institutions have yet to be established in any of the four states that would provide for the training of border guards or customs officials in targeted nonproliferation enforcement.[46]

In summary, the export control development scores for the four Central Asian states remain very low relative to many of the FSU states. The only significant difference among the four is that Kyrgyzstan has made greater progress on the two elements "licensing" and "lists." Kyrgyzstan's higher score on these two elements derives from the existence of a legal framework specifically targeted toward the establishment of a system of nonproliferation export controls. None of the other states currently possesses this.

Analyzing export control development in the Central Asian states therefore becomes more a task of explaining the absence of, rather than the existence or variation in the levels of development. Far from invalidating the purpose of the exercise, however, what this actually provides is a more demanding and rigorous testing ground for each of the theoretical approaches. Thus not only must an approach be capable of explaining variation in development at the higher end of the scale, it must also account for the absence of development at the lower end. What follows, therefore, is a brief examination of each of the four approaches in turn, and a subsequent evaluation of their relative explanatory power.

APPROACHES
The Security Environment

Evaluating the realist/neorealist perspective is complicated in the case of Central Asia. Although certain clear security threats exist, it is far less clear that the implementation of export controls would serve as a means of ameliorating such threats. The most imminent and pressing security threat confronting the region remains the ongoing civil war in Tajikistan. For Tajikistan, it is evident that the conflict constitutes the most acute of threats in that it endangers the very existence of the state itself. For the neighboring states of Uzbekistan and Kyrgyzstan, the primary threat is that of conflict escalation, and associated problems such as refugees and property damage.[47]

The conflict in Afghanistan presents a more potent security threat, at least potentially, to the three bordering states of Turkmenistan, Uzbekistan and Tajikistan. Once again, however, the threat is really much more one of instability as the fighting spreads into the northern sectors of Afghanistan.

As the unofficial sponsors of General Rashid Dostam, an ethnic Uzbek whose army controlled a swathe of territory along the Uzbek-Afghan border, Uzbekistan has been the most directly involved of the four states, and runs the greatest risk of being sucked into an escalating conflict.[48] Attempts by President Karimov to persuade CIS members to channel assistance to Dostam as a means of counteracting the threat of the Taliban have thus far proved unsuccessful.[49] The fact remains, however, that while both conflicts present some degree of security threat, neither would be significantly alleviated by the imposition of nonproliferation export controls. Both are essentially internal struggles which serve to create a climate of instability in the region, but which realistically present only limited threats externally. Arguably, therefore, neither offers a convincing test of the realist perspective.

A more compelling case can be made regarding the role of Iran in the region. The West has long suspected Iran of aspiring to develop a nuclear capability, an eventuality that would have profound implications for the regional balance of power. While all four of the Central Asian states are wary of increasing Iranian influence, this sentiment seems to be most acutely felt in Uzbekistan and Tajikistan. Of the other two, Turkmenistan has maintained a generally good and constructive relationship with Iran. Soon after independence, President Niyazov promulgated his country's defense doctrine of "positive neutrality"[50] and declared the joint border with Iran to be one of "friendship and brotherhood."[51] Early moves to improve lines of communication between the two states culminated in the completion of a railway link between the Iranian border town of Sarakhs and the Turkmen town of Tedzhen in May 1996.[52] Turkmenistan's economic and military contacts with Iran are also far more extensive than any other Central Asian state.[53] It is notable in this context that President Niyazov came out strongly in favor of Iran's right to purchase peaceful nuclear technology from Russia in 1995, and offered sharp criticism of the U.S. decision to implement sanctions.[54]

The major security threats confronting Kyrgyzstan revolve around the instability generated by the Tajik civil war. Relations with China have at times been strained due to a dispute over the joint border inherited from the Soviet era. Recently, however, tension has been diffused following the signing of a border troop reduction agreement in April 1996, and the visit of Chinese President Jiang Zemin to Kyrgyzstan in July, during which it was announced that most of the Kyrgyz-Chinese border had been officially demarcated.[55] While ties with Iran have been extremely limited, there is no evidence to indicate that Kyrgyzstan perceives Iran to constitute a significant threat to its security.

In the case of Tajikistan, openly voiced Iranian opposition to the Rakhmonov regime in Dushanbe, and alleged material and financial support for the UTO (United Tajik Opposition) make the Iranian threat immediate and tangible. Once again, however, it is difficult to see how the implementation of nonproliferation export controls would alleviate this threat. Uzbek perceptions of the Iranian threat are animated mainly by fears of spreading Islamic fundamentalism, and on occasions the connection between this threat and the issue of nuclear nonproliferation has been made explicit. For example, at a November 1993 conference on export controls in Airlie, Virginia, the attending Uzbek delegate made clear his country's primary motivation for supporting export control development:

> Both Iran and Pakistan are relying in no small measure on nuclear power to help consolidate their power in the region. This process on the part of both countries could be significantly accelerated by means of uniting—under the rubric of Islamic solidarity—the high industrial, technical and scientific potential of the Islamic countries of the former Soviet Union in the Central Asian region. . . . Reactionary forces are planning to develop a powerful fist of Muslim states . . . headed by Iran and its nuclear weapons. Such fusion of forces will certainly break the strategic balance of forces in the international arena and will generate a monster which will be waving the Koran and the nuclear bomb.[56]

More recently, Uzbekistan was the only Central Asian state to back the United States in its decision to tighten sanctions against Iran on the grounds of its alleged support for terrorism and its ongoing quest to seek a nuclear capability. The available evidence suggests, therefore, that Uzbekistan perceives Iran to constitute a significant threat, and that this threat would be exacerbated by Iranian acquisition of a nuclear capability.[57]

While it is possible, as some have suggested, that Uzbekistan's President Karimov has deliberately exaggerated the scale of the fundamentalist threat in order to justify his repressive internal policies, it should also be noted that of the four Central Asian states, only Uzbekistan possesses the capability and ambition to evolve into a major regional power.[58] Possessing the largest population in Central Asia (23 million), sizable and competent indigenous armed forces, large reserves of fuel and nonfuel minerals, and a relatively advanced industrial/technological base, Uzbekistan is viewed by many as the natural "superpower" in the Central Asian region.[59] As a potential rival to Iran in terms of regional power and influence, then, one would expect Uzbekistan to be acutely aware of the relative power gain for Iran were it to become a nuclear weapons state. Moreover, of the four Central Asian states, Uzbekistan possesses the most advanced technologies, sensitive materials, and scientific expertise that would be of use to the Iranian nuclear program. According to the realist perspective, therefore, one would expect Uzbekistan to have a relatively well-developed export control system.

At a minimum, one would expect it to be significantly more advanced than those of the other Central Asian states. That neither of these expectations is borne out in practice suggests that realist approaches provide little in the way of explanatory power in the context of Central Asia.

The Role of Material Incentives

From a rational institutionalist perspective, the broad expectation is that states will develop export control systems when the benefits of so doing outweigh the costs. In a purely economic sense, an evaluation of this approach is relatively straightforward. None of the four states has yet received financial assistance directly targeted toward export control development. While the absence of direct financial inducements may help to account for the lack of development in Turkmenistan, Uzbekistan, and Tajikistan, it cannot explain why Kyrgyzstan has made more progress than the others. In addition to specifically targeted incentives, more broadly directed assistance must also be considered.

FREEDOM Support Act (FSA) assistance requires recipient states to implement "responsible security policies" including a commitment to nonproliferation goals. In terms of raw numbers, Uzbekistan has been by far the major beneficiary of FSA.[60] Viewed on a per-capita basis however, Kyrgyzstan has received more support than the other three.[61] On the basis of FSA support received as a percentage of GDP, once again Kyrgyzstan emerges as the major beneficiary.[62] That Kyrgyzstan has received greater FSA aid, and in turn has made greater progress in export controls development, provides support for the idea that financial incentives or side payments are potentially an explanatory factor.

In terms of commitments to the rules and norms of the nonproliferation regime, it is difficult to distinguish among the four states. All four were parties to the 1992 Minsk Accord on CIS export control coordination.[63] Likewise, all four are signatories to the NPT and the Chemical Weapons Convention. Kyrgyzstan remains the only Central Asian state yet to ratify the latter. In addition, no concrete evidence has emerged that any of the states have engaged in the sale or transfer of sensitive materials or technologies to states of proliferation concern.[64] Numerous rumors circulated during 1992 concerning attempts by Tajikistan to sell enriched uranium to states such as Libya and Iran.[65] Tajik authorities consistently denied such accusations, and no irrefutable evidence ever emerged to substantiate the rumors.[66] In terms of formal guarantees and observed behavior, therefore, the four states have displayed consistently strong levels of commitment to the goals of the nonproliferation regime. Further evidence that all four recognize and feel constrained by the rules and norms of the nonproliferation regime came with the signing of a joint Central Asian declaration in September 1997 on the establishment of a nuclear weapons–free zone.[67] On the basis of this analysis, therefore, we would expect both the levels of export control development in all four states to be significantly higher than is the case, and that there would be no cross-state variation. Neither of these expectations is supported by the observed levels of development in Central Asia.

Another possible benefit of developing an export control system is that it provides greater access to Western technology. Once again, the expectation is that a state will develop an export control system if the costs of so doing are outweighed by the benefits derived from access to advanced Western technologies. Of the four, however, only Uzbekistan currently possesses a sufficiently advanced technological/industrial base to derive much in the way of benefit from such access. Some of Uzbekistan's scientific and technological facilities which were inherited following the breakup of the Soviet Union are comparable with anything in the Western world in terms of sophistication. These include the Nuclear Physics Institute, located in Tashkent, which engages in the research and production of advanced radioactive isotopes,[68] and the Scientific-Production Association "Physics Sun" facility, which generates new classes of advanced materials with potential defense applications.[69] Uzbekistan also inherited five significant space research enterprises, which were amalgamated into the Uzbek State Space Agency (Uzbekkosmos) in 1993.[70] Considering the sorts of materials and technologies the West is likely to deny as a consequence of the absence of effective export controls, Uzbekistan remains the only Central Asian state for which this explicit cost/benefit calculus is currently of much relevance. Based on a rational institutionalist approach, therefore, we would expect to see a significantly more developed export control system in Uzbekistan than in the other three Central Asian states. On the basis of the evidence presented in the opening section, however, the facts do not support this expectation.

An analysis of "objective" indicators provides mixed support for the expectations of the rational institutionalist approach. Thus, while the distribution of FSA aid is consistent with export control development in the region, the benefits accruing from access to Western markets would argue for greater development in Uzbekistan than has actually occurred. Moreover, while clear commitments to the norms of the nonproliferation regime have been expressed, these have not yielded positive progress in the direction of export controls. The ambiguity of the evidence is probably due to the fact that export controls is almost invisible as an issue in Central Asia. For Turkmenistan, export controls are basically considered an irrelevance. Officials state that they have nothing sensitive to export, and therefore nothing that warrants establishing an export control system.[71] For Tajikistan, the calculus is also largely hypothetical. For most of its independent existence Tajikistan has been involved in a highly destructive civil war, during which the central government has been consistently unable to exercise authority over large sections of its territory. Regardless of the magnitude of the costs or benefits involved, therefore, Tajikistan has simply been incapable of developing and implementing a viable export control system.[72] Officials in Uzbekistan, while aware of the general importance of the nonproliferation issue to the United States, also do not seem to have conducted explicit cost/benefit calculations with respect to export controls. During interviews by the author with relevant government officials, it was stated repeatedly that Uzbekistan did not produce any weapons, nor would it engage in sales of nuclear-related items.[73] Thus, there was little perceived need to improve the "system" already in place. When questioned about the prospect of Western technology denial, officials seemed unaware that this might be a possibility.[74] For officials in Kyrgyzstan there appears to be a general understanding that export controls are important to the United States, but no clear conception as to how this will benefit Kyrgyzstan tangibly.[75] Given the poor state of the Kyrgyz economy, it seems more accurate to suggest that progress has been made *despite* the prohibitive costs involved.

This analysis suggests that officials in the four Central Asian states have not explicitly weighed up the costs of developing export control systems against the benefits. Rather, officials in Turkmenistan, Uzbekistan, and Tajikistan have simply not considered the issue to be sufficiently important, or relevant, to factor into calculations. Conversely, in Kyrgyzstan, progress has been made in spite of the costs involved and in the absence of a clear understanding of the possible benefits to be gained.

At the same time, some support is provided for the idea that material incentives in the form of side payments are relevant to export control development in Central Asia. Unlike the four nuclear weapon inheritor states (Russia, Ukraine, Kazakhstan, and Belarus), none of the Central Asian states has received financial inducements specifically tied to nonproliferation export control development. However, the allocation of FSA aid is linked to broader nonproliferation goals and is, therefore, relevant in this context. The distribution of FSA aid is consistent with the pattern of export control development across the region. Specifically, Kyrgyzstan has received the largest quantity of aid in per-capita terms and as a percentage of GDP; it has also made the most progress on export controls. The other three states have received equivalent quantities of aid, and in turn, their systems are at comparable levels of development.

The Relevance of Domestic Factors

Relating the various domestic politics approaches to Central Asia reveals that several of the derived expectations must be considered of only marginal relevance to states in the region. In reality, by 1997 all four regimes were highly personalized, with power concentrated in the hands of their respective presidents. At one extreme of the spectrum lie Turkmenistan and Uzbekistan, where repressive state control along former Soviet lines is still much in evidence, and where the states themselves constitute little more than the personal fiefdoms of presidents Niyazov and Karimov respectively.[76] Even in relatively democratic Kyrgyzstan, President Akayev has not been above resorting to undemocratic means to protect and advance economic and political reforms.

In practical terms, what this means is that coherent, stable, and independent bureaucratic structures have yet to develop in any of the Central Asian states. Since the collapse of the Soviet Union in 1991, all four states have had to construct their organs of government from scratch—a task rendered immensely more problematic by the widespread emigration of Russians from the region.[77] Under the Soviet Union, experienced and well-trained Russians occupied many of the higher-level bureaucratic positions. The loss of many of these individuals constituted a serious setback to the Central Asian states as they struggled to create an indigenous bureaucratic apparatus. Assuming that the bureaucratic politics model requires bureaucratic structures to be at least minimally stable and cohesive in order to engage in the "pulling and hauling" characteristic of the model, it is doubtful that bureaucracies in any of the four states provide the necessary conditions for an adequate testing of this approach.[78]

A similar conclusion must be reached for the "pluralist" approach. The pluralist conception stresses policy outcomes as the result of competition between groups of organized interests. Probably the only nonstate interest displaying much in the way of organization in the Central Asian region is the Mafia.[79] In three of the four states (Kyrgyzstan being the exception), meaningful political parties do not exist, let alone a coherent interest-group community. In Kyrgyzstan, opposition political parties are permitted, and an embryonic nongovernmental (NGO) sector seems to be emerging.[80] By the end of 1995 in fact, more than 450 NGOs existed in Kyrgyzstan, providing a stark contrast to the almost complete absence of equivalent groups in the other three states.[81] Ultimately, therefore, the lack of well-developed and organized nonstate interests means that the Central Asian states cannot provide an adequate testing ground for the pluralist perspective.

Locating the four states on a strong-weak continuum yields a fairly clear pattern. Turkmenistan and Uzbekistan can be placed without difficulty at the "strong" end of the spectrum. In both states, economic and political power is highly concentrated in the hands of the respective presidents and their immediate advisers. Moreover, the reluctance of either president to make substantial progress toward a market-driven economy means that all key economic sectors remain under centralized and, hence, presidential control.[82] Kyrgyzstan must be located toward the "weak" end of the scale. Significantly more progress toward political and economic reform is evident in Kyrgyzstan than elsewhere in Central Asia. This in turn means that power is more fragmented and diffuse and thus less susceptible to centralized control. Tajikistan is quite clearly the "weakest" state of all. It is doubtful that Tajikistan would survive without Russian political, military, and economic support. Even with this, large swaths of southern Tajikistan remain beyond the control of the Rakhmonov regime in Dushanbe. As an indication of the lack of central control over the economy, certain regions of Tajikistan (Bashkortostan, for example) have started to bypass the central government altogether and conclude economic agreements directly with other CIS states.[83] Based on the above, therefore, we would expect the two "strongest" states, Turkmenistan and Uzbekistan, to possess more developed export control systems, followed by Kyrgyzstan, then Tajikistan. This expectation is not supported by the empirical evidence.

The domestic approach which best captures the situation in Central Asia is that which stresses the role of elite decision-makers. As noted above, in both Turkmenistan and Uzbekistan, Presidents Niyazov and Karimov continue to exercise tight control over the levers of power. In the more democratic Kyrgyzstan, the elite decision-making model provides a less accurate depiction. Yet even here, President Akayev has, on occasions, assumed "extraconstitutional" powers in order to protect or further the process of reform.[84] Tajikistan presents a more complex picture. On the one hand, the decision-making process within the Tajik government continues to be highly centralized, and concentrated in the hands of President Rakhmonov; on the other, the ability of the government to project power much beyond the capital city and immediate vicinity is severely limited. Another confounding factor is the role of Russia. While it is difficult to gauge accurately the extent of Russian influence over the decision-making process in Tajikistan, one can assume that given the scale of Tajik dependence on Russia, important economic or political decisions are not made entirely free of Russian influence.

Despite these complications, it seems clear that any major policy initiative such as the establishment of an export control system would almost certainly require the personal commitment of the relevant president in order to be successful. The lack of progress made in this area thus far would seem to imply that none of the presidents (with the possible exception of Akayev) considers it to be a high priority, or important for the national interest; this is not entirely surprising. Establishing and sustaining an export control system requires a substantial commitment of material resources. In an environment of chronically scarce resources, it is understandable that more immediate concerns take precedence.

Democracy the Key?

The theoretical approach that arguably offers the most plausible insights into export control development in the Central Asian region is that which stresses the importance of liberal identity. One expectation of the liberal identity approach is difficult to test in the case of Central Asia. That states will target controls toward illiberal states requires that some minimal level of control is actually exercised. Kyrgyzstan possesses the most developed system in the region but has yet to determine who the target of their controls will be. For the other three, controls are not sufficiently systematic to make this a relevant consideration. In terms of the development of democratic institutions, processes, norms, and values, a very clear distinction exists between Kyrgyzstan (the most democratic) on the one hand, and Turkmenistan, Uzbekistan, and Tajikistan on the other. While all three of the latter have drafted nominally democratic constitutions, in reality they remain one-party states in which fundamental political and civil liberties are routinely ignored.[85]

Uzbek President Karimov has continually stressed the primacy of stability over democratic reform. A 1995 opinion poll conducted in the state confirmed that an overwhelming majority of the population shared this priority ordering.[86] President Niyazov meanwhile has given little indication that democratic reform is even on the agenda in Turkmenistan. Since independence, Niyazov has worked hard to generate a cult of personality, and as president, prime minister, and commander in chief of the armed forces, his grip on power remains reminiscent of Soviet times. The prospects for the emergence of democracy in Tajikistan are equally bleak. Following a brief but disastrous flirtation with multiparty democracy immediately after independence, Tajikistan reverted to one-party (Communist) rule, where it has remained ever since. A convenient and reliable comparative index of state "democraticness" is provided on an annual basis by the Freedom House organization. Based on an assessment of political rights and civil liberties, assigned scores can range from 2 (most democratic) to 14 (least democratic). According to the 1995–1996 report, all three of these states rated 14 on the index.[87]

The situation is somewhat different in Kyrgyzstan, where elections are competitive and free (though tainted by corruption), a range of opposition parties is permitted to compete, and basic political and civil freedoms are generally respected.[88] While impossible to establish categorically, most of the available evidence indicates a sincere and genuine commitment to promoting and preserving democratic reforms in the country.[89] It is notable, for example, that President Akayev accepted both the February 1995 parliamentary election results, which went against the president's party and resulted in gains for the Communists, and parliament's rejection of his proposal to hold a referendum on extending his term of office. This willingness to accept unfavorable outcomes of the democratic process suggests that Akayev's commitment to democracy extends beyond mere rhetoric. While Kyrgyzstan would not yet qualify as a full-fledged liberal democracy when judged against Western standards, a Freedom House rating of 8 indicates that a clear distinction can be made between Kyrgyzstan and the other three Central Asian states in terms of the democratic nature of their political systems.[90] Whether Kyrgyzstan's democratic development translates into a "sense of identity" with Western nonproliferation concerns is more difficult to assess. Both the expressed commitment to the basic institutions of the nonproliferation regime and the ubiquitous presence of Kyrgyz representatives at export control conferences provide evidence that Kyrgyzstan's attitude in this respect is unambiguously positive. At the same time, the instability engendered by the simultaneous implementation of meaningful political and economic reforms should, in a practical sense, have made progress on export controls that much more difficult for Kyrgyzstan than elsewhere; in practice however, Kyrgyzstan has made greater progress than the other three.

Gauging the "sincerity" of a commitment to the norms of the liberal community is inherently problematic. Indeed most of the evidence at the level of observed behavior suggests that Uzbekistan is the most pro-American of the four states. Thus, Uzbekistan stood virtually alone in the United Nations in supporting the United States regarding sanctions against both Cuba and Iran.[91] Similarly Uzbek President Karimov has been the driving force behind the recent initiative to establish a nuclear weapons–free zone in Central Asia, suggesting a broader commitment to nonproliferation goals.[92] Finally, both Uzbekistan and Kyrgyzstan have had significantly more extensive interactions with the liberal community than have either Turkmenistan or Tajikistan.[93] However, the superficiality of Uzbekistan's identification with the liberal community is evident in both the paucity of domestic economic and political reform undertaken since independence and the prevailing attitudes of prominent government officials.[94] Looking beyond the rhetorical level, the commitment of Kyrgyzstan to liberal democratic norms appears qualitatively distinct from the other three. A plausible argument can be constructed, therefore, that the liberal identity approach offers an accurate and convincing "match" with the reality of export control development in Central Asia.

ANALYSIS AND CONCLUSIONS

The opening section of this chapter charted in some detail the progress made so far toward the development of systems of nonproliferation export control in the four states of the Central Asian region. It revealed that the region as a whole is characterized by the absence of development, the only important distinction among the four states being that Kyrgyzstan alone possesses a targeted legal framework. Various expectations derived from four theoretical perspectives were then tested against the empirical reality of export controls development in the region. On the basis of this, a number of conclusions can be drawn.

The first of these relates to what cannot be adequately tested in the Central Asian context. Specifically, it must be recognized that the Central Asian states cannot provide an adequate testing ground for certain of the generated expectations. This is particularly true of those stressing the role of domestic politics. In reality, it is likely to be many years before domestic political structures in these states are sufficiently advanced to matter in terms of policy outcomes. This of course does not mean that such approaches are irrelevant to the other states considered in this book, but simply that an analysis of the Central Asian states can neither refute nor provide support for the explanatory power of these perspectives.

In terms of "negative" findings (those which serve to refute or contradict a particular theoretical perspective), probably the most robust is that the realist approach seems to provide little in the way of explanatory power. In many ways, Uzbekistan constitutes a critical test case here. A realist approach would lead us to predict a far higher level of export control development in Uzbekistan than is actually the case. At a minimum, we would expect the system in Uzbekistan to be the most developed in the region. That the Uzbek system is virtually nonexistent, while that in Kyrgyzstan (a state lacking strong threats to security)[95] has made at least some progress, provides convincing evidence that the realist approach can explain little in terms of Central Asian export control development.

Of the "positive" findings (those which provide support for a theoretical perspective), the two most convincing are those which stress the role of material incentives and the importance of liberal identity. In both of these cases, the derived expectations are consistent with the observed variation in export control development across the four states. Bearing in mind the limited variance in terms of system development exhibited across the four Central Asian states, however, it would be unwise to attach undue weight to these positive findings. In reality, the variation displayed hinges on the fact that Kyrgyzstan possesses a legal framework while the others do not. Viewed from an intraregional perspective, the magnitude of this difference appears considerably more significant than when viewed in the context of system development across the FSU as a whole. One of the major advantages of applying the same theoretical approaches to fourteen of the FSU states is precisely that it enables us to put intraregional variance in the proper perspective, thus permitting a more rigorous evaluation of the various hypotheses. For the purposes of this particular case study, it therefore seems more appropriate to conclude that the observed pattern of export control development across the Central Asian region is more consistent with certain expectations than with others.[96]

NOTES

1. Information concerning the contents of the decrees are taken from the original documents, supplied by the Department of International Organizations, Kyrgyz Ministry of Foreign Affairs.

2. Personal communication with export control official, Department of International Organizations, Kyrgyz Ministry of Foreign Affairs, 28 July 1997.

3. Personal communication with officials, Department of International Organizations, Kyrgyz Ministry of Foreign Affairs, 29 July 1997.

4. Personal communication with officials, Department on Science and New Technologies, Ministry of Education, 28–29 July 1997.

5. Personal communication with several officials in the Kyrgyz Ministry of Foreign Affairs and State Customs Inspectorate, 28–29 July 1997.

6. Irina Begjanova and Lisa Palluconi, "Trade with Turkmenistan," *BISNIS Bulletin*, September 1996; published by International Trade Administration, U.S. Department of Commerce, p. 5.

7. "Niyazov Edict Tightens Control Over Foreign Firms," translated in FBIS-SOV-94–233, 5 December 1994, pp. 59–60.

8. "Government Bans Various Import, Export Items," *Interfax*, 18 July 1992, printed in FBIS-SOV-92–349, 21 July 1992.

9. Personal communication with Turkmen delegates to Washington "Forum on Export Controls," September 1996.

10. Information concerning Decree 287 is taken from the original document, supplied by the Uzbek Ministry of Foreign Economic Relations.

11. This was the impression gained by the author during interviews with a variety of government officials (State Committee for Science and Technology, Ministries of Foreign Economic Relations and Foreign Affairs) over the period July 21–25, 1997. When questioned on dual-use items, officials typically stated that Uzbekistan does not produce any defense-related goods, but seemed not to appreciate that certain items designed for peaceful purposes might also be used in the production of WMD.

12. Tajikistan has passed numerous decrees attempting to control the export of critical commodities—particularly aluminum and cotton—none of which has met with much success. (See "Parliament Tells Government to Tighten up Import and Export Controls," *Tajik Radio*, 27 September 1994, translated by BBC Summary of World Broadcasts, 3 October 1994, Nexis; "Government Decree Regulates Export of Goods," *Dushanbe Radio*, 30 January 1995, translated in FBIS-SOV-95–019, 30 January 1995, p. 61). For the inability of Tajik authorities to exercise control over exports, see "Republic Reselling Russian Copper Abroad," *Rossiyskaya Gazeta*, 17 July 1993, p. 6, translated in FBIS-SOV-93–137, 20 July 1993, p. 44.

13. While the Tajik draft law has yet to be officially translated, it transpires that the document is virtually identical to the "Decision of the Russian Federation

Government No. 50" of 15 January 1995, titled "On Procedures for Controlling the Export from the Russian Federation of Chemical Substances and Technologies Which Are Intended for Peaceful Purposes But May Be Used for Developing Chemical Weapons." An English translation of the latter document can be found, "Documents of the NIS," *The Monitor*, Vol. 1, No. 3 (Summer 1995), pp. 26–27, published by the Center for International Trade and Security, University of Georgia.

14. What distinguishes these three states from Kyrgyzstan is that the latter has enacted legislation specifically targeted toward the establishment of a system of export controls. The other three possess legislation for the control of sensitive items only in the most general sense.

15. Interview by author with U.S. Customs officials, 26 September 1996; see also "Special Assessment; Kazakhstan Export Control," unpublished report by United States Customs Service, Office of International Affairs, January 1995, p. 12.

16. "No Question of Russian Border Troop Withdrawal," *Vecherniy Bishkek*, 17 November 1994, p. 2, translated in FBIS-SOV-94–224, 21 November 1994, p. 62.

17. "Country Profile; Kyrgyzstan," *Jane's Sentinel—Commonwealth of Independent States*, 1994 edition, Nexis; Richard Woff, "The Border Troops of the Russian Federation," *Jane's Intelligence Review*, Vol. 7, No. 2, 1 February 1995, p. 70.

18. Ibid, See also Woff, "The Border Troops." For evidence of the unreliability of Kyrgyz conscripts stationed at the Kyrgyz/Chinese border, see, "10 percent of Kyrgyz Servicemen Deserting Unified Army," *Krasnaya Zvezda*, 5 November 1992, translated in FBIS-SOV-92–218, 10 November 1992, p. 64; also, "Mass Desertion of Border Guards on Kyrgyz-Chinese Border," *ITAR-TASS*, 20 December 1993, printed in FBIS-SOV-93–242, 20 December 1993, p. 54.

19. Personal communication with officials, Kyrgyz State Customs Inspectorate, 29 July 1997.

20. Ibid.

21. Michael Specter, "Opium Finds its Silk Road in Chaos of Central Asia," *New York Times*, Tuesday, 2 May 1995, p. A1. For evidence of the extent of corruption, see "Security Official on Widespread Corruption," *Slovo Kyrgyzstana*, 29 November 1994, p. 3, translated in FBIS-SOV-94–235, 7 December 1994, pp. 47–48; "Activity of Drugs Shaykhs Viewed," *Pravda*, 21 September 1994, pp. 1–2, translated in FBIS-SOV-94-185, 23 September 1994, pp. 65–66; "Kyrgyz Sackings," *Financial Times*, 14 September 1996, p. 1.

22. Personal communication, 29 July 1997.

23. For a general overview of Turkmen-Russian military agreements, see Susan Clark, "The Central Asian States; Defining Security Priorities and Developing Military Forces," in Michael Mandelbaum, ed., "Central Asia and the World" (New York: Council on Foreign Relations Press, 1994), pp. 177–206, and "Country Profile; Turkmenistan," *Jane's Sentinel—Commonwealth of Independent States*, 1994 Edition, Nexis; for details of the various agreements and protocols between Turkmenistan and Russia governing the mechanics of border control in Turkmenistan,

see "Officials on Military Treaty with Russia," *Interfax*, 11 June 1992, translated in FBIS-SOV-92–114, 12 June 1992, pp. 82–83; "Decision Made on Dual Control of Border Forces," *Ostankino Television First Program Network*, 28 July 1992, translated in FBIS-SOV-92–029, 29 July 1992, p. 41: "Niyazov, Border Commanders Discuss Cooperation," *ITAR-TASS*, 16 December 1993, printed in FBIS-SOV-93–241, 17 December 1993, p. 82; "Russia, Turkmenistan Sign Accords on Russian Border Guards," *Nezavisimaya Gazeta*, 23 January 1996, translated in FBIS-SOV-96–016, 24 January 1996, p. 70.

24. FBIS-SOV-96–016; Mark Stenhouse, "Central Asia—A Catalyst for Change," *Jane's International Defense Review*, 31 December 1994, p. 46, Nexis.

25. FBIS-SOV-96–016.

26. See "Country Profile: Turkmenistan," *Jane's Sentinel*, also, Stenhouse, "Central Asia—a Catalyst "; Woff, "The Border Troops ."

27. "Niyazov Takes Steps Against Illegal Exports," *Interfax*, 18 June 1992, printed in FBIS-SOV-92–120, 22 June 1992, p. 77.

28. "Turkmenistan State Customs Service Set Up," *Turkmenskaya Iskra*, 29 July 1992, translated in BBC Summary of World Broadcasts, 15 August 1992, Nexis.

29. "Niyazov Issues Decree on Customs Control," *ITAR-TASS*, 29 July 1993, printed in FBIS-SOV-93–145, 30 July 1993, p. 53.

30. "Sarakhs Customs Post Opens Up for Trade and Travel to Turkmenistan," *Vision of the Islamic Republic of Iran Network 1*, 5 January 1995, translated in BBC Summary of World Broadcasts, 17 January 1995, Nexis.

31. Interview by author with U.S. customs officials, 26 September 1996; see also "Kazakhstan Export Control."

32. "Country Profile: Tajikistan," *Jane's Sentinel—Commonwealth of Independent States, 1994 Edition*, Nexis.

33. Ibid.

34. "Interview with General Andrei Nikolaev, director of Russian Federal Border Service," *Moscow News*, No. 8, 29 February–6 March 1996, pp. 5–6.

35. Ibid.

36. Ibid.

37. "Tajikistan Advance Trip Report," report prepared by the Office of International Affairs, U.S. Customs Service, p. 4.

38. Ibid.

39. Clark, "The Central Asian States," p. 195–96.

40. "Country Profile: Uzbekistan," *Jane's Sentinel—Commonwealth of Independent States 1994 Edition*, Nexis.

41. "Uzbekistan to Set Up Customs Agency," *Russia and Commonwealth Business Law Report*, "Briefs," Vol. 3, No. 12, Nexis.

42. Personal communication with officials, Uzbek State Committee for Science and Technology, 24 July 1977.

43. Interview by author with officials from U.S. Customs Service, 26 September 1996. For assessments of the competence of the Uzbek armed forces and border

troops, see, "Country Profile: Uzbekistan," *Jane's Sentinel*; Woff, "The Border Troops"; S. Frederick Starr, "Making Eurasia Stable," *Foreign Affairs*, Vol. 75, No. 1, January/February 1996, pp. 80–92. In addition to customs officials, the National Security Service (SNB) carries out enforcement at Uzbek borders; for this, and evidence as to the effectiveness of the SNB's attempts to counteract cross-border drug smuggling, see, "Uzbekistan: Security Service Official on Fight Against Drugs," *Narodnoye Slove*, 4 May 1992, p. 2, translated in FBIS-SOV-96–089, 7 May 1996, pp. 47–48.

44. Interview with U.S. Customs officials, September 1996; see also, Specter, "Opium Finds its Silk Road"; "UN Official Expresses Concern Over New Drug Routes in Central Asia," *Interfax*, 4 February 1997, printed by BBC Summary of World Broadcasts, 6 February 1997, Nexis; Merril Beattie, "Narcotics Experts Fear Drugs Explosion in CIS," *Reuter Library Report*, 23 June 1992, Nexis. For an examination of the degree of control exercised over Kazakhstan's borders with the other Central Asian states, see, "Kazakhstan Export Control," U.S. Customs Service.

45. Interview with U.S. Customs officials, 26 September 1996. The absence of effective customs controls was also evident during a recent visit by the author to the region. While cursory controls were in operation at a major crossing point on the Uzbek/Kazakh border, no form of control was exercised at crossing points on the Kyrgyz/Kazakh border.

46. Of course this does not mean that Central Asian border troops receive no training; indeed many Central Asian troops are still being trained in Russia, while Uzbekistan has been running a higher military college for the training of border troops ("Uzbek Border Guards Stop Smugglers and Armed Groups," *Uzbek Radio*, 24 March 1996, translated by BBC Summary of World Broadcasts, 24 March 1996, Nexis. The reason why the scores of the four states are so low is that there is no evidence to suggest that indigenous mechanisms are in operation to train officials in proliferation-related enforcement. For details of U.S. Customs efforts to train Central Asian customs officials, see "Nuclear Nonproliferation. U.S. Customs Service Training and Anti-Smuggling Efforts in the Newly Independent Republics," statement of Connie J. Fenchel before the Permanent Subcommittee on Investigations, U.S. Senate, 22 March 1996, attachment 4.

47. "Country Report: Kyrgyz Republic," *Economist Intelligence Unit (EIU)*, 4th quarter 1996, p. 7; Clark, "The Central Asian States," 184–88.

48. According to recent reports, Dostam is currently located in Turkey, and the nature of his future participation in the Afghan conflict is unknown (personal communication with staff at the Uzbek Institute for Strategic and Regional Studies, 22 July 1997).

49. Sanobar Shermatova, "The Southern Flank of the CIS: How Great Is the Threat?" *Moscow News*, 10 October 1996, Nexis.

50. Clark, "The Central Asian States"; Lowell Bezanis, "Turkmenistan on Neutrality," *OMRI Daily Digest*, 13 April 1995.

51. "Extra Checkpoints to Be Opened with Iran, Afghanistan," *ITAR-TASS*, 5

August 1993, printed in FBIS-SOV-93–150, 6 August 1993, p. 39.

52. "Country Report: Turkmenistan," *EIU*, 3rd quarter 1996, p. 33.

53. For examples of economic cooperation, see "Niyazov, Rafsanjani Reach 'Important' Agreements," *ITAR-TASS*, 23 January 1996, printed in FBIS-SOV-95–067, 7 April 1995, p. 74. For details of military cooperation, see "Country Report: Turkmenistan," *EIU*, 1st quarter 1996, p. 28.

54. "Further on Meeting," *Tehran IRNA*, 6 April 1995, transcribed in FBIS-SOV-95–067, 7 April 1995, p. 74.

55. "Country Report: Kyrgyz Republic," *EIU*, 3rd quarter 1996, pp. 7–8.

56. "U.S.-NIS Dialogue on Nonproliferation Export Controls. A Conference Report," transcription of conference held at Airlie, Virginia, 15–17 June 1993, p. 21.

57. An explicit link between the fundamentalist threat and the prospect of a nuclear armed Iran was also made by officials at the Uzbek Ministry of Foreign Affairs. For example, an official of the Division of Political Analysis and Forecasting argued that Iran's acquisition of a nuclear capability would greatly enhance its power and influence in the region and encourage it to exert this influence to promote fundamentalism in the region (interview, 25 July 1997).

58. Concerning the use of Islamic fundamentalism as a policy tool, see Clark, "The Central Asian States," p. 197.

59. For a detailed consideration of Uzbekistan's potential to emerge as a major regional power, see Starr, "Making Eurasia Stable."

60. Total FSA aid to the Central Asian states as of 1996, was as follows: Uzbekistan, $276 million, Kyrgyzstan, $92 million, Turkmenistan, $64 million, and Tajikistan, $42 million.

61. Per-capita dollar amounts of FSA aid are as follows: Kyrgyzstan, $20, Turkmenistan, $14, Uzbekistan, $12, and Tajikistan, $12.

62. GDP figures for the four states in 1996 were as follows (in $ billion): Uzbekistan, 45.1, Turkmenistan, 7, Kyrgyzstan, 6.2, and Tajikistan, 4.1 (source: "Country Report: Russia," *EIU*, 1st quarter 1997, pp. 46–47). FSA aid as a percent of GDP is as follows; Kyrgyzstan, 1.5 percent, Tajikistan, 1 percent, Turkmenistan, .9 percent, and Uzbekistan, .6 percent.

63. "Minsk Summit," *ITAR-TASS*, 26 June 1992, transcribed by BBC Summary of World Broadcasts, 29 June 1992, Nexis.

64. It should be noted, however, that in 1992, President Akayev of Kyrgyzstan openly admitted to considering supplying India with enriched uranium ("Kyrgyz President Explains Uranium Exports," *Izvestya*, 20 March 1992, p. 1, translated in FBIS-SOV-92–058, 25 March 1992, pp. 2–3); subsequently reports emerged that Akayev had negotiated with Pakistan to supply enriched uranium under IAEA safeguards ("Kyrgyzstan Reportedly Offers Enriched Uranium, *Radio Pakistan*, 28 August 1994, transcribed by BBC Summary of World Broadcasts, 31 August 1994, Nexis).

65. See for example, "Uranium Exports Planned; Libyan Group Visits," *Moscow News*, No. 3, 19–26 January 1992, p. 5, reprinted in FBIS-SOV-92–015, 23

January 1992, p. 100; and "Uranium for the Mujahedeen," *Current Digest of the Post-Soviet Press*, Vol. 45, No. 35, 29 September 1993, p. 15, Nexis.

66. For Tajik denials, see "Article Rebuts Uranium Sales 'Canard,'" *Nezavisimaya Gazeta*, 7 January 1992, reprinted in FBIS-SOV-92–016, 24 January 1992, p. 94.

67. Andre Grabot, "Central Asia Pushes on With Nuclear Free Zone Bid," *Agence France Presse*, 16 September 1997.

68. Lilya Strunnikova, "Conference on Radioactive Isotopes Opens in Uzbekistan," *ITAR-TASS*, 24 October 1995, Nexis.

69. The "Physics Sun" facility contains a solar furnace capable of generating temperatures close to 3,000 degrees centigrade; this furnace is used to create new classes of defense-related materials, as well as to conduct ablation studies on high-speed missiles (William B. Scott, "Uzbek Site May Benefit U.S. Surveillance Network," *Aviation Week and Space Technology*, Vol. 142, No. 20, 15 May 1995, p. 68, Nexis.

70. "Uzbekistan: Official Reviews Space, Conversion Projects," *Biznes Vestnik*, 26 April 1996, pp. 1–2, translated in FBIS-SOV-96–086, 2 May 1996, pp. 52–54.

71. Personal communication with Turkmen delegates to Washington Forum on Export Controls, September 1996.

72. This point was clearly stated by Tajik delegates to the Washington Forum. While agreeing with the broad aims of the nonproliferation regime, they maintained that export controls would be impossible to implement while the civil war continued (personal communication, September 1996).

73. Personal communication with various Uzbek government officials, July 21–25, 1997.

74. Personal communication with officials, Uzbek State Committee for Science and Technology, 24 July 1997.

75. It is notable in this context that Kyrgyz export control officials did not anticipate receiving future financial assistance from the United States for the development of their system, nor did they make the connection between export controls and access to Western technology (personal communication with various Kyrgyz government officials, 28–30 July 1997).

76. Carey Goldberg, "Niyazov; Capitalism via a Cult?" *New York Times*, 23 August 1993, p. A1; Michael Ustingov, "Uzbekistan," unpublished paper, December 1995.

77. For recent figures on Russian emigration from Central Asia, see Lowell Bezanis, "Forecasts on Emigration from Central Asia," *OMRI Daily Digest*, 23 May 1995. The state most affected by Russian emigration has been Kyrgyzstan. For figures and analysis of the impact of Russian emigration, see "Country Report: Kyrgyz Republic," *EIU*, 1st quarter 1994, p. 55, 2nd quarter 1994, p. 50, and 3rd quarter 1994, p. 53. For Uzbekistan, see "Country Report: Uzbekistan," *EIU*, 3rd quarter 1994, p. 72. For Tajikistan, see Andreas Ryeesch, "Conflict and Collapse in Tajik-

istan," *Swiss Review of World Affairs*, 1 March 1994, Nexis.

78. One of the key factors working against the evolution of stable, coherent bureaucratic entities has been the extremely high turnover of officials at all levels. In Tajikistan, for example, between December 1995 and September 1996, ten of the seventeen heads of key ministries were replaced. In Uzbekistan over the same period, ministerial turnover ran close to 50 percent (figures calculated from "Key Ministries" sections of the EIU Country Reports for Tajikistan and Uzbekistan). The high turnover of officials in Kyrgyzstan is viewed as one of the major barriers to the establishment of a coherent cadre of export control experts. The locus of responsibility for the coordination of the Kyrgyz system is now the Department of International Organizations within the Ministry of Foreign Affairs. Since 1992, however, five separate agencies have been charged with this responsibility (personal communication with officials, Department of International Organizations, 28 July 1997).

79. Copious evidence exists as to the widespread influence of Mafia groupings throughout the Central Asian region. See for example, "Dismissal Follows Mafia Exposure," *ITAR-TASS*, 3 April 1993, transcribed in FBIS-SOV-93–063, 5 April 1993, p. 74; "Instability, Drugs from Tajikistan Viewed," *Kyrgyz Radio*, 27 September 1994, transcribed in FBIS-SOV-94–188, 28 September 1994, pp. 67–68; "Akayev Proposes Purge on Law Enforcement Bodies," *INTERFAX*, 25 March 1995, transcribed in FBIS-SOV-95–058, 27 March 1995, p. 70.

80. Raymond D. Gastil, "Freedom in the World 1995–1996" (New York: Freedom House, 1996), p. 299.

81. Attempts by the U.S. government to stimulate the NGO sector in Central Asia include financial assistance provided under the USAID program. For a summary of recent activities and an indication of the poverty of the NGO sector in Central Asia, see "Statement of Thomas A. Dine before the Subcommittee on Foreign Operations," 11 March 1997, *Federal News Service*, 9 April 1997, Nexis.

82. In Uzbekistan, for example, by 1995 the private sector accounted for only 25 percent of GDP (EBRD figures, quoted in "Country Profile: Kazakhstan, Kyrgyz Republic, Tajikistan, Turkmenistan, Uzbekistan, 1995–1996," *EIU*, p. 112). Even less progress has been made in Turkmenistan, where the oil/gas and cotton sectors account for about 80 percent of export earnings and are still predominantly state owned ("Country Report: Turkmenistan," *EIU*, 4th quarter 1996, p. 2). The EBRD estimated that by the end of 1995, the private sector in Turkmenistan accounted for less than 15 percent of GDP ("Country Profile," *EIU*).

83. "Bashkotostan's Economic Ties Bypass Center," *ITAR-TASS*, 8 September 1993, printed in FBIS-SOV-93–174, 10 September 1993, p. 45.

84. In late 1994 for example, parliamentary government effectively collapsed in Kyrgyzstan for a period of time. Some have suggested that Akayev deliberately precipitated the crisis which led to the collapse, thus giving him free reign to rule by decree. Whatever the truth, Akayev's rule by decree lasted from 5 September 1994 until 31 March 1995 ("Country Report: Kyrgyz Republic," *EIU* 2nd quarter 1995, p. 22). That Akayev chose to exploit this opportunity to further the process of

reform rather than enhance his own long-term power position relative to parliament, however, suggests that this incident should not be interpreted as evidence of anti-democratic sentiment on the part of Akayev.

85. Roger D. Kangas, "Uzbekistan: Evolving Authoritarianism," *Current History*, April 1994, pp. 178–82; Christopher J. Panico, "Turkmenistan Unaffected by Winds of Democratic Change," *RFE/RL Research Report*, Vol. 2, No. 4, 22 January 1993, pp. 6–10; David Nissman, "Turkmenistan (Un)transformed," *Current History*, April 1994, pp. 183–86.

86. The opinion poll, conducted by the U.S. Institute of Peace in 1995, revealed a striking lack of concern amongst the general population of Uzbekistan for democratic reforms and associated values, Nancy Lubin, "Central Asians Take Stock: Reform, Corruption and Identity," (Washington, D.C.: U.S. Institute of Peace, 1995); see especially pp. 4–5.

87. "Freedom in the World 1995–1996."

88. On the corruption of Kyrgyz elections, see Sanobar Shermatova, "Enigmas of Central Asian Democracy," *Moscow News*, 7 April 1995, Nexis. For assessments of civil and political liberties in Kyrgyzstan, see "Freedom in the World 1995–1996," pp. 297–99, and "Amnesty International Report 1996" (London: Amnesty International Publications), p. 204.

89. Graham E. Fuller, "Central Asia: The New Geopolitics," 1992 (Santa Monica, CA: Rand); Bess Brown, "Central Asia: the Economic Crisis Deepens," *RFE/RL Research Report*, Vol. 3, No. 1, 7 January 1994, p. 63.

90. "Freedom in the World 1995–1996," p. 297.

91. The most recent vote condemning the continuation of U.S. sanctions against Cuba was proposed by Libya in November 1996. The vote was carried 56 to 4, with only Uzbekistan, Israel, and Micronesia supporting the U.S. position; see "General Assembly Adopts Libyan Draft," *Reuters*, 27 November 1996, Nexis. During 1996, Uzbekistan also had one of the most pro-American voting records of all the U.N. states, opposing the United States on only 24 percent of recorded votes. (Bryan Johnson, "Does Foreign Aid Serve U.S. Interests?" *Heritage Foundation*, 15 April 1997, Nexis.)

92. Grabot, "Central Asia Pushes."

93. During 1996 and 1997, for example, U.S. government interagency teams visited both Uzbekistan and Kyrgyzstan to assist with export controls. Subsequently, a delegation from Uzbekistan traveled to the United States for a follow-up meeting in May 1997, followed by a Kyrgyz delegation in July 1997. Neither Turkmenistan nor Tajikistan has participated in similar programs—the former due to lack of interest, and the latter due to problems relating to the civil war (personal communication with U.S. government officials, April 1997).

94. During interviews with a variety of officials in the Ministry of Foreign Affairs, Institute of Strategic Studies, and Office of the President, it soon became evident that Uzbek support for the United States is rooted in calculations of strategic self-interest. Thus, by publicly supporting the United States Uzbekistan is able to

send an unambiguous message to Russia regarding its determination to remain independent of Russian influence. Regarding the glacial rate of progress on democracy, officials were virtually unanimous in asserting that the Uzbek people are simply not ready for democracy, and could not be trusted with extensive civil liberties (interviews conducted 21–25 July 1997).

95. The important point here is that while certain threats to Kyrgyz security do exist (Tajik civil war, the Afghan conflict, and even fears of Uzbek expansionism), the implementation of a system of export controls would do nothing to reduce the threat.

96. The same argument does not apply with equal force for the "negative" findings based on the Central Asian case. If certain derived expectations are seriously at odds with observed behavior (as in the case the realist approach), then the relevant null hypothesis can be rejected with relative confidence.

EIGHT

SECURITY DIMENSIONS OF NONPROLIFERATION
Export Control Development in the Caucasus

CASSADY CRAFT

This chapter provides data and analysis for important, and yet understudied, states of the FSU—the Caucasus republics of Armenia, Azerbaijan, and Georgia—and their attempts to control the spread of weapons of mass destruction (WMD). Nonproliferation issues in these states have thus far received scant scholarly attention and very little Western assistance, and yet these countries have the potential to play vital roles in the proliferation, or nonproliferation, of WMD. Despite the fact that countries in the Caucasus did not inherit a share of the Soviet nuclear arsenal, they did inherit significant component parts of its WMD-producing infrastructure, such as nuclear reactors, production facilities, and military industrial enterprises. This study suggests that security issues dominate the Caucasus states' development of nonproliferation policies, or lack thereof, at this time. In order to promote greater capabilities in controlling the proliferation of WMD via this critical region, much more needs to be done by the many interested parties in the region.

The Caucasus states are often seen as areas ripe for proliferation activities due to internal instability, being described by one analyst as "mafia 'hotbeds,' [areas of] ethnic strife, ethnic cleansing, [and] border clashes."[1] Of attendant importance, though, is these states' geographic location. Their location makes them ideal transit points for legal commerce and illegal smuggling to other regions of the world—especially regions such as Iran and Iraq, which pose the greatest proliferation concern to the West. It is, therefore, important to assess the magnitude of the Caucasus states' proliferation threat.

This chapter looks first at the strategic threat of the Caucasus states in terms of their potential to promote or inhibit the spread of WMD. Next, it

examines the level of export control development in the Caucasus. After an
element-by-element description of export control development, an overall
assessment of the progress of nonproliferation efforts—especially focusing
on export controls—is offered. Next, the theoretical framework developed
in chapter 1 is applied to the states of the Caucasus. After a presentation of
the evidence for each approach, the study's findings are presented and interpreted.

THE STRATEGIC THREAT FROM THE CAUCASUS

The geographic location of the Caucasus states makes them a primary concern to the West. While Armenia, Azerbaijan, and Georgia have only limited
weapons production capabilities, they can and do serve as conduits for
products like drugs, conventional weapons, or WMD materials and technologies going elsewhere. They thus serve as threats to Western security.[2]
Along these lines, the U.S. State Department in 1996 notified Congress, for
example, that "we have periodically received reports of proliferation-related
transfers of weapons of mass destruction involving Armenia."[3] Striking in
this regard is the "friendliness" of relations between Armenia and Russia,
and Armenia and Iran, along with the potential for Russian products to
transit the Caucasus (especially Armenia, Nagorno-Karabakh, and the
Georgian enclaves of Abkhazia and Ajeria) territory en route to Iranian
markets.[4] Likewise, Turkish officials have arrested several individuals who
claim that the original supplier of the HEU that they were caught trying to
sell was Georgian President Eduard Shevardnadze's chief bodyguard.[5] Despite the somewhat sensationalist character of some of the claims surrounding the transfer of WMD or materials in the Caucasus, the potential or real
proliferation problem is serious because the flow of weapons, materials, and
technology—if it does take place—is to the southeast. Iran and other Middle
Eastern states of proliferation concern that are likely recipients of any WMD
"leakage" from the FSU have foreign policies sometimes violently averse to
Western interests.[6]

Of further importance, but ranking slightly behind their potential as
transhipment points, are the indigenous production facilities and expertise
in the Caucasus that have potential for WMD proliferation. It must be
stressed here that much of this threat is not from the activities of the governments themselves, but again from the activities of criminal elements who
may have the wherewithal to divert important materials to the "wrong people." Armenia's type 440 VVER V230 nuclear power plant at Metsamor
represents a low-level proliferation threat due to the expertise of its scientists, who could be of use in an advisory capacity in Iranian attempts to
master the intricacies of operating a nuclear power plant. Further, the low
enriched uranium in Armenia, as well as materials contained in spent fuel

and storage facilities, represent possible sources of radiological weapons material.[7] There is also a slight danger that any enriched or reprocessed uranium fuel being transited from Russia to the Metsamor plant could be hijacked or otherwise diverted.[8] However, Armenia is probably not a significant nuclear proliferation threat itself in terms of its own acquisition of nuclear weapons. Light water reactors, as noted by Hannerz and Segerberg, are not an attractive means of obtaining fissile materials for this use due to the substantial technical obstacles, economic costs, and difficulty in hiding clandestine reprocessing or enrichment facilities necessary to convert the spent fuel to weapons-grade materials.[9] This is especially true if—as in the case at Metsamor—the facilities are subject to IAEA safeguards and inspections.

Armenia has, however, recently proved to be a proliferation threat in terms of ballistic missiles. During the 1993–1996 period, there were perhaps $1 billion worth of weapons clandestinely transferred from Russia to Armenia.[10] Included in these transfers were thirty-two Russian-made SCUD-B ballistic missiles, which were allegedly shipped through Georgia or across the Caspian and Black Seas and then through Iran without the knowledge of the Russian, Georgian, or Iranian governments.[11] These missiles are a serious proliferation threat because they represent a new weapon type introduced into an area where there is a simmering, if not boiling, conflict between Armenia and Azerbaijan over the Nagorno-Karabakh enclave. In addition, Azerbaijani officials have made corresponding allegations that these weapons are chemical-warhead capable, and that Armenian engineers had recently been trained in Russia to make such adjustments for combat usage.[12] If these rumors are true, then these transfers would again represent a dangerous escalation of military capabilities in a region that plays an important role in the national security of Russia, Iran, and Turkey.[13] Given that Iran is an aspiring regional nuclear power, Turkey a member of nuclear weapons–armed NATO, and Russia a former superpower, any instability caused by weapons transfers into the Caucasus has important ramifications for *international* security, as well.

Of the Transcaucasian states, only Azerbaijan possesses few industries or facilities vital in the production of WMD.[14] At the same time, however, a former Azerbaijani interior minister, Iskendor Khamidov, has made claims that Azerbaijan possesses the capability to produce or acquire nuclear weapons, and on another occasion that he "has a pair of nuclear weapons in the trunk of his car."[15] Most observers in Baku and elsewhere do not take such claims seriously, however.

The state of Georgia also has facilities that represent a WMD proliferation threat. Georgia possesses an IRT-M nuclear research reactor in Tbilisi at the Institute of Physics, which was shut down in 1988 but contained 4 to 8 kilograms of weapons-grade uranium.[17] Georgia also has nuclear research and training facilities, including two isotope-production reactors, and several locations rumored to contain radioactive waste.[18]

In addition, each state in the Caucasus is a member of the Joint Institute of Nuclear Research (JINR), a former Soviet-bloc nuclear training facility that remains active in training nuclear scientists and engineers in the post–Cold War era. While membership and activity in JINR is certainly not indicative of proliferation activity, the development of such scientific expertise can *potentially* become a proliferation threat if the member states cannot, or will not, control the movement of these scientists. While much has been written about the potential "brain drain" from the Russian Federation, the same dynamic operates, albeit on a smaller scale, in the Caucasus.

General instability in the Transcaucasian region is obvious because of the civil conflict in Georgia over Abkhazia and Ajeria and the sporadic warfare between the Azerbaijani military and ethnic Armenians in the enclave of Nagorno-Karabakh. These conflicts result in weakened political and economic structures that leave each of these states underdeveloped in terms of their security structures. This underdevelopment requires increased attention from the West, given the harsh political and economic climates, growing and strengthening organized criminal elements, and incentives offered by Iran and other relatively affluent Islamic states near their borders. Furthermore, these conflicts raise security issues that concern where borders are drawn between current states and regions that have aspirations toward statehood. The problems of control are also exacerbated by the influx of conventional weapons into the region.[19] The internal instability of the Caucasus societies has also spawned militarists groups and criminal elements. The rise of rebel, separatist, and paramilitary groups in the region has led one scholar to describe the Caucasus as "the most militarized area in the world."[20]

EXPORT CONTROL DEVELOPMENT IN THE CAUCASUS

In the Caucasus states, just as in the other non-Russian former Soviet states, export control systems had to be created from scratch. As of yet, these countries have been unable to develop systems that approximate the well-developed export control systems of the West. In fact, it may be argued that the countries of the Caucasus cannot be seen to have export control *systems* at all. It is more realistic to state that these countries have partial development of individual export control elements, but lack the necessary channels of interaction between elements that typify a well-developed system in comparison with Western models.

Probably the most immediate and pressing concern of the Caucasus states after their independence and consolidation periods has been the development of border controls. Border controls in the Caucasus have received considerable governmental and international attention in light of the potential and actual transit of drugs and weapons through the region. However, relatively little emphasis has been placed on border controls for WMD proliferation materials. Despite the importance of this element in terms of WMD nonproliferation, border controls in these regions are haphazard, rife with corruption, tied to important elements of foreign policy which favor states of high proliferation concern such as Iran and Russia, and generally controversial.[21]

Corruption is rampant in the Caucasus with complete border posts being abolished in periodic shakedowns. For example, according to the former Customs Department chairman of Georgia, by May 1994 the entire staffs at three of the country's border posts and a fourth post's chief of operations had been fired due to evidence of corruption.[22] The role of organized and unorganized crime in the Caucasus region cannot, and should not, be ignored. As part of what can be viewed as either transnational criminal groups or petty, local thugs, criminal elements by nature undermine the sovereignty of states. In doing so, they perpetuate the weakness of states and thus serve to enhance the proliferation potential of the region. If criminal groups have successfully integrated themselves into the governing coalition of the state, their influence on state policies will necessarily be to the detriment of nonproliferation efforts. This is especially true in the Caucasus where nonproliferation efforts, such as those sponsored by the U.S. FBI, DOD, and Customs Service, are closely tied to programs to control the black markets in conventional weapons or drugs.

Throughout the young histories of the Caucasus states, the Russian Federation has played an important role in border control. After the fall of the USSR, the Transcaucasian Border Troops district was disbanded, and responsibility for controlling former borders of the Soviet Union was transferred to the new states of Armenia, Azerbaijan, and Georgia. Because of the dearth of technical and financial resources, lack of experienced personnel and the extraordinarily tenuous control that these states have over their geopolitical space, they proved largely incapable of performing the most basic border control functions. Thus, Russian troops continued their occupation of border control bases in the Caucasus, with the North Caucasus Border Troops District first being formed and then abandoned.[23] In March 1994, Russia created the Caucasus Special Border District stretching from the Black to Caspian Seas and maintaining troops in both Armenia and Georgia. However, Azerbaijan has staunchly resisted the stationing of Russian troops in the country, either for the purposes of border control or as CIS peacekeepers deployed to implement the cease-fire in Nagorno-Karabakh. At this time, it is the only state in the Caucasus where Russian forces do not provide border patrols, although Georgian commitment to this Russian "service" has waned. During a recent Commonwealth of Independent States meeting of the "Council of Border Forces," Azerbaijan and Georgia did not sign the resulting declaration.

If the Russian Federation's provision of border control forces provides a commonality, of sorts, for the customs authority for the states considered here, in respect to many of the other elements there are few similarities. Those that exist, however, can be summarized succinctly: a) export control functions are levied by decree from the executive branch, and b) most elements are either wholly undeveloped or severely underdeveloped.

Armenia represents the zenith of export control development among the states examined here, with a system that is about 50 percent compatible with Western common standards.[24] However, enforcement and implementation of these controls, as in the rest of the Caucasus, are less than uniform. On paper, the Armenian export control system is relatively sophisticated. Decrees issued in 1992 and 1993 require special permission to export radioactive materials and establish a Commission on Export Control, which includes the deputy prime minister, the head of the State Department on National Security, and the first deputy of the Military and Industrial Commission.[25] While the actual structure of the Armenian system was in the process of being reconstructed due to a shakeup of the Ter-Petrosian government in mid-1997, in functional terms the export control system is expected to be the same.[26] On September 27, 1993, the Armenian government adopted an itemized export control list, which has four main divisions of materials, substances, devices, and dual-use technologies: bacteriological and poisonous weapons-related; nuclear-related; rocket weapons-related; and chemical weapons-related.[27] These decrees required that exporters of sensitive materials, which are all government-owned industries, provide full technical specifications and supporting documentation with any export application before it is processed by an "export controls working group," which was formerly housed in the Ministry of Finance.[28] A "council of experts" made up of academics, scientists, and industry officials was created to give technical support for this processing. Munitions and dual-use items can be exported only to prescribed destinations while exports to all end-users and countries subject to "international embargo" are banned, according to Armenian officials.[29] All illegal exports of items included in the control list are to be viewed as violations of criminal law with penalties ranging from three to eight years of imprisonment.[30] According to Armenian officials, however, there have been no illegal attempts to export controlled materials to date.

In addition, Armenia has developed lists of proscribed items which cannot be imported or transshipped through the country.[31] Transit items include all types of weapons, ammunition, army equipment, components for their production, explosives, nuclear materials, and sources of ionized radiation. Customs units are responsible for verifying the contents of transit loads when transit of prohibited items is suspected, and have the legal power to inspect and seize suspect transit shipments if there is any doubt as to their veracity. However, there have been no such detainments to date, which is perplexing given the amount of weaponry commonly accepted to have transited Armenian territory on the way to Nagorno-Karabakh, or less commonly, to Iran and to Kurds in Turkey. Dual-use items require an export certificate from the country of destination to guarantee that the imported items will not be used for military purposes. Items prohibited from import (and thus, reexport) include weapons, explosives, and army equipment.

Armenia's intelligence and security forces are tasked with the verification of end-users of imports and exports. However, given the scarcity of government resources for such activity, there are questions as to whether this function is being performed. Training facilities where licensing, customs, and law enforcement officials can be trained in the technical aspects of nonproliferation policy have not been established, although Armenian officials are quick to point out that their border forces are trained, in part, by security officers of other states such as Russia and France.[32] Finally, the Armenian export control apparatus lacks a "catch-all" clause which would prohibit exports to states or end-users who are suspected of being involved in clandestine WMD programs.[33]

The other Caucasus states lag behind in terms of nonproliferation export control development. Georgia lies somewhat below Armenia in terms of the development of an export control structure with a score of about 24 percent (i.e., compatibility with Western common standards). As is the case in other states covered here, exports are controlled by decree.[34] On September 8, 1992, the Georgian government issued a decree, "On Provisional Rules for Restricting and Licensing the Export and Import of Goods (Works, Services) on the Territory of the Republic of Georgia," which controls the export and import of all goods, presumably including those of proliferation potential.[35] This document indicated that a list of goods would be established, provided licensing procedures and institutional responsibilities, and it established the State Department of State Border Forces as the enforcement body.[36] Georgia also has provisions for the control of all weapons and military hardware exports.

This level of control in Georgia is, however, questionable. An example of the inconsistency of the early efforts to control the export of weapons in Georgia is provided by the case of Tbilisi Aviation Enterprise. The State Parliamentary Committee of Defense and Security accused this company, the most important defense industry in the country, of having produced and delivered equipment to both domestic and international purchasers without a customer's order.[37] Inspections also revealed that some related documents were illicit. Further complicating matters, the government of Georgia does not control, nor do its border forces patrol, its entire geographical space.

The areas of Abkhazia and Ajeria are both under the control of nongovernment forces, and border controls are enforced by the Russian Federation. There have also been disputes between Georgian border control forces and their Russian counterparts in the ports of Poti and Bakumi, where Russian forces are present under the mandate of the CIS agreement on border forces. Finally, disputes in Abkhazia are unlikely to be over, either between the Georgian government and the breakaway region, or Georgia and Russia. The Russian Federation had committed to withdraw all its peacekeeping forces from Georgia by July 31, 1997. As this deadline approached, Georgian President Shevardnadze backed down, and the Russians remain. Although this probably does preserve the nascent peace between Georgia and Abkhaz rebels, it remains a source of tension in the region.[38] Even if Russian forces were to leave, given the political state of affairs in Abkhazia and Ajeria and the lack of political desire in Tbilisi to force the issue of these regions' independence, the Georgian government could probably not attain political or military control over its territory.[39]

Azerbaijan is about even with Georgia in developing an export control policy and an effective border and customs regime. Few laws exist on export controls, customs, or trade, although a 1992 decree introduced customs regulations and border controls.[40] Azerbaijan prohibits the export of weapons, explosives, radioactive materials and wastes, narcotics, and psychotropic drugs. It also requires that importers provide certain information concerning imports, and prohibits outright the import of radioactive wastes and narcotics, and requires special permission for the import of weapons, explosives, and certain "radioactive equipment" used in the oil industry. This decree establishes the illegality of the sale of weapons, although the sale of conventional weapons in Azerbaijan is, at least in Nagorno-Karabakh, without doubt a regular event. The Ministry of Foreign Economic Relations controls the export of all goods from Azerbaijan and is charged with export license evaluation, while the customs service is charged with implementation of border controls.

COMPETING EXPLANATIONS FOR EXPORT CONTROL DEVELOPMENTS IN THE CAUCASUS
Realism

Realist explanations for development of nonproliferation export controls apply to the Caucasus in varying degrees. These states uniformly have legal decrees that prohibit the sale, transfer, or transshipment of any type of weapons through their territories. These decrees fit with realist expectations of state behavior in terms of concerns about external threats, balancing the power of others, or preventing gains in others' military capabilities only in Armenia. Because these expectations are of a secondary nature insofar as they presume that the state has established territorial integrity, they clearly do not apply to either Azerbaijan, which has no control over Nagorno-Karabakh and the "occupied territories," or in Georgia where both the regions of Abkhazia and Ajaria dispute the sovereignty of the government in Tbilisi. These goals are thus in important ways beyond the scope of government thinking in the period immediately after independence. Export control development, however, has throughout the Caucasus served to enhance state security in important ways.

Only Armenia saw fit to establish immediate controls over WMD technologies, and it apparently did so for at least three reasons (two of which are clearly realist).[41] First, the Armenian government established export controls because of its desires to secure the dangerous materials at the Metsamor site from internal and external enemies. Second, the government quickly saw the need for restarting the power reactors at Metsamor and surmised that establishing proper materials control would be a necessary precondition. This fits the rational institutionalist, not realist, perspective. Finally, Armenian officials viewed Turkey, which is part of the nuclear-weapons–armed NATO alliance, as the biggest threat to their security. This security concern in many ways forms the basis of Armenia's defense posture, as the only means by which this country can balance the power of Turkey is through alliance with Russia. An additional factor in Armenia's efforts to secure the Metsamor site was undoubtedly the conflict with Azerbaijan and the resultant possibility of Azerbaijani terrorist attacks.

In the other states of the Caucasus, export controls play an important role in enhancing state security in the more fundamental sense of providing resources to governments trying to establish control over their constituent borders. Especially problematic in this region is the flow of conventional weapons, refugees, and drugs.[42] Because these states have no nuclear, chemical, or biological weapons and have little indigenous capability of proliferation concern, they did not initially see WMD proliferation as posing a great risk to their national well-beings. In turn, their governments saw little reason to devote scarce resources to the development of nonproliferation export controls beyond their immediate concerns over the ability of the states to guarantee their borders.[43] In Georgia, government officials described the potential of the state as a "transportation corridor" as the impetus behind developing export controls.[44] Rather than linking such a corridor and export control development with increased trade with the West (as rational institutionalism would suggest), the Georgians spoke instead of the potential transit of illicit materials through the state and the attendant threats to law and order that such criminal activities would pose. In describing the importance of these priorities, an Armenian government official stated, "We do not have the luxury of leisure by which to ponder the best way to develop an export control system. We are fighting wars and trying to stabilize an inherently unstable region."[45]

Perversely, in terms of developing nonproliferation export controls in the region, obtaining WMD may be an attractive means to obtain such stability via creating a situation in which a clear preponderance of power rests with one side.[46] According to this logic, Armenia may have acquired ballistic missiles and perhaps chemical weapons capability in order to deter Azerbaijan from renewing its attempt to regain control of Nagorno-Karabakh and the other "occupied territories" under the military and political control of Karabakh forces.[47] According to other realist thinkers, however, such activity should *incite* Azerbaijan to develop, buy, or steal its own WMD capability in order to balance the power of Armenia. Thus, rather than promoting the development of nonproliferation policies, norms, or export controls, acquisitions of ballistic missiles serve to undermine such development. Worse, because of the intricate dynamics of the rivalries in the Caucasus, and the presence of military forces of a WMD-reliant Russia, imports of high-technology weapons could undermine nonproliferation efforts in the entire region if Iran and/or Turkey were to become involved.

Finally, there is another realist argument to be considered when analyzing Caucasian export control development. As noted by many scholars, the role of "small powers" in the international system is contingent on the interests of the powerful.[48] Their survival is due to the calculation of larger states who have need to keep smaller states "alive" in order to retain geopolitical influence over politico-economic space. According to Goldenberg, this influence is obvious in the Caucasus, especially in the terms established between their leaders and Moscow. She posits that both presidents Aliev of Azerbaijan and Shevardnadze of Georgia were installed with little domestic support but ample covert support from Russia.[49] The signing of Russian military-basing agreements with Armenia symbolizes the importance of Moscow's influence on the Ter-Petrosian government, which also is a strong supporter of the Russian-dominated CIS.[50] In turn, the small states must assess their options in terms of the interests of the large. As Alexander Rondeli asserts,

> Russia's small neighbors . . . have realized that the norms and principles of international community are not working in the so-called "near abroad" and they are left unprotected vis-à-vis the most powerful state in the post-communist space [Russia]. [A] small country has to take into consideration the national security interests of its powerful neighbor and conduct diplomatic relations with Russia and other former Soviet Republics according to the existing geopolitical and economic conditions in order to ensure future survival and development. Thus, [they] have to accept the rules of the game that dominate international relations in the post-Soviet space. Small states neighboring Russia find

themselves . . . in a net of harsh and merciless politico-economic relations, where the leader or the hegemon [Russia] is holding its weak neighbors and is busy "amputating" their vitally important organs.[51]

We can extend this argument to examine the influence that the Russian Federation may wield over nonproliferation export control development in the Caucasus. Accordingly, export control development in the small states of these regions will be driven by their calculation of *Russian* interests in their doing so. Is it in Russia's interest for states on its perimeter to strictly control the movement of products, goods, and services? When one considers the Russian Federation's economic difficulties, desire to export weapons and other products for hard currency, and its carefully stated non-enmity with states that the West considers "pariahs," quite possibly it is not.

While the drastic difference between Russian nonproliferation export control development and that in the states of the Caucasus belies this theory, it should not be disregarded completely at this time, given Russian transgressions (noted by Michael Beck in chapter 2) in transferring conventional and WMD weapons and technology to areas such as China, North Korea, India, Iran, Armenia, and Nagorno-Karabakh.[52] This is true especially if Beck is correct and Russian export control development is *not* driven by its own strong concern for national security. Viewed in this light, *lack of nonproliferation export control development* along the transit routes to profitable legal and illicit markets may well constitute the Russian interest. There is certainly the potential that Russian border officials in two of the three republics under consideration here provide economic efficiencies to illicit trade in addition to undermining the creation of national nonproliferation export control capability in these regions.[53]

To summarize, realist expectations provide considerable explanatory power in terms of the development of nonproliferation export controls in the Caucasus states. This theory may also provide important insights into why these states may *not* develop their export control systems, as scarce resources may be better devoted to more pressing security needs. The dynamics of a potential WMD or conventional weapons arms race, and the indisputable influence of Russia in these regions of its "near abroad" are important considerations as policy-makers in the West seek to promote export control development in the Caucasus.

Rational Institutionalism

According to rational institutionalist expectations, states develop nonproliferation export control systems if they value future interactions with nonproliferation regime member states, are interested in inducing reciprocity, receive directly targeted aid and side payments, and otherwise calculate that the costs and benefits involved in doing so emerge as positive. As none of the states considered here was able to "cash in" on U.S. nonproliferation export control aid provided by the Cooperative Threat Reduction (CTR, or Nunn-Lugar) programs for money directly given for the development of export controls, it is necessary to look for less direct links between inducements and export control development.[54]

In Armenia, the only state in the region with a nuclear power plant and the state in the region with the most sophisticated nonproliferation export control system, we see evidence of such indirect linkages. Nonproliferation export control development in Armenia is linked in important ways to the Metsamor nuclear power plant, which has been subjected to IAEA safeguards since its restart in 1995. These safeguards perform dual functions in terms of nuclear safety and nonproliferation concerning such items as nuclear fuel storage procedures. In turn, satisfying IAEA inspections is important in terms of side payments to Armenia, with $57 million of European Bank for Reconstruction and Development (EBRD) money being committed to the plant over several years and $6 million of U.S. FREEDOM Support Act money committed to the plant in 1997.[55] This represents a sizable amount of aid to a country with a total annual budget of $325 million and a defense budget of $65 million. With the other states under consideration, perhaps the best statement of indirect linkage is between FREEDOM Support Act aid and development of nonproliferation export controls because of the former's stipulations that the U.S. State Department must assure Congress that the potential recipient is not a proliferant of WMD or conventional weapons. Armenia, for example, has been given roughly five times the amount of aid given Georgia. The U.S. government has found it virtually impossible to give aid to Azerbaijan due to its ongoing blockade of Armenia and involvement in the conflict in Nagorno-Karabakh.[56] Comparing the rank ordering of these states according to the export control development and their level of FSA aid reveals that this is an inadequate means of predicting such development.

The views of defense and security officials raise a final and important point in terms of nonproliferation export control development due to cost and benefit calculations. In many ways, the potential costs of *not* developing export controls dominated discussion of the issue (rather than the assessment of costs for developing export control policies). First, if they do not develop such measures, it is clear to officials from the NIS that their access to technologies and other forms of aid will be inhibited.[57] Experiences from the Cold War era, when the Soviet republics were likewise "locked out" from this type of trade with and aid from the West, reveal that the costs of such policies are astronomical. The debilitated economic structures, atrophied service programs, and unstable political systems of today are a testament to these costs.

The second rational institutionalist expectation concerning the development of export controls is that states will do so in order to gain access to material, economic, and technological aid from the West. It is clear from interviews with government officials and nongovernment defense experts in the Caucasus that restrictions on such access will inevitably lead to continued dominance by Russia in all aspects of political and economic life. Simply put, development of any mechanisms which promise long- or short-term benefits vis-à-vis Russian penetration and influence in politico-economic affairs promises to produce enormous dividends in the future. This is especially true in Georgia and Azerbaijan, which both resent the Russian influence in military, economic, and political affairs.

When analyzed in this light, the rational institutionalist approach to nonproliferation export control development in the Caucasus provides good explanatory power compared to the other approaches examined in this work. However, when the author questioned government officials about the relative relationship between export control development and rational institutionalist or realist concerns, they immediately answered that security interests were more important. It is clear that Caucasus officials make rational, if "fuzzy," calculations concerning the costs and benefits of developing export controls and other measures. In turn, government officials in the Caucasus see the development of nonproliferation policies as one means of showing that their governments are capable of effectively and efficiently managing the state.[58] However, these calculations certainly contain elements of realist expectations, including fear of Russian dominance and exploitation and the need to develop border controls in order to enhance the viability of the state.

Domestic Politics

The domestic political approach to nonproliferation export control development posits that government policies are strongly influenced by the structure, goals, and power of domestic groups operating within the confines of the political system. In regard to expectations derived from theories of domestic politics, we see little evidence to indicate that this approach is a viable means of explaining export control development in the Caucasus region.[59]

The states of the Caucasus have very immature governments that are largely dominated by powerful presidents. Legislatures and interest groups play very little role in these societies at all, much less in the realm of export controls. It is obvious that the elites in these states do not see nonproliferation export control policies as priorities in terms of the "national interest." Rather, their security interests are preoccupied with issues in which export controls play a secondary role: consolidating hold over territory, preventing the flow of narcotics, refugees, and conventional weapons across their bor-

ders, battling organized criminal groups and corruption, and maintaining
or removing Russian troops on their soil. It is certain that the somewhat inconsistent Western orientation of these states has built a constituency within
their governments in terms of providing offices and officials to negotiate
with the West and to implement parts of resultant nonproliferation programs. It is unclear, however, what influence these groups have within their
respective political systems.

Although these countries qualify as centralized states, this is a commonality within the NIS as a whole and therefore does little to help us explain why some states have developed nonproliferation export control
systems while others have not. In fact, the above-noted occurrence of the illicit arms transfers in the region calls into question the proposition that
states with centralized authority are better equipped to control exports. This
is especially true in the case of Armenia, where one expert has noted that
the Ter-Petrosian government maintains complete control over both the co-
ercive and economic aspects of the state, but does so through corrupt political practices and extortion.[60] As Armenia is not the sole example of an NIS
state allegedly dominated by corruption, it is possible to speculate that
criminal elements represent some of the strongest domestic interest groups
within these countries. These groups, as noted earlier, are probably interested in preventing the development of nonproliferation export controls, especially when such efforts are linked to controlling other types of illicit
trade.

Privatization of the economies of the region has proceeded only haltingly, and it is unclear in any case whether this would create constituencies
that would support, or oppose, the creation of export control policies. Indeed, the state with the most industry of sensitive nature, Armenia, has followed a policy similar to that of the Russian Federation in not privatizing
major industries of this sort. Many segments of the privatized economies
will seek trade and profits wherever they may be found. This is especially
noteworthy in the Caucasus because of the proximity and wealth of states
such as Iran, Iraq, and the other Persian Gulf and Middle Eastern states that
do not have a uniform commitment to nonproliferation.

Conversely, other groups in these societies may see the development of
nonproliferation export control policies as in the state's economic interests
because such policies enhance their ability to trade with the West due to the
relaxation of trade restrictions. It is unclear at this time how influential such
interest groups are. It is clear, however, that companies which could export
moderate- to high-technology products that would be of concern to Western
nonproliferation export control regime members are few in number in the
Caucasus. Their lack of numbers may make their influence relatively weak
despite the fact that these states place great emphasis on exporting in order
to gain economic viability.[61]

All or most of the above evidence mitigates against the development of nonproliferation export controls in the Caucasus. Yet, these states *have* started to develop such systems, even if ever so slightly. Because of the limited development, however, we are left to ponder whether these countries may have developed their systems of nonproliferation export controls further if domestic political influences were not so negative. Additional research is needed to determine why or why not.

Liberal Identity

The Caucasus states have since before their independence associated "democracy" with the "West" and with the idea of a counterbalance to Russian imperialistic dictatorship.[62] After the euphoria of independence wore off, however, the unfamiliarity with democracy and civil liberties in the Western sense became evident. A powerful political figure in the early history of Georgia coldly proclaimed, "Democracy is not a picnic. We will shoot the enemies of democracy on the spot."[63] Similarly, an Azerbaijani leader insisted that he would "prefer 'nationalist dictatorship to non-nationalist democracy.'"[64] Despite such inconsistencies, or perhaps because of them, the final approach employed to attempt to explain nonproliferation export control development in the NIS is that of liberal identity. It is apparent that little evidence exists in the Caucasus to support liberal identity expectations. These countries have exhibited little "sense of community," until recent years, with Western states in export control matters.[65]

The importance that policy-makers place on regular interaction with the liberal community and its advocacy of nonproliferation export controls is very difficult to gauge given that they have seldom interacted with the international nonproliferation regime. Most policy-making is instead focused on internal problems and civil strife. Perhaps some evidence for liberal identity does exist in the fact that all of these states have signed and ratified the Nuclear Nonproliferation Treaty, and committed themselves to non-nuclear status. However, when one looks at the direction of their respective foreign policies, there may be less credibility given by Western members of the nonproliferation regime to states that identify strongly with Iran (both Azerbaijan and Armenia, at times), with Turkey (Azerbaijan),[66] and with Russia (Armenia), and in states in which Iran recruits scientists for work on its nuclear power and purported weapons projects (Georgia and Armenia).[67]

Indeed, the strongest evidence for an explanation of export control development based on liberal identification is found in Georgia and Armenia. Some Georgian officials, when asked, responded that they believed that identification with the West was the most important reason for the development of their nonproliferation policies.[68] However, more senior officials were uniform in their assessment of the major influences on the creation of the draft export control law. First, border controls were the most important aspect of their export control system because they would increase the viability of the state. Second, the "transportation corridor" was the most important driving force behind further development of export controls. Neither of these explanations support the identity approach.

In Armenia, identity takes another form. Just as the Armenian export control system is designed along Russian lines, so is the state's reasons for developing export controls. While apparently copying the Russian export control system, the Armenians also apparently copied the Russian desire for regional political leadership. As stated by an Armenian official, "Armenia wishes to be the leader of the Caucasus states in the development of nonproliferation policies."[69] Indeed, this leadership is an extension of Armenian leadership within the Caucasus and in the Russian-dominated CIS. Even though Russia is a long-standing participant in the nonproliferation regime as a signatory of the NPT and a member of the Nuclear Suppliers Group, identification with the Russian Federation does not yet—and it is questionable if it ever will—qualify as liberal identification.[70] Finally, in terms of showing interest in controlling the flow of sensitive materials toward illiberal states, there seems to be very little evidence.[71] Indeed, the strategic importance of the Caucasus states (as well as the Central Asian states) for most U.S. policy-makers and analysts seems to be the potential that they have, also noted above, as transit routes *to* the pariah states on their borders.[72]

In addition, these countries have moved only haltingly toward creating the normative and institutional bases of liberal, democratic governments.[73] The Ter-Petrosian government in Armenia has been accused often of corruption, election fraud, and other tendencies toward authoritarianism. The regime perceived in the West as the most "democratic," the Shevardnadze regime in Georgia, was put into power by Russian interests, sought to put down political unrest by use of military force, and has been described as a "one-man democracy."[74]

At the same time, Armenia and Azerbaijan have each applied for full membership in the Council of Europe, and Georgia is, according to most observers, the most European of the Caucasus states.[75] All of these states have launched intensive campaigns to convince the West, especially the United States, that they are indeed part of the democratic-capitalist community. For example, in visits to the United States in January and April 1997, Armenian Prime Minister Sarkissian and Ambassador to the United States Shugarian claimed that Armenia had "held to its commitments to reform and liberalize the economy"; that "democracy . . . is our highest priority"; and that "Democracy, with all its political and economic consequences, has not become just a way of life, but a means of survival for us."[76]

While the evidence presented here does not convince one to attribute the bulk of nonproliferation export control development in the Caucasus to aspects of liberal identification, it does seem that this approach may need to be kept in mind in order to promote further development in the future. Certainly, Western nonproliferation regime members will want to heighten the liberal identification of the Caucasus states in order to promote nonproliferation.

CONCLUSION

To summarize these findings for the Caucasus, realist approaches provide the most compelling explanations for nonproliferation export control development in the region. Many officials stated that nonproliferation export controls played an important role in the security of the state because export controls inherently place emphasis on the control of a state's borders. Because of the security environment in the Caucasus, which is fraught with breakaway regions, irredentist and multinationalist tendencies, control over geographical space is still the paramount, and unfulfilled, function of the state. While nonproliferation export controls play a small role in the terms of political debate surrounding these issues, government leaders in each state in the Caucasus recognize the potential for transit of WMD-related materials or technology through the region. Additionally, in the one state which has established territorial integrity, Armenia, export controls seem to play a somewhat more important role in what is termed here as the secondary function of the state: maintaining a military/political balance with rivals such as Turkey and preventing the increase in power of enemies (in this case, via the diversion of radiological material to Azerbaijan). Realist explanations provide definite insight as to why nonproliferation export controls have not been developed further. First, the fact that other security priorities are more important has inhibited the development of export control structures. Second, states that possess little in the way of WMD technologies have little incentive to think of export controls as a means of balancing the power of others. Finally, states that must consider the interests and reactions of a powerful and potentially domineering regional hegemon may have little interest in developing export controls if they see that hegemon as consistently and willfully circumventing its own control system in order to provide sensitive technologies to states such as Iran. Finally, the fact that this hegemon has been an active player in the proliferation of an extraordinary amount of conventional weapons, as well as of chemical weapons–capable ballistic missiles, into the region may send signals about its desire to see development of export controls in these states and breakaway regions.

A note of caution is in order concerning the role of realist expectations and the development of nonproliferation export controls in the Caucasus. While it best explains such development for the first five years of statehood in the region, evidence presented in the above analysis may indicate that security issues will *not* promote *further* development of export controls. As the

Caucasus governments only see nonproliferation as of secondary importance in terms of national priorities (behind such issues as establishing sovereignty over their territory or protecting irredentist groups), further development may languish if these states devote resources in accordance to such priorities. In addition, security concerns, such as the problems over Nagorno-Karabakh and Abkhazia, which in 1997 are latent, may again flare up. If so, the proliferation of light and heavy conventional weapons into the region, as well as the transfer of weapons of mass destruction in the form of Russian ballistic missiles sold to Armenia, will probably work against the development of export controls in any meaningful sense.

Fortunately, perhaps, realism is not alone in providing some explanatory power in terms of nonproliferation development in the Caucasus. Rational institutionalist approaches are also credible, albeit to a lesser extent. In Armenia, much of the basis for export controls seem indirectly linked to nuclear safety issues of concern to the IAEA, the European Bank for Recovery and Development, and the United States. However, for the most part, Armenia has been unable to turn this into increased high-technology investment from the West.[77] In Georgia, export control development is important to the state because of the security threats inherent in the future "transportation corridor" that Georgian officials hope will make the country a major trade artery between East and West. While this has been interpreted above as largely a security factor in terms of nonproliferation export control development, it is inescapable that lack of an export control system would make this "corridor" a "one-way street," i.e., an outlet for raw materials from the Central Asian republics rather than a "two-way street" which could bring about the movement of high-technology goods and investment from the West.

The domestic politics and liberal identity approaches seemed to play a lesser role in explaining the development of nonproliferation policies in the Caucasus due to the absence of political constituencies that support such efforts and tenuous patterns of identification with the West (as opposed to Russia, Iran, or Turkey). Policy efforts based on their tenets, such as encouragement of nonproliferation-related interest groups and the promotion of democratic norms, should not be neglected. Indeed, the security, political, and economic dynamics of the Caucasus region probably will demand a multifaceted approach by the West in promoting nonproliferation export controls there. The West has a stake in the success of such efforts. As noted by U.S. Deputy Secretary of State Strobe Talbot, "If economic and political reform in the countries of the Caucasus . . . does not succeed—if internal and cross-border conflicts simmer and flare—the region could become a breeding ground of terrorism, a hotbed of religious and political extremism, and a battleground for outright war."[78]

NOTES

1. Nicholas Awde, "Introduction," in John Wright, Suzanne Goldenberg, and Richard Schofield, eds., *Transcaucasian Boundaries* (London: UCL, 1996), p. 1.

2. Concerning drugs, see Bureau for International Narcotics and Law Enforcement Affairs, "U.S. Department of State International Narcotics Control Strategy Report," March 1996. Other types of transits are covered in the text.

3. FY 1995 Annual Report on "U.S. Government Assistance to and Cooperative Activities with the New Independent States of the Former Soviet Union," April 1996. Prepared by the Office of the Coordinator of U.S. Assistance to the NIS submitted pursuant to section 104 of the FREEDOM Support Act (Public Law 102–511), p. 4.

4. Azerbaijan is positioned to serve a similar role as a "roadway to Iran" for Russian goods except that the Aliev government there has strained relations with the Yeltsin regime, which includes disagreements between the two governments concerning whether Russian military units should be stationed in Nagorno-Karabakh as CIS-mandated peacekeepers. This may not matter in terms of illicit transfers of materials, although the fact that Azerbaijan is the only one of the countries covered here which does not rely on Russian troops for border control makes it probable that illicit transfers from Russia to Iran via this route would require additional payoffs within the Azerbaijani government. Even if relations between the two states remain sour, Russian products may in any case transit unimpeded across the Caspian Sea to Iran.

5. "Georgia with Libya, Russia, Switzerland and Turkey," *Nonproliferation Review* 4 (Fall 1996), p. 121. Georgian officials assert that 600 grams of HEU from Sukhumi have turned up missing or are unaccounted for. It is unclear what their sources of information are, given that the government does not control the Abkhaz region (personal interviews with Georgian Ministry of Foreign Affairs officials, July 1997).

6. See the Statement of Glenn E. Schweitzer before the Permanent Subcommittee on Investigations, Committee on Government Affairs, U.S. Senate, 13 March 1996.

7. Ibid. See also Center for Nonproliferation Studies, Commonwealth of Independent States Nuclear Databases (CNS Database), Armenia (Monterey, CA: Monterey Institute for International Studies, 1995), and Robert S. Norris, "The Soviet Nuclear Archipelago," *Arms Control Today* 1–2 (1992). Spent fuel from reactors of this type, which would necessarily contain plutonium, cannot be directly used in nuclear weapons and is highly radioactive. See Anthony Nero, *A Guidebook to Nuclear Reactors* (Berkeley: University of California Press, 1979), pp. 186–99; and K. Hannerz and F. Segerberg, "Paper 5. Proliferation Risks Associated with Different Back-end Fuel Cycles for Light Water Reactors," in SIPRI, *Nuclear Energy and Nuclear Weapon Proliferation* (London: Taylor and Francis, 1979), pp. 91–103. According to Rotblat, this material is not useful to a nonstate adversary unless the group is,

"large, very well financed, [and] technically competent . . . with a secure base of operations and a few members willing to risk radiation injury." See J. Rotblat, "Nuclear Energy and Nuclear Weapon Proliferation," in SIPRI, *Nuclear Energy and Nuclear Weapon Proliferation*, pp. 373–435.

8. Such a theft might be attractive for a group with black market contacts in a country with a clandestine nuclear weapons program and an established enrichment plant. See Rotblat, "Nuclear Energy," p. 403.

9. Hannerz and Segerberg, "Proliferation Risks," pp. 91–92.

10. See Paul Goble, "Russia: Analysis from Washington—Using Minsk in the Caucasus," *RFE/RL Features*, 8 April 1997; "Baku Alarmed by Moscow Arms Supplies to Armenia," *Reuter* 4, April 1997; and "Russian Parliament to Investigate Alleged Illegal Arms Supplies to Armenia," *OMRI Daily Digest*, 21 February 1997.

11. Information on arms transfers from Russia to Armenia is available from various sources. Prominent among these are the Stockholm International Peace Research Institute's SIPRI Arms Transfer Database (1997), and *Jane's Defense Weekly*, April 1997, p. 15.

12. See "More Fallout from 'Yerevangate' Arms Scandal," *RFE/RL Newsline* 1, 17 April 1997.

13. For views of Russian, Iranian, and Turkish historical and contemporary interests in the Caucasus, see Margot Light, "Russia and Transcaucasia," in Wright *et al.*, pp. 34–53; and Suzanne Goldenberg, *Pride of Small Nations: The Caucasus and Post-Soviet Disorder* (London: Zed, 1994), pp. 46–69; Shireen Hunter, *The Caucasus in Transition: Nation-Building and Conflict* (Washington, D.C.: The Center for Strategic and International Studies, 1994), pp. 142–78; William Hale, "Turkey, the Black Sea and Transcaucasia," in Wright et al., pp. 54–70; and Fred Halliday, "Condemned to React, Unable to Influence: Iran and Transcaucasia," in Wright et al., pp. 71–88.

14. Azerbaijan does, however, have several nuclear waste storage sites as well as a small chemical industry that could be capable of weaponization. See CNS Database; interview with U.S. State Department official, 7 August 1997.

15. "Khamidov Says Baku has Nuclear Weapons, Delivery Means," *FBIS-SOV*-92-236, 7 December 1992; discussions with Turan Experts Group, Turan News Agency, July 1997.

17. International Atomic Energy Agency, *Nuclear Research Reactors in the World*, Reference Data Series No. 3 (Vienna: IAEA, 1991). There have been reports in the open source literature that Georgia sold part of its cache of HEU from this reactor to Uzbekistan, which personal interviews with Georgian government officials confirm. Also, the United States apparently made a deal to purchase this uranium at market value and have it reprocessed in Russia. However this deal was held up, apparently, by Russian protests over the United States not paying $1 million in reprocessing costs. See Misha Dzhindzhikhashvili, "Georgia Uranium Sale," *Associated Press* wire report, 7 January 1997; personal interviews with Georgian Ministry of Foreign Affairs officials, July 1997; and "Moscow Said Ready to Thwart Nuclear

Safety Deal," *Reuter*, 6 January 1997, and "Russia Ready to Accept Uranium from Georgia," *OMRI Daily Digest*, 13 January 1997. Georgian government officials are puzzled as to why the United States has not offered to buy this HEU from Georgia outright. They assert that this could probably be done for less than the inflated price that the Russians are insisting upon to reprocess the material (interviews with Georgian Ministry of Foreign Affairs officials, July 1997). U.S. Department of Energy officials claim that protections on this material are "cost effective and successful." However, no defining criteria for how such assessments are made have been forthcoming (personal correspondence with Department of Energy officials, September-October 1997).

18. CNS Database.

19. Conventional weapons, both small arms and heavy equipment, find their way to the Caucasus states in several ways. Besides the sensational sales of Russian equipment to Armenia noted above and discussed further below, and illicit transfers which we know little about, there have apparently been a large number of weapons transfers from Russian border and "peacekeeping" units to governments and insurgents in the region. Personal interviews with Georgian and Azerbaijani government and nongovernment analysts confirm this. Armenian officials deny any transfer of Russian weapons to or through their country or Nagorno-Karabakh. See Aves, "Politics, Parties and Presidents"; Light, "Russia and Transcaucasia," pp. 51–52; *Moskovskie Novosti*, 20 December 1992; and personal interviews with Azerbaijani, Georgian, and Armenian officials, July 1997.

20. Light, "Russia and Transcaucasia," p. 51.

21. Personal experience indicates that passage may be occasioned between states in the region without inspection of vehicles. How commonplace this type of transit is remains open to question.

22. "Customs Official Outlines Efforts to Curb Corruption," *FBIS-USR*-94–048, 5 May 1994.

23. See Richard Woff, "The Border Troops of the Russian Federation," *Jane's Intelligence Review* 7, 1 February 1995, p. 70.

24. See Craft and Grillot, "Tools and Methods."

25. Government Enactment 537 "On the Establishment of a Commission for Export Controls on Primary Products, Materials, Equipment, Technologies and Services Used in the Creation of Weapons of Mass Destruction," 3 November 1992; and Enactment 121 "On Matters of Export Controls on Primary Products, Materials, Equipment, Technologies and Services Used in the Creation of Weapons of Mass Destruction and Missile Delivery Systems," 19 March 1993. See also *JPRS* "Nonproliferation Issues," 10 May 1992, pp. 10–11, and *FBIS-SOV*-93–085 "Commission to Oversee Export Control of Weapons Materials," 5 May 1993.

26. Interviews with Armenian government officials from the former Ministry of Finance and Ministry of Foreign Affairs, July 1997.

27. "List of Materials, Substances, Equipment, and Dual-Use Technologies Export of Which Must be Licensed," described in U.S. Department of State, "Armenia

Country Commercial Guide," Office of Coordinator for Business Affairs, June 1995.

28. According to Armenian officials, there are at most one or two exports per year which fall under these controls. Despite this small number, no Armenian official was willing or able to say to what countries or end-users such exports had been made in the past. Personal interviews with Armenian Ministry of Foreign Affairs and Ministry of Finance officials, July 1997.

29. Personal interviews with members of export controls working group, government of Armenia, July 1997.

30. "List of Materials, Substances, Equipment, and Dual-Use Technologies Export of Which Must be Licensed," described in U.S. Department of State, "Armenia Country Commercial Guide," Office of Coordinator for Business Affairs, June 1995.

31. Ibid.

32. Personal interviews with Armenian government officials, July 1997.

33. Armenian officials described the authority given to their border controls officials as a "catch-all" mechanism on the basis of their empowerment to stop any export, import, or transit that was "suspicious" (personal interviews with Armenian Export Control Working Group officials, July 1997).

34. This is scheduled to change. In the spring of 1997, the Georgian parliament was presented with a draft export control law which had been constructed by the Military-Industrial Subcommittee of the Committee on Defense and Security (with the assistance of the Commission on Export Controls, Ministry of Trade and Foreign Economic Relations, Ministry of Foreign Affairs, and State Department of State Border Forces). Personal interviews with officials in these offices (including parliament) indicate that they see little threat of serious alteration of this bill when it is voted on in the next session of parliament (fall 1997).

35. "Government Decree Restricts Exports, Imports," *FBIS-SOV*-92–190, 30 September 1992.

36. Georgian officials assumed that the Ministry of Trade and Foreign Economic Relations would retain all licensing and list maintenance functions under the new law. This staff, according to the chairman of the Export Control Commission, would be about six to eight people. These officials also assumed that the border forces would retain the enforcement function, and that the Ministry of Foreign Affairs would handle all bilateral and multilateral issues concerning nonproliferation aid and cooperation as well as compliance with dictates of the various arrangements of the nonproliferation regime (NPT, IAEA, Wassenaar Arrangement, NSG, MTCR, CWC, BWC, Australia Group). From personal interviews and correspondence, July–August 1997.

37. Tbilisi Aviation Enterprise has operated since 1941 in the construction of various aircraft types, including its current product, the SU-25 TK (a ground attack aircraft). The Aviation Enterprise also produced K-10 wing rockets, which were designed to carry nuclear warheads delivered by TU-16 and TU-95 strategic bombers. See Irakli Aladashvili, "Problems of Developing a Military Industrial

Structure in Georgia," *Army and Society in Georgia* 4, November 1996.

38. Interviews with Georgian Ministry of Foreign Affairs officials, July 1997. See also "Abkhaz Peacekeepers' Future Unclear," *RFE/RL Newsline*, 1 August 1997.

39. Interviews with Georgian State Department of State Border Forces and Ministry of Foreign Affairs officials, July 1997.

40. See U.S. Department of State, "Azerbaijan Country Commercial Guide," Office of Coordinator for Business Affairs, June 1995.

41. Interviews with Armenian Ministry of Foreign Affairs officials and non-government defense experts, July 1997.

42. Control of conventional weapons makes sense, in realist terms especially, because in all but one of these states (the exception being Armenia), internal security problems threaten the very survival of the state. Azerbaijan has been involved in a terrible civil and interstate war (with Armenia) in the Nagorno-Karabakh region, Georgia does not have control over Ajeria or Abkhazia. All have severe problems with organized criminal groups, which are largely outside the control of government, but have led to allegations of rampant corruption among government officials. See Craft, "The Caucasus States," Gary Bertsch, ed., *Restraining the Spread of the Soviet Arsenal: NIS Nonproliferation Export Controls Status Report* (Athens, GA: Center for International Trade and Security, 1997), 64–73, for more on these issues.

43. It could be argued that the focus on conventional weapons control more effectively meets the security needs of these countries, and therefore explains the *lack* of development of nonproliferation export controls in a region where governmental resources are extremely scarce.

44. Interviews with Georgian government officials from the Ministry of Foreign Affairs, State Department of State Border Forces, Ministry of Trade and Foreign Economic Relations, Committee on Export Controls, and the Military and Industrial Subcommittee of the Committee on Defense and Security (parliament). When in August 1997, the Georgian government hosted an international conference, "Black Sea Coast: Historical, Ecological, Ethnographical and Defense Aspects," export controls were covered in terms of how they affected state strategies on border control in the presentation "Relationship of Nonproliferation and Export Controls with Border Defense (Overview of Present Situation)," by Mamuka Kudava, head of Disarmament and Arms Control Department, Military-Political Directorate, Ministry of Foreign Affairs.

45. Personal interview with official from the Bilateral Economic Affairs section of the Armenian Ministry of Foreign Affairs, by Scott Jones (CITS), at the Hotel Washington, 25 September 1996.

46. For an argument that WMD do not provide stability in unstable regions, see Peter Lavoy, "Nuclear Myths and the Causes of Nuclear Proliferation," *Security Studies* 2 (Spring/Summer 1993), pp. 192–212.

47. It is important to note that the military forces of the breakaway Karabakh region, in their quest for independence from Azerbaijan (as perhaps a first step in political unification with Armenia) have seen fit to occupy what constitutes of one-fifth of all Azerbaijani territory.

48. See, for instance, Sheila Harden, ed., *Small is Dangerous: Micro States in a Macro World* (New York: St. Martin's, 1985); Charles Morrison and Astri Suhrke, *Strategies of Survival: The Foreign Policy Dilemmas of Smaller Asian States* (New York: St. Martin's, 1979); and Michael Handel, *Weak States in the International System* (London: Frank Cass, 1981).

49. See Goldenberg, *Pride of Small Nations*, pp. 92–94; and Goldenberg, "Background Note: Reflections on Cockney," in Wright et al., *Transcaucasian Boundaries*, pp. 11–14.

50. According to Armenian officials, the presence of Russian forces in Armenia is a necessary precondition to security of Armenia and peace in the Caucasus. Russian forces serve to deter hostile actions by Turkey, which would presumably result from the military and political defeat of that state's staunch ally in the region, Azerbaijan. Interviews with Armenian officials, Ministry of Foreign Affairs, July 1997.

51. Alexander Rondeli, "Georgia in the Post-Soviet Space," *Caucasian Regional Studies* 1 (1996), 96–100. Accordingly, the Georgian Ministry of Foreign Affairs has created an Analytical Center to help "figure out" what Russia's interests in the Caucasus are, and what actions the Russian Federation will take to preserve those interests. Rondeli is the head.

52. For more evidence of Russian transgressions on WMD and conventional weapons control norms, see Richard Speier, "Statement before the Subcommittee on International Security, Proliferation, and Federal Services of the Committee on Governmental Affairs, U.S. Senate, 5 June 1997 (reprinted in *The Monitor: Nonproliferation, Demilitarization and Arms Control* 3, Summer 1997).

53. The concern in these countries over the influence of Russia in the region and the potential for Russian interference in regional affairs (including the difficulties of ousting Russian military forces from the region) is explored in Paul Goble, "Outflanked on CFE," *RFE/RL Newsline*, 2 May 1997. In this article, Goble argues that each of these states, despite their concerns over the prospects that the CFE flank modification agreement "may have the effect of legitimizing Russian dominance over the territory of a country that no longer exists, namely, the Soviet Union," have agreed to the proposed modifications.

54. Conversations with U.S. Department of State officials reveal that money from the U.S. Nonproliferation Disarmament Fund can be used to develop nonproliferation programs in the Caucasus states based on the "indiscretion term" of this funding; i.e., the money can be spent despite restrictions on other aid such as FREEDOM Support Act.

55. See "Second Unit of Armenian Nuclear Power Plant Back in Service Yerevan," *OMRI Daily Digest*, 5 February 1997; "U.S. Aid to Armenia," *OMRI Daily Digest*, 5 February 1997; and "Safety of Armenian Nuclear Plant Key Topic in Talks with EBRD," *OMRI Daily Digest*, 20 December 1996. In regard to U.S. aid, it should be noted that the $95 million in FSA aid to Armenia in 1997 (down from $150 million in 1996) is subject to Section 498A(a)(6) of the FREEDOM Support Act.

56. See Office of the Coordinator of U.S. Assistance to the NIS, FY 1995 Annual Report on "U.S. Government Assistance to and Cooperative Activities with the New Independent States of the Former Soviet Union," April 1996. U.S. efforts to give assistance to Azerbaijan have not been promoted by statements of former Interior Minister of Azerbaijan Iskendor Hamidov, who claims that the country has been able to produce or buy nuclear weapons ("Khamidov Says Baku has Nuclear Weapons, Delivery 'Means,'" *FBIS-SOV-92-236*, 7 December 1992).

57. Interviews with U.S. State Department officials.

58. Interviews and correspondence with Azerbaijani, Armenian, and Georgian government officials, April-August 1997.

59. Georgian Ministry of Foreign Affairs officials were quick to point out that the lack of domestic pressure may well help to explain the lack of export control development in Georgia. Interviews conducted July 1997.

60. For allegations concerning Armenian political practices, see Jonathan Aves, "Politics, Parties and Presidents in Transcaucasia," *Caucasian Regional Studies* 1 (1996), pp. 5–23. The Ter-Petrosian government is also suspected of distorting the results of the last parliamentary elections (in the summer of 1995) and the last presidential election (in the fall of 1996); see, for example, Aves, "Politics, Parties and Presidents," fn. 25, p. 13, and "European Parliament Condemns Presidential Elections in Armenia," *OMRI Daily Digest*, 21 November 1996.

61. According to one Armenian official, the sensitive industry in the country, because they are government owned and not in a position to export much of their technology, have very little chance of influencing government in terms of exports. Interview with Ministry of Foreign Affairs officials, July 1997.

62. See David Zurabishvili, "Shevardnadze's One-Man Democracy," *War Report* (September 1996).

63. Statement of Dzhabi Ioseliani, leader of the powerful military-criminal organization "Mkhedrioni," quoted in Zurabishvili, "Shevardnadze's One-Man Democracy."

64. Azerbaijani leader quoted in Hunter, p. 79.

65. Furthermore, it seems problematic to classify the institutions that these states do identify with (the Commonwealth of Independent States in terms of foreign policy, which is exemplified by its members' acceptance of the Minsk Accord on Export Controls) as "liberal." In every one of these states important aspects of their export control system—especially with regard to border patrols most notably in the Georgian regions of Ajeria and Abkhazia)—are performed by armed forces of the Russian Federation, giving further pause to such a classification. Finally, the fact that these states were historically the *target* of the international nonproliferation regime has led to real difficulties in terms of their liberal identification.

66. Illustrative of the region's tenuous identity with the West is a 1996 poll conducted by the Turan News Agency. In this poll, fifty experts (analysts, political scientists, party members, and media) were asked which countries were considered allies of Azerbaijan. Their rank orderings were (Western countries are included for

comparative purposes): 1) Turkey; 2) Georgia; 3) Ukraine; 4) Israel; 5) United States (Russia—12th; China—13th; Iran—15th). In the top 10, only 3 were Western states (United States, United Kingdom—6th; Germany—7th). When asked which countries they *would like* Azerbaijan to be strategic partners with, the rank orderings were: 1) Turkey; 2) Turkmenistan; 3) Georgia; 4) Ukraine; 5) Kazakhstan (United States—8th; Russia—10th; Iran—11th; China—14th). In the top 10, again, 2 were Western (Germany—6th, United States—7th), with Japan also included (8th). See Turan Expert Group, "Search of Partners for Azerbaijan," *Turan News Agency*, Analytical Review by Turan, Issue 267; see also Suzanne Goldenberg, *Pride of Small Nations* (London: Zed, 1994).

67. See the statement of Glenn Schweitzer before the Permanent Subcommittee on Investigations, Committee on Government Affairs, U.S. Senate, 13 March 1996.

68. In Georgia and Armenia, this typically took the form of noting the common Christian heritage and long history of interaction with Europe.

69. Statement by Ministry of Foreign Affairs official, Armenia, July 1997.

70. It is hard to discount the notion that Armenian "identity with the West" has ulterior motives, such as the denial of approval, aid, and assistance to Azerbaijan. In effect, it seems that Armenian officials are eager to recruit the West as the West is to recruit Armenia. The difference is important. In the Armenian case, the "enemy" or "other" is Azerbaijan and Turkey, and therefore pan-Turkism. Turkey, while hardly being in a cultural or political sense an integral part of the West, is nonetheless included in most Western political and security arrangements. For the West, the "other" includes Iran, which is for Armenia its second-greatest trading partner and an important ally against Turkey—and one that Armenia guards jealously because of Iran's large ethnically Azerbaijani population, which Armenians perceive could throw Iran into Azerbaijan's arms at any time.

71. See, for instance, Misha Dzhindzhikhashvili, "Georgia Offers Uranium for Sale," *Associated Press* wire report, 7 January 1997. The United States was attempting to buy highly enriched uranium from the government of Georgia, with Russian concurrence, probably because of the intensity of Iranian interest in the nuclear expertise of Georgian officials associated with the Tbilisi Institute of Physics. U.S. efforts were deemed necessary due to the absence of nonproliferation export controls and materials protection capabilities of Georgia.

72. See, for example, the statement of U.S. Deputy Secretary of State Strobe Talbot, "A Farewell to Flashman: American Policy in the Caucasus and Central Asia," at the Johns Hopkins School of Advanced International Studies, 21 July 1997. See also the many accounts of illicit weapons and WMD materials proliferation through the Caucasus region noted by Richard Speier before Congress (note 52 above), in the Monterey Institute for International Studies database "CNS Illicit Transactions Involving Nuclear Materials from the Former Soviet Union," and the report by William Potter, director, Center for Nonproliferation Studies, "Less Well-Known Cases of Nuclear Terrorism and Nuclear Diversion in the Former Soviet Union," August 1997.

73. Freedom House scores for these countries are as follows (political rights/civil liberties ratings): Armenia 4/4 "partly free," Azerbaijan 6/6 "not free," Georgia 4/5 "partly free." See Freedom House, *Freedom in the World: The Annual Survey of Political Rights and Civil Liberties, 1995–1996.*

74. Zurabishvili, "Shevardnadze's One-Man Democracy."

75. See "Council of Europe Official on Azerbaijan's Membership Chances," *RFE/RL Newsline* 5 May 1997. In addition, Azerbaijan was praised by the International Monetary Fund for its cooperation with that organization, and in May 1997 a loan of $230 million was confirmed. At the same time, Armenia has had difficulties in obtaining portions of the $150 million credit approved from the IMF in 1996, "IMF Confirms New Loan to Azerbaijan, Sets Conditions for Armenia," *RFE/RL Newsline* 5 May 1997.

76. See "Address by His Excellency Dr. Armen Sarkissian, Prime Minister of the Republic of Armenia" at the Center for Strategic and International Studies, Washington D.C., 10 January 1997; and speech by Armenian Ambassador to the United States Rouben Shugarian, "Armenia Today: the Commonwealth of Independent States and Regional Reality," to the Fletcher School of Law and Diplomacy, Boston, 16 April 1997.

77. Interview with Economic Department, Ministry of Foreign Affairs, Republic of Armenia, July 1997.

78. Talbot, "Farewell to Flashman."

NINE

FSU EXPORT CONTROL DEVELOPMENT
The Factors That Matter

SUZETTE R. GRILLOT, KEITH D. WOLFE,
AND MICHAEL BECK

The preceding chapters of this book help us to better understand the status of efforts to construct nonproliferation export control systems in the states of the former Soviet Union, and to assess how useful four international relations approaches are for explaining the export control development observed. We believe the case studies offer important policy, methodological, and theoretical insights. First, those in the policy community should gain a greater appreciation of the proliferation threats and nonproliferation opportunities in the region. Second, the book offers a method for more objectively measuring export control development in states of the FSU, and across states. Third, practitioners gain an understanding of the forces motivating decision-makers in the FSU, and can use this to more effectively promote export control development both in the former Soviet Union and globally. Finally, the study determines the relative utility of various theories of international relations for understanding export control development.

While the Soviet period limited study in the region, the post-breakup period afforded analysts exceptional research opportunities. For the contributors to this study, the political changes in the former Soviet Union allowed in-depth examinations of export control development as a part of ongoing state-building efforts. Moreover, because nonproliferation initiatives in the West have focused on enhancing the ability of the FSU to control strategic technology, the study affords the possibility of assessing the impact of these efforts. By examining the driving forces behind the development of nonproliferation export control policies, practices, and procedures, we come to better appreciate what is prompting these governments to address the potential leakage of weapons and weapons-related items from their territories. In particular, we can ascertain the importance of varying factors, such as security threats, democracy, identity, material inducements, and domestic politics, for explaining the development of nonproliferation policies.

This concluding chapter synthesizes the findings of the individual case studies presented in this volume, and puts into context their implications for policy-makers and analysts. First, we review the trends of export control development in the states of the former Soviet Union. Next, we discuss and compare the driving forces behind export control development in light of the theoretical approaches employed. In closing, the theoretical and policy implications of the study's findings are suggested and some final observations regarding the future of export control development in the FSU are offered.

TRENDS OF EXPORT CONTROL DEVELOPMENT IN THE FSU

All the states of the former Soviet Union possess at least some elements of a national export control system. They differ, however, in the degree to which they have developed all elements of an export control system, which include: licensing procedures, control lists, international regime participation, catch-all provisions, training mechanisms, bureaucratic process, customs authority, verification procedures, penalties for export control violators, and information-gathering and -sharing methods. They also differ in the extent to which they have moved beyond mere policies for each of these elements toward actual implementation.

Based on the empirical evidence presented throughout this volume, it is apparent that some elements of an export control system are consistently more developed throughout the FSU (see Table 1). A clear example of this can be seen in the "Licensing" and "Control Lists" elements, which across the fourteen cases are among the most developed of all export control structures. This is not especially revealing given that an export control system lacks a foundation without a licensing system for sensitive exports and some type of control list that specifies the items requiring an export license. In fact, in all the states that exhibit a medium to high level of export control development, both the licensing and control list elements are highly developed. The states with the lowest levels of development on these elements are those of Central Asia and Georgia, and their lower scores are indicative of this missing foundation of an export control system. It is worth noting that most states develop licensing mechanisms in order to regulate the foreign trade of other commodities, such as short-supply items. The presence of export licensing mechanisms in some states may have more to do with controlling these commodities than with controlling strategic trade.

Enforcement mechanisms also represent a critical component of any export control system. We find that the export control systems in the FSU

TABLE 1

Comparison of Element Scores Across Cases, 1997
(Percentage of Ideal Score)

	Licensing	Lists Regimes	Int'l	Catch-All	Training Process	Bureaucratic Authority	Customs	Verification	Penalties	Information
Russia	92%	100%	96%	0%	89%	92%	83%	50%	67%	80%
Ukraine	100%	100%	100%	50%	66%	100%	66%	66%	90%	90%
Belarus	100%	100%	83%	0%	50%	100%	66%	33%	50%	62%
Kazakhstan	100%	83%	33%	0%	83%	80%	66%	33%	58%	58%
Estonia	83%	100%	58%	0%	50%	83%	66%	50%	50%	50%
Latvia	83%	100%	63%	0%	66%	83%	66%	77%	50%	66%
Lithuania	83%	100%	58%	0%	44%	83%	66%	33%	50%	33%
Kyrgyzstan	66%	66%	0%	0%	0%	17%	58%	0%	25%	0%
Tajikistan	17%	0%	0%	0%	0%	0%	50%	0%	25%	0%
Turkmenistan	17%	0%	0%	0%	0%	0%	50%	0%	25%	0%
Uzbekistan	33%	0%	0%	0%	0%	17%	67%	0%	25%	0%
Armenia	100%	100%	37%	0%	0%	75%	50%	17%	33%	12%
Azerbaijan	42%	100%	4%	0%	0%	33%	66%	0%	33%	12%
Georgia	33%	33%	0%	0%	0%	0%	66%	0%	33%	15%

have relatively underdeveloped enforcement structures—which include "Customs Authority," "Verification," "Penalties," and "Catch-All"—in comparison to other aspects of their systems. Interestingly, the customs authorities in the states with the lowest level of overall development actually compare quite well with Western standards. Because customs control often serves as an important line of defense for export control, such a finding may prove heartening. However, as both the chapters on the Caucasus and Central Asia point out, customs plays more of a role in broader security initiatives and in duty collection than in export control functions, such as searching for illicit or illegal transfers of materials and technologies. In both of these regions, states are more concerned with intercepting drugs and contraband than dual-use and weapons-related technologies.

Domestic agencies also play a central role in determining the level of export control development. Concerning the closely related elements of "Bureaucratic Process" and "Information Gathering and Sharing," we find that they are strongly correlated with overall levels of export control development. For example, in states such as Ukraine and Russia, which have higher levels of overall development, bureaucratic processes are relatively elaborate and decision-making is often interagency in nature. In states with exceptionally low levels of export control development, such as Georgia and the states of Central Asia, there are few agencies that have competence in export control, and there are no formal mechanisms for states to resolve disputes or to implement policy.

In the area of information gathering and sharing, most of the states score comparatively low, which may reflect the legacy of Soviet secrecy. Many of the FSU states are hesitant to share information with other states about the number of licenses issued and denied, and prosecutions of export control violations. This may stem from fear that such information could reflect poorly on their export control systems if, for example, there have been no prosecutions and few license denials. Even in Russia, information on export licenses of strategic technology is regarded as "sensitive." Russia has yet to report any denials of export control violations to the NSG and it lobbied against important information sharing provisions that were to have been introduced into the Wassenaar Arrangement. However, some states, such as Russia and Ukraine, have undertaken educational efforts designed to inform exporters of strategic technology about national export control laws and regulations. Until exporters in the FSU come to understand export control procedures, there remains the very real threat that they will unknowingly provide technology, equipment, and other items to proliferants. Throughout the FSU, the majority of enterprises exporting strategic technology remain to varying degrees under state control, which should make efforts to regulate exports more manageable. The challenge, however, comes in the legal structure of the FSU which gives these enterprises greater freedom to pursue international contracts and to market their wares abroad. Moreover, many enterprises that struggle in efforts to find foreign buyers employ the services of middlemen and export consultants who are adept at eluding regulations of all kinds, including export controls.

Although the information-sharing element remains underdeveloped throughout the FSU, an even more pressing task is training export control personnel. Only Russia, which inherited a small Soviet export control cadre, had a personnel base upon which to build. Other states have been faced with learning the many facets of export control from scratch. The United States and other Western countries have provided training (through seminars, conferences, on-site training, the provision of equipment, etc.) for many agencies and officials in the FSU. The existence of most training efforts in the FSU can largely be attributed to these assistance efforts. Not surprisingly, the Caucasus and Central Asian states lack trained officials and training programs, largely because the United States and other states have yet to provide it. Some states, such as Kyrgyzstan, have requested assistance in training customs officers and other export control officials, but had received very little in the way of assistance as of 1997.

The final element concerns "International Regimes." The case studies suggest that states with the most sophisticated export control systems tend to have higher scores for this element owing to either outright membership in, or adherence to, the multilateral export control arrangements. Becoming a member in the export control arrangements requires that states develop other aspects of an export control system. In other words, a relatively developed export control system is a prerequisite for membership in most of the export control arrangements. Russia, for example, was able to gain membership in the MTCR and Wassenaar Arrangement only after convincing member states that it had taken steps to develop an effective export control system. Ukraine also gained membership in the Wassenaar Arrangement and the NSG once it had taken measures to develop the national basis for an export control system. Other FSU states, which seldom export strategic technologies, are unlikely to become members of these regimes. Latvia, however, which hardly represents a major supplier of nuclear technology, has been admitted into the NSG.

Export Control Policy, Institutions, and Behavior

While this comparison of export control development based on the ten elements used in this study provides a useful framework for cross-case analysis, it is important to note that there are also significant differences between states (e.g., Ukraine and Kazakhstan, or Armenia and Georgia) in the extent to which declared policies have been implemented. The method used to measure export control development in this study also allows us to separate export control systems into subparts to gauge the extent to which policies have been implemented. The subparts may demonstrate differences in the existence of export control (a) policy; (b) institutions and procedures; and (c) actual implementation. From such an analysis of export control development, we can assess whether or not words have been translated into deeds and the extent of actual commitment to export control.

We find that in all the FSU states, policy scores are notably higher than scores for export control behavior (see Table 2). This marked difference between the level of policy development and the level of implementation increases for states with less developed systems. It is clearly the case that export control policies are not only first steps in export control development, but are much easier and less costly to create than to implement. Implementation of policies would require some states such as Georgia and Azerbaijan, for example, to allocate resources they simply do not possess. Even Russia, which has the highest score for overall export control development, finds implementing certain measures difficult and must sometimes rely on external assistance. The United States, for example, has funded several meetings designed to inform Russian industrialists about export control regulations so that these exporters do not unknowingly export strategic technology without first acquiring a license.

Overall, the data in Tables 1 and 2 demonstrate that all the states of the FSU have developed and implemented at least some elements of an export control system. In the case of Georgia, Uzbekistan, Turkmenistan,

TABLE 2			
FSU Export Control Development by Subpart, 1997			
	Policy	Institutions	Behavior
Russia	92%	90%	50%
Ukraine	90%	87%	58%
Belarus	70%	66%	58%
Kazakhstan	76%	59%	31%
Estonia	70%	54%	50%
Latvia	92%	60%	50%
Lithuania	70%	56%	42%
Kyrgyzstan	29%	21%	4%
Tajikistan	21%	4%	4%
Turkmenistan	21%	4%	4%
Uzbekistan	25%	15%	4%
Armenia	65%	36%	26%
Azerbaijan	53%	25%	12%
Georgia	35%	4%	4%

Tajikistan, and Kyrgyzstan, however, the presence of some export control elements may not be linked directly to nonproliferation goals. These states may have developed several elements of an export control system to accomplish other tasks. For example, the customs bodies in these states could theoretically aid nonproliferation export control efforts, but they were established primarily to regulate trade and to interdict contraband. Licensing agencies also exist in these states, but they exist more because of economic imperative (regulation of foreign economic trade) than a desire to regulate strategic trade. While export control development in these states may not be attributed directly to nonproliferation goals, such developments should not be entirely dismissed given that they can serve as the basis for strengthening nonproliferation controls in the future. Moreover, other states of the FSU have made noteworthy progress in developing nonproliferation export controls.

ALTERNATIVE EXPLANATIONS

The analyses presented throughout this volume allows us to draw a number of conclusions regarding the relative strengths and weaknesses of the various theoretical explanations for export control development (see Table 3). First, the expectations drawn from the realist/neorealist approach, which emphasizes the role of military security, largely failed to explain export control development in the former Soviet Union. Realist factors, in other words, did not motivate export control developments in most of the states studied here. No state developed its controls to balance the power or prevent the military gains of other states. External security threats seemed to influence export control behavior in Armenia only, although Armenian, Azerbaijani and Georgian officials all indicated that export control allowed them to address their countries' internal security needs. The internal and external conflicts in these three countries, in other words, necessitates the control of military items for their immediate security. Moreover, Armenia's historical enmity with Turkey affected its leaders' perceptions of export control activities and their utility. Although a number of other former Soviet officials expressed concerns about their security, they did not suggest that their security threats could be alleviated through the development of export control systems.

Our case studies' strong and consistent findings regarding realist expectations suggest that military security concerns play little role in state export control decision-making in the FSU.[1] Moreover, such consistent findings do little to explain the variance in export control development across the former Soviet states. Realist expectations, in other words, failed to explain export control behavior in states with the highest levels of development (Russia, Ukraine, Belarus, and the Baltics), as well as in states with

TABLE 3

Explanations of Export Control Development: Theory and Evidence

	Russia	Ukraine	Belarus	Kazakhstan	Baltics	Central Asia	Caucasus
Realism							
• external security threats	negative	negative	negative	negative	negative	negative	negative/positive[1]
• balance power of others	negative	negative	negative	negative	negative	negative	negative
• prevent gains of others	negative	negative	negative	negative	negative	negative	negative
• export control for security enhancement	negative	negative	negative	negative	negative	negative	positive
Rational Institutionalism							
• explicit cost/benefit calculations	positive	positive	mixed	positive	positive	negative	mixed
• regime rules/norms constrain behavior	mixed	negative	positive	negative	positive	negative	negative
• transaction costs, uncertainty, future reciprocity	positive	positive	mixed	positive	positive	negative	negative
• material direct and side payments	positive	positive	positive	positive	positive	positive	mixed/positive[2]
Domestic Politics							
• interest group pressures	mixed	negative	negative	negative	negative	negative	negative
• elite perceptions of national interest	positive	positive	mixed	negative	mixed	negative	negative
• centralized state/society relations	negative	negative	negative	negative	negative	negative	negative
• export control agencies influential	positive	mixed	negative	mixed	mixed	negative	negative
Liberal Identity							
• sense of community with liberal states	mixed	positive	negative	mixed	positive	positive	mixed
• interaction with liberal community	positive	positive	positive	positive	positive	negative	mixed
• liberal, democratic government	mixed	mixed	negative	negative	mixed	negative/mixed[3]	negative
• target illiberal states	negative	mixed	negative	negative	positive	negative	negative

1. The positive result is for Armenia.
2. The positive result is for Armenia.
3. The mixed result is for Kyrgyzstan.

the lowest levels of development (Tajikistan, Turkmenistan, and Uzbekistan). The overall utility of the realist/neorealist approach for explaining export control development is, therefore, weak.

The rational institutionalist approach provides the strongest explanation for export control development in, as well as for the variance within, the FSU. In the states with the least developed systems, there was little if any evidence that explicit calculations of costs and benefits were made. Such calculations were, however, important factors for those states with more developed systems. Transaction costs, uncertainty, future interaction, and reciprocity were also important factors for the states with more developed export controls, and were not for the less developed. Nonproliferation regime rules and norms, however, played virtually no role in affecting export control development throughout the FSU. Only in Belarus and the Baltic countries were such rules and norms important factors driving decisions related to export control. Belarus, Estonia, Latvia, and Lithuania are fairly similar in terms of their export control development (all are on the middle to high end of the development scale), but it is unclear why the other states with more developed systems were not as affected by nonproliferation rules and norms as well. In the case of Russia, nonproliferation rules and norms were used occasionally to rationalize export control policy decisions (the decision to renege on the agreement to transfer cryogenic missile technology to India is an example) to domestic critics, and therefore served an instrumental role. Rules and norms were not, however, among the most important factors influencing development.

The receipt of material incentives in the form of direct and/or side payments (e.g., U.S. assistance through the Nunn-Lugar program) proved to have an overwhelmingly positive effect on the development of export controls in all the former Soviet states with the exception of Azerbaijan and Georgia, where the amount of aid was so scant that its impact was marginal. Although there is a clear link between material aid from the West and the level of export control development, it is important to note that there was considerable variance in the amounts and types of aid flowing to these countries individually. The countries with the most developed export control systems, for example, received the most aid both specifically for export control activities as well as for general nonproliferation and other purposes. Those countries receiving less aid, which was often not directly connected to export control development, have less developed export control systems. Although direct payments explicitly linked to export control policies, practices and procedures are important determinants affecting state behavior, the evidence suggests that side payments made with implicit connections to responsible security policies were also important factors influencing some state decisions. For Russia and Ukraine, these side payments took the form of access to Western markets and technology. The United States and other

Western countries made it clear that if Russia and other states of the FSU wanted to market strategic technology and services in the West, and if they wanted Western technology, they would first need to develop effective export control systems.

The authors of this volume found that domestic political approaches failed to explain adequately export control motivations and behavior in the former Soviet Union. For example, interest groups, at least as understood in the West, are largely nonexistent in the former Soviet countries and were not, therefore, significant factors influencing export control development or the lack thereof. Likewise, the institutional constructs within these states, in terms of degree of centralization, did not positively affect their export control ambitions. Although all of these countries do indeed operate under highly centralized government processes, there is significant variance in their degree of centralization. The finding that centralized state/societal relations had no impact on the export control behavior of any former Soviet state is, therefore, puzzling.

Expectations derived from the domestic political approaches do, however, provide some assistance in explaining variance in the level of export control development in the region. Elite perceptions of the national interest and the relative power of export control agencies were relevant factors for states with higher, but not for those with lower, levels of export control development. In Russia, for example, the establishment of the Federal Service for Currency and Export Control, an agency dedicated exclusively to overseeing nonproliferation export controls, has prevented other domestic commercial interests and other agencies from promoting a very loose system of control. Moreover, government elites in Russia, and to a lesser degree in Ukraine, Belarus, and the Baltics, argued that export control development was in the "national interest" and called for the creation of agencies with responsibilities for regulating strategic trade. It is worth noting that these states are the more industrialized of the former Soviet Union and perhaps stand to gain the most from developing export control systems because such systems would allow them access to Western technology for enhancing their domestic infrastructures. We see, therefore, that the elite perceptions of export control being in the "national interest" are largely tied to external considerations—namely the fact that full and normalized trade relations and uninhibited technology transfer with the West required the development of export control systems. Although the evidence suggests that these factors did influence export control behavior in the states with more developed systems of export controls, the overall strength of the domestic politics approach in explaining export control development is less robust than the rational institutionalist approach.

Finally, the liberal identity approach offers some general understanding of export control behavior in the FSU, but does not explain well the observed variance in the level of export control development within the FSU. Nearly all states investigated here, with the exception of Belarus, expressed some sense of community with Western, liberal states concerning export control matters. However, this "sense of community" and identification with the West provides little insight into the varying levels of export control development in the former Soviet region given that both the states with well developed export control systems and the states with lesser developed systems expressed such a sense of community.

All the former Soviet states suggested that interaction with the liberal community, especially the United States, played a role in their efforts to develop national systems of export control. There also appears to be a correlation between the amount of interaction (export control conferences, training seminars, etc.) with Western states and the level of export control development. The Baltic states, Belarus, Ukraine, Russia, and Kazakhstan, which have been the focus of Western export control training efforts also have more developed export control systems. Conversely, the states of Central Asia and the Caucasus have had limited interaction with the West in export control activities and have the least developed export control systems. It seems, however, that the material and personal benefits (e.g., travel to the West) that such interaction provided were of great importance.[2]

We also find that nearly all the states of the FSU opposed export controls that were targeted toward illiberal states. Only the Baltic countries, perhaps because they are most oriented toward the Western liberal community and Western institutions, were likely to support the restriction of exports specifically to countries deemed illiberal by the West. The targeting expectation derived from the liberal identity approach, therefore, does not help to explain export control variance in the FSU.

The liberal identity approach does direct our attention to the importance of democratic government processes for explaining variance in the level of export control development in the FSU. The evidence demonstrates that the countries that have made more progress toward establishing a liberal, democratic government (e.g., Russia) tended to have made more headway in developing national export control systems. Nevertheless, a state such as Belarus, which moved in 1996 and 1997 toward dictatorship rather than democracy, challenges this finding given that it has a more developed system of export control than many of the more democratic states of the FSU. Belarus did begin its export control development efforts before 1996 when it was still making some progress in implementing democratic reforms, but continued its efforts after 1996 when it began to move away from them. Moreover, struggles with democratic reform have often sidelined export control activities in the states seeking such reform. Nonetheless, the states that have not accepted democratic practices in some way have in most cases made less progress in export control development.

Implications

The case studies presented in this volume were guided by theories of international relations. The researchers employed four theoretical approaches to determine their relative strengths and weaknesses and to illuminate forces motivating nonproliferation efforts in the former Soviet Union. Based on the analyses, the findings may be generalized to other regions of the world dealing with similar nonproliferation export control issues. Given that the array of states analyzed in this volume range from the moderately developed, such as the Baltics and Russia, to the much less developed, such as Tajikistan and Turkmenistan, the findings may be extended to export control developments across the globe from Latin America to Africa to Southeast Asia.

Concerning this study's specific findings, the rational institutionalist approach best explained export control variance in the FSU. Three of the four behavioral expectations derived from the approach (cost/benefit calculations; transaction costs/uncertainty/future reciprocity; and material payments) were found to have been important factors affecting export control development in those states with more developed export control systems. Access to Western markets and Western technology also proved to be a key incentive motivating some states to develop export controls. In the states with less developed systems of export control, we find that fewer "carrots" or material payments were offered.

To a lesser degree, the domestic politics and liberal identity approaches enhance understanding of export control development in the FSU. Domestically, elite perceptions of the national interest and bureaucratic power asymmetries seemed to have a greater impact on export control behavior in those states exhibiting more export control development than in those with less developed systems. Elitist and bureaucratic approaches to state behavior are, therefore, enhanced. Moreover, the existence of liberal democratizing governments seemingly affected export control behavior in those states with more developed export controls. Theoretical approaches highlighting the importance of liberal democracy and its impact on state behavior are, therefore, supported and strengthened.

In a practical sense, these studies highlight the various factors that contribute to general export control development in the FSU. The material costs and benefits associated with, and the inducements or side payments received for, export control development were important considerations motivating the FSU states. Moreover, a growing "sense of community," positive, nonmaterial, or value-oriented interaction with Western liberal states, and efforts to implement democratic reforms greatly affected former Soviet interest in, and support for, export control development.

Because these factors tended to influence constructively export control behavior in the FSU, Western decision-makers interested in facilitating, achieving, and maintaining nonproliferation export control behavior in the region should further incorporate such factors into ongoing policy initiatives. Current export control aid programs, such as the U.S. Cooperative Threat Reduction and Nonproliferation Disarmament Fund programs, should be continued in states receiving such funds, and expanded to those that are not, while emphasizing *implementation* of export controls so that they are capable of serving the cause of nonproliferation. Implicit export control goals should also be attached to additional nonproliferation assistance and other aid flowing to the region. In addition, Western leaders should further engage their former Soviet counterparts in consistent interaction. Such efforts will undoubtedly foster the budding "sense of community" between FSU and Western officials and enhance nonproliferation activities. Moreover, the Western community should further encourage the development of liberal democratic governments throughout the former Soviet region.

Based on the case studies presented in this book, a couple of additional conclusions may be drawn concerning export control development in the region. First, one might note that the FSU states of European origin have more developed export control systems than those of non-European origin. Such differences reflect the fact that Western states interact and trade most often with states that are closer geographically and which have common political values. Second, one may argue that because Russia, Ukraine, and Belarus possess more strategic technologies, they have developed more advanced export control systems. In other words, the more strategic technologies a state possesses, the more advanced its export control system will be. It is no secret that the nuclear successor states, for example, were the primary focus of U.S. assistance efforts upon the collapse of the Soviet Union. The Baltic states, however, have made considerable progress in developing national systems of export control despite the fact that they do not possess many strategic commodities. Moreover, the Baltics have received extensive nonproliferation assistance from both the United States and other Western neighbors seeking to develop closer commercial relations. Furthermore, Uzbekistan arguably possesses a more extensive technological base than Azerbaijan, Georgia, and Kyrgyzstan, yet its export control system is less developed than those in any of these three states. Indeed, there are a myriad of potential historical, cultural, and political insights and explanations that warrant attention in future studies of export control decision-making in the former Soviet region.

THE FUTURE OF EXPORT CONTROL DEVELOPMENT IN THE FSU

While this book has emphasized the advances made in the development of nonproliferation export controls in the FSU, it is quite clear that a great deal of work remains to be done. The states of Central Asia and the Caucasus have yet to establish functioning export control systems compatible with Western standards. These are precisely the states on the southern tier that are the most likely to serve as transit points for diversion efforts to "hot spots" in the Middle East and Asia. With what amounts to largely unprotected internal borders within the CIS, export controls in the FSU are really only as strong as the weakest link in the chain.[3] This reality requires one to reassess the overall level of export control development in the FSU and to recognize that the lack of controls in some states may undermine the best efforts of other states. Even for states with the highest levels of export control development, a great deal of work is still needed in informing exporters of their responsibilities, in formalizing export control structures and procedures through law, and in minimizing corruption in the system.

Despite the many export control developments we have witnessed in the FSU, several issues may affect future efforts to enhance export controls there. First, the inducements the West has provided to these countries do not always result in better export control policy and export control implementation. These states, in other words, may have an incentive to build an export control system on paper, but not to develop the relevant institutions and see to it that they work. They may calculate, therefore, that the best way to placate vital trading partners in the West, receive much needed assistance, and minimize internal costs, is to create export control policies, practices, and procedures that are only as strong as the paper on which they are printed.

Given the economic plight of the FSU states, they are sensitive to the possibility of losing trade revenues as a result of nonproliferation goals that may be of less concern. U.S. demands that Russia halt the sale of nuclear power technology to Iran as well as stop the sale of cryogenic rocket engines to India in the name of nonproliferation are just two examples of the lost revenue export controls can cause. The other costs associated with export control are more direct in nature. States must allocate resources to establish bureaucratic agencies and personnel to implement export regulations. Resources within these governments are extremely limited, and export controls require the use of precious resources in an area many do not consider a priority. Finally, there are real domestic political costs for the advocates of nonproliferation export control policy. These advocates face political assault from opponents within the government and from the powerful military-industrial complex who see export control as inhibiting an important source of state revenue. For all these reasons, the FSU may find it difficult to continue and enhance the export control development they have begun.

Another reason for possible reluctance stems from the view among FSU policy-makers that the United States and other Western countries are imposing export controls on them. Export controls were once a major tool of the West to slow economic and technological development in the FSU during the days of the Cold War. Institutions such as COCOM, for example, governed Western attempts to control trade with and to the Soviet Union throughout that era.[4] The issue of export control development, therefore, is often met with great skepticism in the FSU. Many FSU officials feel that they are now being asked to participate in technology denial efforts that once had severe domestic implications for their societies. Despite such feelings, most leaders in the region have committed to export control development. Future leaders, however, may not be as cooperative, and export controls, if not well institutionalized, may be subject to their whims.

An additional point of reluctance involves the difference in threat perceptions between the West and the FSU. U.S. conceptions of "rogue" states are not necessarily acceptable to many in the FSU.[5] Many FSU states, for example, have established close political and economic relations with countries such as Iran, India, and China—countries which some in the West, particularly the United States, consider to be violators of international nonproliferation norms. These differing perceptions may lead to serious discord with Western states, and especially the United States, concerning targets of export controls, because the former Soviet states often see such targets as vital trading partners and believe that they can simply no longer afford to turn their backs on much-needed trade.[6]

Finally, this study has demonstrated that many FSU policy-makers do not see export control as a means to reduce security threats. The future of nonproliferation export control efforts may very well hinge on whether or not some agreement can be made concerning the "real" threats to national and international security, and whether the control of sensitive exports addresses these threats. Because this study has shown that liberal identification between the West and states of the FSU has had a marginal effect on export control development, the lack of agreement on the nature of national and international security threats must be addressed. Common perceptions of threats, in other words, may enhance nonproliferation export control efforts in the absence of other factors that encourage international cooperation, such as a shared liberal, democratic identity.

Although there may be reasons for the FSU states to discontinue their export control development efforts, there are many reasons why they may not abandon them. Past, present, and future export control activities are likely to become more and more institutionalized as standard policy practices. Once institutionalized, export control efforts will be less likely to disappear. Moreover, along with the development of export control systems in the states of the FSU has come a budding nonproliferation culture that is being embedded in their political operations. Such a culture may ensure the longevity of export control development throughout the FSU, if it is adequately nurtured. Ultimately, these states have come a long way toward developing nonproliferation export controls given the numerous impediments to their efforts. For the sake of international nonproliferation efforts, the states of the West and the FSU can and should work together to minimize the obstacles and maximize the incentives the FSU states are likely to face on their way to truly effective export control development.

NOTES

1. For some states of the FSU, the primary security threat comes from Russia. Export control does not offer an effective tool, however, for addressing this threat. On the other hand, Russia could use export control or an embargo as a form of economic or political coercion designed to bring about policy changes in other states of the FSU.

2. For specific information on U.S. efforts to promote export control in the FSU and perceptions of this assistance see National Research Council, Office of International Affairs, *Proliferation Concerns: Assessing U.S. Efforts to Help Contain Nuclear and Other Dangerous Materials and Technologies in the former Soviet Union* (Washington, D.C.: National Academy Press, 1997), especially pp. 99–108.

3. CIS states refer to their borders with fellow CIS states as "internal," to which they appropriate fewer resources to customs posts and security checkpoints for control purposes. Moreover, the Customs Union, of which Belarus, Russia, Kazakhstan, and Kyrgyzstan are members, allows for free trade between these states with only minimal checks. This raises the concern that Russian technology, weapons, equipment, and materials may be exported to Kyrgyzstan, and subsequently reexported to any location worldwide due to the less stringent system of export control there. Kazakhstani officials, for example, confirmed this as a real possibility and area of concern. Personal interview conducted in September 1996.

4. For more on the role of COCOM, see Richard T. Cupitt and Suzette R. Grillot, "COCOM is Dead, Long Live COCOM: Persistence and Change in Multilateral Security Institutions," *British Journal of Political Science* 27 (July 1997), pp. 361–89.

5. For more on the different conceptions of rogueness, see Richard T. Cupitt, "Target Rogue *Behavior*, Not Rogue States," *The Nonproliferation Review* 3, 2 (Winter 1996), pp. 46–54.

6. It is important to note that the 1990s have seen many disputes between the United States and other members of supply-side nonproliferation arrangements surrounding the targets of export control and sanctions. Russia and the FSU states are not alone in questioning U.S. policy on the choice of targets (e.g., Iran).

LIAM ANDERSON is a researcher at the Center for International Trade and Security at the University of Georgia. He has studied politics at the University of Nottingham, the University of Cambridge, and the University of Georgia. His major area of research is concerned with issues relating to nuclear nonproliferation, with a specific focus on the proliferation threat from the southern tier states of the former Soviet Union. He has presented his research at regional, national, and international conferences, and has recently published in *Jane's Intelligence Review* and *Geojournal*. He is coauthor of the book *Strategic Minerals in a Changing Environment*, published in May 1997.

MICHAEL BECK is a researcher at the Center for International Trade and Security at the University of Georgia. He has studied political science at Emory University and the University of Georgia. He spent six months in Moscow during 1996 as a Staff Research Assistant with Los Alamos National Laboratory where he helped in launching a compendium of Russian export regulations and an export control newsletter designed to inform Russian industry on the need to control "sensitive" technologies. In addition, he has attended and spoken at numerous conferences in Russia on international aspects of nonproliferation and technology control. His work on Russian export control issues has been published in *World Affairs* and other scholarly and policy journals.

CHRIS BEHAN is a researcher for the Center for International Trade and Security at the University of Georgia. He has served as a research assistant for the Congressional Research Service and for the Lawyers Alliance for World Security, both in Washington, D.C. He spent the first half of 1997 in Washington where he served as a research assistant in the export control offices of the U.S. Departments of Energy, State, Defense, Commerce, and Customs. In 1997, he spent six months in Almaty, Kazakhstan where he coordinated U.S. export control initiatives as a liaison for Los Alamos National Laboratory. His research interests focus mainly on nuclear nonproliferation issues in the former Soviet Union, with a specific focus on the Baltic region.

GARY K. BERTSCH is the University Professor of Political Science and Director of the Center for International Trade and Security. Professor Bertsch has served as a Fulbright Professor in England and an IREX (International Research and Exchanges Board) Professor in the former Yugoslavia. Professor Bertsch directs the Center for International Trade and Security's longterm project on "Export Controls in the 1990s" and codirects the Center's two projects on nonproliferation and export controls in the former Soviet Union and Asia. He recently served on the National Research Council's Committee on Dual-Use Technologies, Export Controls, Materials Protection Control, and Accounting. He has published fifteen books, including: *International Cooperation on Nonproliferation Export Controls* (University of Michigan Press, 1994), coeditor and contributor; *Export Controls in Transition* (Duke University Press, 1992), coeditor; *After the Revolutions: East-West Trade and Technology Transfer in the 1990s* (Westview, 1991), coeditor and contributor; and *Controlling East-West Trade and Technology Transfer: Power, Politics, and Policies* (Duke University Press, 1988), editor and contributor.

CASSADY CRAFT is a researcher for the Center for International Trade and Security at the University of Georgia. His research includes developing formal and informal means of assessing the development of nonproliferation policies in the NIS, arms control policies in the United States, and weapons transfer policies globally. He currently teaches in the Department of Political Science and conducts research for the Center for International Trade and Security. He has worked previously for the Nonproliferation and International Security Division of Los Alamos National Laboratory and with the Southern Center for International Studies in Atlanta. He is active in academic and policy communities, publishing in policy and scholarly journals, and presenting research before both governmental and academic audiences. His research is supported by the National Council for Eurasian and East European Research.

SUZETTE R. GRILLOT is Assistant Director and Senior Research Associate for the Center for International Trade and Security, and Adjunct Professor of Political Science at the University of Georgia. She previously served as a graduate research assistant at the Los Alamos National Laboratory where she also spent several months rotating through the export control divisions of the U.S. Departments of Energy, State, Defense, Commerce, and Customs. She has authored and coauthored several published articles, including articles most recently published in *The British Journal of Political Science* and *Political Psychology*. She has attended and presented her research on nonproliferation and export control issues at many regional, national, and international conferences. Her research has been supported by the National Council for Eurasian and East European Research, the U.S. Arms Control and Disarmament Agency, and the Consortium for Multi-Party Conflict Resolution and Negotiation.

SCOTT A. JONES is a researcher for the Center for International Trade and Security at the University of Georgia. He has studied politics at the University of Georgia and Lancaster University in England. He spent part of 1997 in

Kiev, Ukraine, as part of the Department of Energy/Los Alamos National Laboratory Graduate Student Facilitator Program. Over the past two years, he has resided in Los Alamos, New Mexico, undergoing technical training on nuclear nonproliferation, and in Washington, D.C., serving several U.S. governmental agencies involved in nonproliferation export control issues. His research interests include post-Soviet political economy, U.S. foreign policy, and political theory.

SAM NUNN is a former U.S. senator from the state of Georgia. While in the Senate, Senator Nunn served as the ranking Democrat on the Senate Armed Services Committee and the Senate Permanent Subcommittee on Investigations. He also served on the Senate Small Business Committee. Senator Nunn has focused his efforts on strengthening America's defenses and reducing the threat of nuclear war, and is internationally recognized as a leading expert on U.S. defense, national security, and foreign policy. He is coauthor, along with Senator Richard Lugar (R-Ind.), of legislation to fund nuclear weapons dismantlement activities in the former Soviet Union. Senator Nunn is now involved in several projects to address the proliferation threats related to weapons of mass destruction. In April 1997, he and colleagues at the University of Georgia's Center for International Trade and Security hosted a major conference on "Terrorism, Weapons of Mass Destruction, and U.S. Security."

KEITH D. WOLFE is a researcher for the Center for International Trade and Security at the University of Georgia. He has studied political science at the University of Michigan and the University of Georgia. His research focuses on issues of nonproliferation and export control in the region of the former Soviet Union. He previously served as a research assistant for Los Alamos National Laboratory where he spent eight months working within the Atomic Energy Agency and the Kazakhstani National Nuclear Center on issues of export control development, and eight months in Moscow with a nongovernmental organization, the Center on Export Controls, working on project development and industry outreach programs. His research interests include NIS security and political affairs and policy studies.

INDEX